THE HIDDEN ISAAC
BASHEVIS
SINGER

Literary Modernism Series

Thomas F. Staley, Editor

THE HIDDEN ISAAC

BASHEVIS

SINGER

EDITED
BY SETH L.
WOLITZ

UNIVERSITY
OF TEXAS
PRESS,
AUSTIN

Requests for permission to reproduce material from this work should be sent
to Permissions, University of Texas Press, P.O. Box 7819, Austin, TX
78713-7819.

♾ The paper used in this book meets the minimum requirements of
ANSI/NISO Z39.48-1992 (R1997) (Permanence of Paper).

Library of Congress Cataloging-in-Publication Data

The hidden Isaac Bashevis Singer / edited by Seth L. Wolitz.

p.   cm. — (The literary modernism series)

Includes bibliographical references and index.

ISBN 0-292-79147-x (cloth : alk. paper)

1. Singer, Isaac Bashevis, 1904—Criticism and interpretation.

I. Wolitz, Seth L.   II. Series.

PJ5129.S49 Z697   2002

839'.133—dc21

2001027586

Dedication

This volume of original essays on the works of Isaac Bashevis Singer and a newly translated unpublished text by this Yiddish prose master is dedicated to my family, who handed down to me their library of Yiddish and Hebrew texts lovingly acquired across three generations amidst all the vicissitudes of the late nineteenth and twentieth centuries from the Pripet Marshes of tsarist Russia via New York City to Austin, Texas, U.S.A.

To my paternal grandparents, Benjamin and Hennie Feyge (née Shterman) Wolitz (Ellis Island changed the family name from Volinets to Wolitz) of Antepolie (Antopol), Grodno Province, and to my maternal grandparents, Dovid Leyb and Tonie Bella (Becky, née Spector) Rubin (originally Dubinsky, another Ellis Island creation) of Vysoke-Litovsk and Kamenets-Litovsk, in Grodno Province in tsarist Russia and at present in Belarus.

To my parents, Morris (Motche, the Yiddish White Russian dialectal form of Mordecai) and Gertrude (Gishe) Wolitz, who named me after my mother's grandfather, Shmuel Eleazar (in Hebrew on his tombstone), called Shmoyl Leyzer Spector in spoken daily Yiddish. This Ashkenazic Jewish tradition of carrying on the name of the deceased is a noble one. I bear his name in Hebrew, and my grandparents addressed me in its Yiddish pronunciation, as Shmoyl Leyzer. However, I am Seth Leslie Wolitz in America, following the Jewish-American tradition of maintaining the initial Hebrew or Yiddish letter and finding an American equivalent: Seth (Shmoyl) for the Yankee traditional clock Seth Thomas, which my mother stared at in the long process of giving birth to me and which had a solid American ring, the L from Leyzer for Leslie Howard, my mother's movie heartthrob — Jewish, by the way — who died tragically while returning to England during World War II. My bilingual parents always considered Yiddish a valid language and culture and with pride spoke it freely; they brought me up in New York with English, French, and Yiddish as part of their vision of a civilized world.

To my wife, Louise Berman, whose family is from the same Grodno Province as my Litvak ancestors and whose family proudly contributed their volumes of Yiddish literature to our library for our children.

To our children, Rabbi Rebecca (named after my maternal grandmother) Wolitz Sirbu and David Israel Berman Wolitz (named David after my maternal grandfather and Israel Berman after my beloved wife's paternal grandfather), who, carrying on both the Jewish and American traditions, inherit the spiritual library of Israel and humankind.

Contents

III. BASHEVIS'S INTERFACE WITH OTHER TIMES AND CULTURES

IV. INTERPRETATIONS OF BASHEVIS'S AUTOBIOGRAPHICAL WRITINGS

V. BASHEVIS'S UNTRANSLATED "GANGSTER" NOVEL: <ins>YARME UN KEYLE</ins>

Acknowledgments

Walking with my family up the main street of Wengen, a mountain resort high in the Swiss Alps, in the summer of 1983, I swore I had just seen Isaac Bashevis Singer pass us by. My wife—an economist—scoffed. What would he be doing here? She slyly suggested I must be affected by the pure mountain air. In fact I had just delivered a paper at Oxford on Bashevis Singer's occult novel *Satan in Goray*. No! It was Bashevis Singer, I insisted, and ran off to find him. But he was nowhere to be seen. Gone! Disappeared—as in his own stories! Did my eyes deceive me? Was I prepared to return crestfallen to my attentive wife and mumble: "You were right, darling"? No! I *did* see him. But where did he go? Desperate, I looked up and down this one long street and suddenly noticed a small alley. I raced into the alley, which soon opened into a small square where the Hotel Victoria stood like some half-Gothic horror. I dashed in and asked, "Is Herr Singer here?" "Yes," replied the clerk. "He just went up in the elevator." Hotel Victoria indeed! I immediately wrote a note in Yiddish explaining that I had given a paper on Bashevis Singer's novel *Satan in Goray* and his use of parody (actually I had called it creative plagiarism) and would be honored to meet him. He called shortly later and invited me to join him for dinner—vegetarian—at the hotel.

Bashevis Singer was in good form, but his wife, Alma, was ill. He liked to hide in Wengen, he told me, so that he could write in peace and correct proofs. He wanted to know in great detail what occurred at the Oxford conference of Yiddish Studies, who was there, and the quality of the papers and the Yiddish. He was delighted to learn that there was a movement to study his writings from the Yiddish and not from the English. I promised him that one day I should like to publish a book of critical articles based entirely on the texts written in Yiddish. He wondered if that would be possible given the passing of Yiddish. But he wished me well, and we pursued other topics such as why he would never set foot in Germany or Poland and why he believed in vegetarianism. The memory of the days spent at Wengen seeing him twice more has served as a goad to produce this first volume of critical studies entirely based on his original Yiddish texts.

The idea became feasible when my friend and colleague Professor Joseph Sherman of the University of Witwatersrand, South Africa, came to the University of Texas to organize the manuscripts of Isaac Bashevis Singer housed in the Harry Ransom Humanities Research Center. These rare manuscripts and realia were obtained through the active support of the HRC director, Thomas F. Staley; the ingenuity of Robert King, the former dean and specialist in German and Yiddish linguistics; and the generous donations of Texan philanthropists.

I proposed to Professor Sherman, who was already well known as a superb translator of Bashevis Singer, that if he were to translate some unpublished material and perhaps write a critical article, I would bring together other Yiddish scholars to create and publish new interpretations of Isaac Bashevis Singer based finally on the original texts, many of which were now available at the Harry Ransom Humanities Research Center at the University of Texas. Professor Sherman was most enthused and took up this idea. He also performed a splendid task in clarifying the contents of the Bashevis archives. I wish to acknowledge fully how often he volunteered his help and services for this volume, which is as much an expression of his profound appreciation of Yiddish literature as of my own and that of our colleagues. His is perhaps of a special intensity, for he has toiled with Singer's works not only in manuscripts but in translations, in ordering his archives but also in editing his works and those of others. Indeed, Joseph Sherman is a scholar who joins other unsung heroes in Jewish history like Professor Nissan Babalikashvili of Tiblisi, Georgia, and Professor Alexander Scheiber of Budapest, Hungary, engaged in the bitter task of closing the intellectual and cultural accounts of their dying communities. His work for South African Yiddish literature and Yiddish literature in general places his name in the Scroll of Righteous Men.

It was Thomas F. Staley who gave the green light to proceed on such an undertaking, for he supported my efforts to create this volume, which underscores that Bashevis Singer is unique as a Yiddish writer who instinctively provides the mental imaginary both of Polish Jewry and of immigrant American life in Yiddish, which belongs to a new class of literature called American literature in a non-English language. Much has been translated, but more remains to be brought into English, and much that was deleted from the English needs to be restored. Thomas F. Staley, therefore, must be acknowledged for his advanced vision in collecting the

The Hidden Isaac Bashevis Singer

manuscript works of Isaac Bashevis Singer and his constant encouragement for this volume.

I wish to express my deep appreciation to the Slavic Department of the University of Texas at Austin and especially to its staff for constant support in so many ways to bring this book to fulfillment. The staff members took on tasks which added to their already heavy secretarial burdens. I should like to single out particularly Clint Schneider, who brought his computer skills to the fore and his diplomatic skills to happy conclusions.

I want to thank the various personnel in the University of Texas Libraries, who have unstintingly helped me acquire texts over the years, who have tracked down rare materials, and who have provided support and encouragement in every way possible. Let me thank especially the Hebrew cataloguer, Nathan Snyder, who has found rare and difficult texts and helped elucidate them whether in Aramaic, Greek, or rabbinic Hebrew. For this volume, he made special efforts to find the sources of Bashevis's religious allusions and kabbalistic lore. The library has also provided a most generous man by the name of James Wieferman who helped track down rare maps of Poland, which have proved invaluable.

Let me express my special appreciation to Professor Monika Adamczyk-Garbowska of the Marie Curie-Skladowska University of Lublin, Poland, who has supported this project from the very beginning, offering information obtainable nowhere else, and whose friendship I hold dear.

Each contributor to this volume sensed the historical importance of this critical undertaking, and I wish to thank them all for their devotion and constancy in completing this noble task: scholars and archaeologists of Yiddish culture.

I should like to conclude these acknowledgments with a special expression of appreciation to the Gale family of Beaumont, Texas: to the memory of Edwin Gale and to his widow, Becky Gale, who have been the major initiators and benefactors of the growth of Jewish Studies on the campus of the University of Texas at Austin and have helped underwrite most of the lectures, programs, and international congresses treating Jewish subjects which have taken place at the university.

Seth L. Wolitz
Gale Chair of Jewish Studies
University of Texas at Austin

Introduction

The fiction in English translation of Isaac Bashevis Singer (1904–1991), winner of the 1978 Nobel Prize for Literature, has long been known to general readers and literary critics alike. Less well known are the original Yiddish texts from which these works in English derive. This volume of essays attempts to resurrect, recover, and restore the authentic voice and vision of the writer known to his Yiddish readers as Yitskhok Bashevis.

From the time Bashevis's fiction first appeared in English in 1950, Yiddish literary critics have drawn attention to the differences that exist between these two strangely different corpuses of work. The English versions are generally shortened, often shorn of much description and religious matter, and their perspectives and denouements are altered significantly. A need has now arisen to pay more critical attention to the Yiddish texts, to appreciate the significant differences between the originals and the translations, and to recognize the implication of these differences for the literary achievement of their creator.

At this juncture of scholarly appreciation of Isaac Bashevis Singer's oeuvre, this book seeks to establish that the Yiddish original should be the primary source for study of the master's fictions. To be sure, subsequent translations and transformations from the original Yiddish reflect the differences of perceptions of other linguistic cultures, but they obscure—if they do not entirely eclipse—the original Yiddish creation and the uniquely Jewish culture it elaborates and interprets. Serious scholarship in any literature always starts with the original text in its original language, and the Yiddish texts of Bashevis Singer should be no exception. All the essays in this book, for the first time in the scholarly evaluation of this writer's work, are by specialists in Yiddish literature and linguistics; their studies are all based on the Yiddish originals, which have at times been rigorously compared with their English versions. These studies therefore offer a reinterpretation of the writer from a perspective not often taken and thus underscore his identity as a distinctively Yiddish voice and an empowered interpreter of his own Jewish culture. This book seeks clearly to establish that Bashevis belongs first and foremost to Yiddish language and culture and only secondarily to the broad and great stream of twentieth-century American literature. Bashevis Singer's ambivalent dual position is entirely due to the surgical skills of translators, publishers, editors, and, indeed, Singer himself, who was never opposed to any changes in his English translations that would enhance his popularity among readers.

The studies published here seek to clarify the distinct Yiddish environments in which Bashevis lived, observed, and created. The textured vitality of his Yiddish-speaking milieux emerges in his Yiddish writings, whether anchored in the traditionally observant village of Bilgoray, seething through Warsaw's Krochmalna Street, swirling along the exilic blocks of New York City, or loping about the retirement community of Art Deco Miami Beach. These new essays view Bashevis from a perspective that differs from that of most earlier critics. Reading their author only in English, the majority of these earlier critics remove the writer from his Yiddish-language-based culture, make him marginal to his own linguistic milieu, construct of him an American writer of Jewish origins, and thus invent an English prose master, Isaac Bashevis Singer, out of a subsumed Yiddish writer, Yitskhok Bashevis.

By deliberate contrast, the critics in this new volume focus directly on the Yiddish culture that produced this Yiddish writer and his Yiddish works. Their essays identify Yitskhok Bashevis the man, the artist, and his culture as part of a vibrant Yiddish way of life that was massacred in its prime. Struggling on determinedly, fully aware that he is among the last voices of a Yiddish universe that had been dealt a mortal blow, Bashevis projects through his art a vision of that exterminated world, validates its existence, and offers a uniquely personal interpretation of it.

Bashevis was the pen-name he himself chose when he started writing, to distinguish his own voice and vision from those of his older brother Israel Joshua Singer (1893–1944), then still alive, famous, respected, and widely read. Unlike I. J. Singer, Bashevis writes not as an ideologue of some political persuasion, nor as a prophet with a didactic moral stance, but as an author functioning within, and drawing inspiration from, the linguistic and cultural parameters of his own Eastern European Ashkenazic Jewry—a people basically disenfranchised, but possessing an ancient heritage, a distinctive religious perspective, and a unique lifestyle.

Bashevis's personal existential condition mirrors the conflict within modern

European Jewish culture, which fractured itself between traditional religious observance decreed by its Halakhic world view and secular accommodation to Westernization. Many Jews sought to unburden themselves of intense if unsatisfactory religious practice in order to participate in the modern secularism of the surrounding majority, but they tried to do this within a Jewish *Weltanschauung*. In the newly emerged Yiddish-speaking secular culture of 1900, art as an esthetic undertaking was problematic for a significant sector of this linguistic community.

This dichotomy in Ashkenazic culture at the beginning of the twentieth century reflects the powerful inroads made by the Haskala (Jewish Enlightenment movement), imported into Eastern Europe from Germany throughout the nineteenth century. This movement encouraged modernization, secularization, and the invention of a new national identity which decentered, altered, and deflected the spiritually ideal encounter between Jews and their God to the politically real encounter of Jews joining other Jews to create a national and cultural renewal rooted in ethics, history, blood, and language.

Secularism—and its most dangerous expression, esthetic production in theater, literature, the plastic arts, music, and dance—had already established important benchmarks among Eastern European Jewry. With Abraham Goldfadn and Esther-Rokhl Kaminska in the theater, Mendele Moykher Sforim, Y. L. Peretz, and Sholem Aleykhem in literature, Mark Antokolsky in sculpture, Maurycy Gottlieb and Marc Chagall in painting, and Ida Rubenstein in dance, a *de facto* Yiddish secular culture came into being, burgeoning and expressive. Mordecai Ze'ev Feierberg (1874–1899) in his Hebrew novella *La'an* (Whither, 1899) captures the quandary of young men like Bashevis, riven by conflicting emotions over the Enlightenment and wrenched between the choices of rejecting a world of rigid traditionalism or embracing the new secular Yiddish culture with its lack of a meaningful spiritual compass.

Bashevis and his sister Hinde-Esther and brother Israel Joshua were new participants in the arguments that had long stirred their Yiddish world. Young Bashevis recognized the value of the critical appreciation of his older brother's literary work by the Yiddish readership of urban Warsaw, but his father, a rabbi and a Hasidic traditionalist, considered such secular literary performances frivolous and irresponsible, if not outright sinful. Nevertheless, Bashevis followed the path trodden by his brother and so many others of his generation and entered secular life, daring to encounter Westernization, fearful of being appropriated, yet fully con-

xv

Seth L. Wolitz

scious that this Western secularism masked the old/new Hellenic foe of the world as traditional Jews conceived it.

The essays in this collection underscore the primacy of Isaac Bashevis Singer as a Yiddish author by examining his own angle of vision on his culture, one that generally eschews an exclusively positivist depiction of the Ashkenazic world. Instead it emphasizes both the daily lived reality and the imaginative boundaries of that culture, drawing not only on its folk memories and mystical traditions, but also on the influences of the surrounding Polish Gentile world. Unlike such earlier Yiddish prose masters as Sholem Aleykhem (1859–1916), who with a humorist's eye lovingly portrayed *shtetl* (market town) people grappling with daily life; Sholem Asch (1880–1957), who, though he recorded the raw aspects of *shtetl* life, the roughness of urban existence, and the pain of historical vicissitudes, kept a strictly realist and neutral narrative style; or Dovid Bergelson (1884–1952), who meticulously constructed an impressionistic and symbolist style inherited from the Russian Silver Age, Bashevis moved dramatically across the literary spectrum from harsh realism to the fantastic, tapping the Ashkenazic Id, as it were, fearlessly uncovering unholy dreams and profane desires.

Bashevis could take it for granted that his Yiddish readers would follow his allusions and rich descriptions, especially in Poland, where *kheyder* and *yeshive* (Jewish religious primary school and seminary) education and heritage, no matter how beleaguered or even abandoned, still reverberated in the body of Yiddish speakers. Bashevis represents the last major resistant generation of strictly religious Polish Jewry dipping its feet for the first time into modernity. Isaac Babel (1894–1941), the master Russian-Jewish novelist, in his collection of short stories *Red Cavalry* (1926) makes the Jewish Communist narrator, Lyutov, stand in anthropological awe, trapped in a time warp, when he first encounters religious Polish Jews. Bashevis emerged from the same religious rearguard, many of whose youth sought to find an accommodation with the new. From a rearguard they would have liked to become an avant-garde. Not matriculants from the secular *gymnasia* but autodidacts of Western literature and thought, they needed both to catch up with their secular Jewish contemporaries and to outflank them with their own perspective.

Bashevis created a *nouveau frisson* in Yiddish literature because he dared initiate for his own Yiddish society a radical reactionary backlash. By the skill of his pen, he pulled into the foreground of his fiction the lurking memories, fears, and lusts quivering just behind this new Westernizing Yiddish culture, determined to remind it of its historical uniqueness, moral concerns, and precarious reality. Deep inside the cultural volcano that was Yiddish life in Poland before the Shoah (the Jewish/Hebrew term for the Holocaust), Bashevis preserved as if in amber the ideological battles of the secularists against the religious, the assimilationists against the nationalists, and the utopians against the pessimists. He continued to dramatize these conflicts in his presentation of the survivors of Adolf Hitler's genocide, disoriented in the New World, haunted by their immediate past, struggling with the American reality, disquieted by the complex inheritance of their traditional Ashkenazic world, and inevitably still at the mercy of their smoldering human passions; all this, for Bashevis, argues for self-restraint and the recognition of human limits.

In the first instance, Bashevis wrote for and spoke to his linguistic community, the Yiddish-speaking Jews who had shared his inheritance and experienced the cataclysmic destruction of their world. In the aftermath of this annihilation, the Yiddish language and culture became the life-raft to which Bashevis and his readers clung, set adrift by a nightmare of history that overtook them and perhaps overtook even their God.

When a culture is destroyed by violent conquest — like Provence conquered by the medieval French or the Aztecs and the Incas crushed by the Spaniards — there are always some remains that endure after the ruin. Yiddish culture, utterly laid waste by genocide after World War II, experienced a last flicker of creativity in New York, in Buenos Aires, and finally in Israel. Bashevis and other Yiddish artists, certainly at that time more famous than himself, produced a few lasting works in these outposts of Yiddish life before they too succumbed. They were all haunted by an appalled awareness that they were facing the end of their language, their culture, and their world. To cite an illustration from my personal experience, I helped lift to his feet the incomparable Yiddish poet Itzik Manger, drunk in a Brooklyn stairwell, as he clutched onto me shouting, *ikh bin a dikhter far toyte,* "I'm a poet for the dead!" Each Yiddish speaker who dies, newspaper subscription canceled, marks another grain of Yiddish existence running out of the hourglass: the attrition inflicts continuous pain.

Bashevis, like many of the Yiddish writers before him, sought a bridge to another linguistic community, and he certainly desired to reach an English-speaking Jewry, the descendants of immigrants from Eastern Europe, and anyone else who would read a translated text. Such a want — if not a need — after the Shoah was

Seth L. Wolitz

stoked as much by a sense of the historical debacle, a drive for esthetic appreciation from a larger audience, a longing for fame and immortality, as by the reality of pecuniary necessity. Of the earlier Yiddish writers, Sholem Asch could probably claim the greatest crossover success in English, for his novels and short stories were published by good houses in acceptable translations and sold well among both Jews and Gentiles. Bashevis may have had Asch in mind when he encouraged his own earliest large-scale family novel to be the first of his major works to be translated into English.

The Family Moskat appeared in 1950 in English garb, with pages and paragraphs trimmed and, more significantly, with its tonality and message altered.[1] Translations from Yiddish into English had always taken liberties by reducing descriptions, speeding the syntactic rhythms, and tightening the plot pacing. But this translation mode would in time become the means of transforming the Yiddish Yitskhok Bashevis into his English literary persona, Isaac Bashevis Singer. What appeared as the original Yiddish text in *Forverts* (Forward) or other Yiddish literary or cultural journals became significantly transmogrified in English by intense and conscious labor on the part of hired translators working with the Yiddish master. The massive success of "Gimpel the Fool," translated by Saul Bellow in the *Partisan Review* of May 1953, established Bashevis on the American literary scene as an amazing new voice from the Yiddish. In 1955 *Satan in Goray* appeared, followed by *Gimpel the Fool and Other Stories* in 1957 and *The Magician of Lublin* in 1960, all in English translation. In consequence I. B. Singer's voice in English extended, deepened, and enriched the full blossoming of Jewish-American fiction so brilliantly marked, in their time, by such artists as Bernard Malamud, Saul Bellow, and Philip Roth.

Bashevis had tested himself in various genres and seemed determined to write the successful well-made nineteenth-century-style historical novel, of which *The Manor* and *The Estate* are other examples. These were generally well received in English dress. With *Enemies: A Love Story*—and the posthumously translated *Shadows on the Hudson*—Bashevis moved his Yiddish-speaking survivors to the New World, but the generic form of these later novels remains the well-made realist novel so remote from his early experimental and brilliant *Satan in Goray*. He also took to writing memoirs, *In My Father's Court* being the most outstanding of these texts. What he serialized under his Yiddish nom de plume Bashevis in *Forverts* after 1960 tended routinely to be translated into English, and this no doubt affected his choice of genre and subject matter. The Nobel Prize of 1978 confirmed his literary stature and affirmed his persona, Isaac Bashevis Singer, to the non-Yiddish world. His prize and fame derive therefore from the English translations, not from the original Yiddish texts.

When the Yiddish Yitskhok Bashevis became the English I. B. Singer, he assumed the iconic stature of a living grandfather just as, sixty years earlier, Mendele Moykher Sforim had been ratcheted upward to this rank by the newly emergent writers Y. L. Peretz and Sholem Aleykhem. Singer's translated writings and his New World persona soon became fused in American letters. The presence of Bashevis Singer undoubtedly widened the spectrum of Jewish literature in general, and provided an added resonance to American Jewish literature in particular, by revealing an Eastern European Yiddish imagination never experienced before. Earlier Yiddish writings rendered into English had presented the harsh satires of Mendele, the heartfelt but humorous folk characters of Sholem Aleykhem, and the bourgeois historical realism of Sholem Asch and Joseph Opatoshu, overlaid with a patina of nostalgia. But Bashevis Singer's texts move from the external depiction and social critique typical of these earlier writers to the inward, moral, imaginative, and speculative elements of the Yiddish cultural whole. Bashevis uses imagery and concepts derived from kabbalistic texts and Hasidic tales, as well as from materials absorbed from Slavic folklore and literature. From very early in his career, he showed full awareness of modernist multiple points of view and unreliable narrators—the diverse voices heard throughout *Satan in Goray* illustrate this perfectly.

Demonic imps and other-worldly figures populate and narrate many of Bashevis's tales, enabling the reader to experience the interpenetration of one world into another with the stylistic ease of the German Romantic tales of Achim von Arnim or E. T. A. Hoffmann. Bashevis offered his English readers what American Jewish writers could not: the authenticity and authority of the past, an intact Jewish civilization, still alive in the organic experience of the last survivors of the Holocaust. And what an unexpected past this proved to be! The tired old water-carrier and exhausted cobbler share center-stage with demonic peddlers of talismans and diabolic representatives of the *yeytser-hore* (Evil Inclination); in observant Jewish households venerable rabbis succumb to *accidie* or lust in the densely populated cities of Warsaw or Lublin as easily as they do in some forsaken *shtetl* encircled by swampy Polish fields and sinister pine forests where pagan and Jewish demons

Seth L. Wolitz

together rule the night. On his literary canvas, Bashevis paints a community in the manner of Hieronymus Bosch, forcing Jewish notables of law and business, like their more ordinary fellow Jews, into the snares of immoral enticements, teasing games, and agonizing tortures devised by Jewish demons and imps: dark folk fantasy is interwoven with mystical imagery to legitimize and authenticate a people with a place, an inheritance, and a past.

Bashevis's Yiddish texts depict an Eastern European Jewish visionary world that situates their author firmly in a Yiddish literary tradition derived from Hasidic hagiographies and a Jewish mystical legacy that moves through the *Tales* of Rabbi Nakhman of Bratslav (1815) to Peretz's Hasidic stories and Der Nister's transcendental meditations. For the non-Yiddish reader, the translated texts can appear attractive as well as exotic and opaque. They contain no assured point of reference in the familiar Western world. The same sense of defamiliarization can occur when a Western, non-Jewish viewer encounters a Chagall painting, for example, in which an artist is portrayed with a hand comprising seven fingers. To the Yiddish speaker there is no mystery: the seven fingers visually translate the idiom *mit ale zibn finger,* literally "with all seven fingers," meaning with intense creative energy. Critics who know no Yiddish and are unaware of Yiddish culture see a surrealist painting and praise the painter's fanciful and gifted imagination. Both readings are possible, but knowledge of Yiddish authenticates the one over the other.

From the time the first works of Bashevis were translated into English, a substantial number of critical and scholarly articles and books have emerged which base their prooftexts exclusively on the translations and not on the original Yiddish texts. This tradition hides behind Singer's own often-repeated comment that his English versions can serve as "a second original." Under that protective guise, the English translation is made to appear not only equal to the Yiddish original, but even canonical, for according to Singer's own public claim, restated many times, it represents his own further reworking of his literary text. Unobtrusively, the Yiddish text becomes subsumed under the English text and is reduced to an appendix if it is noticed at all. Wittingly or unwittingly, this erasure becomes an act of cultural imperialism. Through it, Yiddish language and culture is made to appear moribund and parochial, serving as a mere chrysalis from which the Yiddish writer Yitskhok Bashevis can burst forth as the full-flighted English author I. B. Singer, the Nobel Prize winner who uses English as the universal tongue that carries his universal message. Singer, of course, was never innocent of working in tandem with his critics in this process of Americanizing him. If his motives were not ethically sterling, they were certainly grounded in the realistic recognition that his native constituency was dwindling, and in consequence he was not prepared to enter the shades of linguistic oblivion or poverty.[2]

In *Critical Essays on Isaac Bashevis Singer,* a recent collection that brings together some of the most widely quoted critical writings published over the last three decades, the volume's editor, Grace Farrell, articulates a sophisticated position which allows a postmodernist indeterminacy to resolve the so-called conundrum of these two corpuses of work by arguing that Bashevis Singer wanted both a Yiddish version and an English version and neither therefore can stand alone.[3] But this, it seems clear, is begging the question. Close comparative studies of the available Yiddish texts with their English translations reveal that the English has deliberately omitted many of the Jewish—and even Slavic—allusions. The loss of such iconic elements affects the works' esthetic value and cultural meaning. Above all, there are serious ethical implications involved in not closely following the Yiddish master-text.[4] The English version is at best an elegant reworking of Yiddish into American English with the plain intention of gripping an American readership. Charles Baudelaire's magnificent translations of Edgar Allan Poe do not make the French version canonical any more than Friedrich Schlegel's great German translations of William Shakespeare can supersede the unsurpassable original English. Singer's work appears as the only case in literary history where it is currently argued that the translation not only can, but in reality does, assume a greater validity than the original.

The argument is then advanced that Singer himself made the translations. That assertion can now be proved to be less than accurate. Most critics agree that the single best English translation of Singer's work into English is Jacob Sloan's version of *Satan in Goray,* which, for all its elegance, pruned the text judiciously—and Singer had little hand in its transformation. Singer did indeed participate in the English versions of later texts, but much had already been prepared by his hired helpers. Singer knew English well enough as a medium of oral communication, but editors at his most frequent publishers, Farrar, Straus and Giroux, as well as those at the *New Yorker,* a magazine which for many years held the first refusal rights to all of Singer's stories in English translation, were conscientious in their continued buffing. A comparison between the earlier translations by professionals and the later translations "by committee," as it were, reveals stylistic differentiations. The

xxi

Seth L. Wolitz

English version of *Shadows on the Hudson,* translated by Joseph Sherman, ran into difficulties at times because of publishing house rules regarding what was considered the Singer style and tonality.[5] Cuts were made. This happens in translation all the time. Constance Garnett's splendid translations of Fyodor Dostoevsky are justly highly praised for their skilled tonality even if they do contain not only howlers but also page and paragraph condensations. The original language of the text, however, must always remain the basis of sober scholarship. No serious scholar would study the work of Dostoevsky in Garnett's English versions.

Another favorite ploy in the defense line of the primacy of the English text of Singer's writing is to deny that Bashevis has a place in the Jewish canonical tradition. Grace Farrell asserts this clearly in her introduction: "Throughout his career Singer would be criticized, particularly by scholars of Yiddish, for not continuing the tradition of sentiment [*sic*] established by that literature."[6] This assertion can only appear as something of an impertinence when it is made by a scholar who admits to knowing no Yiddish. Even if Singer himself regularly pretended otherwise to an American readership largely ignorant of the Yiddish literary tradition, his own place in that tradition—by no means "a tradition of sentiment" in the work of its greatest exponents—was perfectly clear to himself, and his extensive borrowing from it in any number of forms and guises is the most convincing proof we have of his inextricable interconnection with it. Moreover, this is an argument that uses the old canard that if Jewish Americans say that Singer was outside the Yiddish tradition, then surely he must be. To support this position, as eminent a Jewish literary critic as Irving Howe is invoked,[7] and a Jewish-American playwright like Paddy Chayefsky is quoted to argue that Singer is an "alien figure" in Yiddish literary history.[8] However, it is then forgotten or overlooked that these critics and commentators are not scholars of Yiddish literature or of the literary world around which that literature revolved. These critics depended a good deal on their "advisers." Irving Howe, for example, looked to the critical sensibilities of the Yiddish poet Eliezer Greenberg for guidance, and it was Greenberg who insisted on the worth of translating "Gimpel tam" by reading it aloud to Howe and then spared no effort to convince Saul Bellow to translate this famous trademark Bashevis tale into English.

Many of the Jewish-American critics and scholars of the 1950s, 1960s, and 1970s knew Yiddish as a kitchen language of childhood—and some of them knew it very well indeed—but none of them were academic specialists in Yiddish. There were no chairs of Yiddish language and literature in American universities in those days. Indeed, Jewish Studies per se hardly existed on American campuses. Consequently most critics and commentators of these decades read and wrote about Singer in English, using the published English translations of his work. Very few—perhaps a handful—obtained copies of the Yiddish originals they wrote about. Significantly, most of Bashevis's Yiddish texts existed only in newspaper columns, for—remarkably enough—he permitted few of his Yiddish texts actually to be published between hard covers.

Most of the so-called Yiddishists whose opinions are invoked to judge Bashevis's place in "the Yiddish literary tradition" were Yiddish newspaper critics and Yiddish writers of *belles-lettres*. They were rarely professional academics. At best there were Jewish professors of English or German, like Joseph Landis or Eli Katz, who had a solid scholarly control of the Yiddish language and its literature. In general the most vocal Yiddishists were a polemical lot who recognized Bashevis's strong points but did not pull their punches in exposing what, from their perspective, they regarded as his weaknesses. But among them there was no unanimity of hostility—on the contrary. If Yankev Glatshteyn, the distinguished modernist Yiddish poet, was less than pleased with Bashevis's writings, Judd Teller, another modernist poet, admired his art. In the introduction to her book, Farrell has set up the "Yiddishists" as straw men, and she obtains their putative negativity from critics whom she has read only in English. In short, Farrell has heard only one side.[9] The ignorance and dismissiveness expressed by English-language critics who have read neither Bashevis in the original nor his critics' analytical essays in Yiddish reveal a cultural arrogance and a transparent appropriation of Singer's oeuvre that has now been made part of English-language-based American literature. It is regrettable, to say the least, that the subtext of this process seems to suggest that English-language critics were saving this supreme Yiddish writer from a Yiddishist crucifixion.

We can now appreciate all the more the importance of this collection of essays, for this is the first assemblage of texts in English by academic specialists in Yiddish language, literature, and culture. The scholars who wrote these papers are professionals, Jews and Gentiles alike, who live and work in many different countries, but who are all committed to the serious study of Yiddish culture and its institutional expression at their respective universities. They are not ideologues of Yiddishism, nor propagandists for their own ideological persuasions. Rather they

Seth L. Wolitz

are academics who share a deep interest in the Yiddish texts of a master Yiddish writer, Yitskhok Bashevis. Most of them have already published essays and larger studies on his works and related subjects. They do not have a hagiographical vision of the writer: they are all fully aware of the controversial aspects of his oeuvre. They all know both his Yiddish originals and their English translations and have engaged with the problematics these different texts raise. Some have written on his biography, others on his bibliography, and most of them on his works and their relationship with the surrounding environment in which they were produced.

In this volume the essays have been arranged in five sections that permit different angles of vision and frame the intellectual problematizations of Bashevis's achievement:

1. The Yiddish language and the Yiddish cultural experience in Bashevis's writings
2. Thematic approaches to the study of Bashevis's fiction
3. Bashevis's interface with other times and cultures
4. Interpretations of Bashevis's autobiographical writings
5. Bashevis's untranslated "gangster" novel.

The first section brings together essays which consider the accomplishment of the writer in his native tongue and the culture from which he derives his material. Each of these essays highlights some aspect of the differences that occur when the original Yiddish text passes into English translation. Irving Saposnik's elegiac essay, "A Canticle for Isaac: A *Kaddish* for Bashevis," confronts the question of cultural difference as posited in its very title. He argues suggestively that the English variant "served as a commentary on the original." Joseph Sherman, in his study, "Bashevis/Singer and the Jewish Pope," uses the short story "Zeidlus the Pope" to illustrate the significant differences that occur when the Yiddish text is performed in English dress. In this persuasive analysis, the English text is shown to vitiate the complexity, everywhere present in the Yiddish text, of Bashevis's questionings and doubtings. In "History, Messianism, and Apocalypse in Bashevis's Work," Avrom Noversztern explores Bashevis's political engagement with the messianic and apocalyptic motifs prevalent in much modern Yiddish literature, in work he wrote immediately prior to and immediately after the Shoah. From a linguistic perspective, Mark Louden, in "Sociolinguistic Views of Isaac Bashevis Singer," notes the significance of the artist's attitude to Yiddish in all its registers and the richness of their incorporation into the dynamics of text. In Bashevis's hands, Yiddish emerges as a remarkably subtle instrument incapable of being transmitted in English translation.

The essays in the second section focus on key themes in Yiddish culture and the ways in which Bashevis interrogated these themes in his writing. Leonard Prager, in "Bilom in Bashevis's *Der knekht* (The Slave)," explores the role of animals, especially dogs, in Yiddish culture. Prager uses theme, role, and metaphor to study Bashevis's handling of the way fear of dogs traditionally affected Jewish-Gentile relations and became a pivotal signifier in defining Jewish accommodation to the Gentile world. Alan Astro's study, "Art and Religion in *Der bal-tshuve* (The Penitent)," analyzes what is probably the most controversial of Bashevis's novels to point out that Bashevis may permit a mockery of the esthetic condition by the "penitent" who is the novel's virtual monologist, but that in the end he validates the centrality of art for the modern Jewish condition. In "'Death Is the Only Messiah': Three Supernatural Stories by Yitskhok Bashevis," Jan Schwarz expresses his disappointment with Bashevis's static world view and the passivity of his characters across forty years of writing. By studying the theme of death, Schwarz perceives Bashevis as a Wandering Jew figure whose passive, exilic condition leads himself and his community to a doom without restitution.

The third section recognizes the historical and intercultural forces which affected not only the whole of Yiddish culture but the singular art of Bashevis. There has been a tendency to treat Yiddish culture in general, and Bashevis's work in particular, in isolation, but the present studies set in clear relief the importance of time and place for a work of art and the straddled culture from which it emerges. In "Bashevis's Interactions with the *Mayse-bukh* (Book of Tales)," Astrid Starck-Adler reveals the interface between Old Yiddish stories in the often-reprinted *Mayse-bukh* (1602) and Bashevis's reworking of some of these medieval *topoi:* first, the marriage of a demon with a human being in "Taibele and Her Demon"; second, dybbuk possession in "The Dead Fiddler" and "Two Corpses Go Dancing"; and third, the Jewish pope in "Zeidlus the Pope." This study appreciates both consonances and incongruities between the texts, to prove that Bashevis read and drew from a great deal more than simply Hasidic materials or current Yiddish, Polish, and German novels. Monika Adamczyk-Garbowska's essay, "The Role of Polish Language and Literature in Bashevis's Fiction," provides us at last with examples and proofs of what Singer read and learned from Polish language, fiction, and cul-

Seth L. Wolitz

tural life. This essay posits that the Polish cultural realm holds a significant place in understanding the works, the writer, and Polish-Yiddish culture itself.

Part four of this book explores the place of autobiographical writing in Bashevis's life and works, an exploration that offers a unique penetration of the Polish-Yiddish world. Many readers and critics have been led to believe that Bashevis began to compose such efforts late in life, but Nathan Cohen in "Revealing Bashevis's Earliest Autobiographical Novel, *Varshe 1914–1918* (Warsaw 1914–1918)" proves that this work, partially published in 1936 in a Yiddish newspaper in Poland, contains many of the first accounts of incidents in Bashevis's boyhood that would later be reworked and developed in his autobiographical writings like *In My Father's Court,* in his fictions such as *Shosha,* and in such short stories as "Menashe and Rachel" and "Growing Up." Itzik Gottesman explores the representation of Bashevis's Yiddish-speaking world through the folklore lurking on every page of his memoiristic writing in "Folk and Folklore in the Work of Bashevis." The interplay of religious high culture and folk culture living in tandem in the Singer family apartment on Krochmalna Street in Warsaw provides rich insights into the complexity of a traditional culture encountering the harsh winds of change. Janet Hadda, whose recent comprehensive biography of Bashevis Singer explores his complex psychological life choices, interprets a central moment in Bashevis's creative life in "Bashevis at *Forverts,*" the New York Yiddish newspaper in which he published most of his literary works. Bashevis found himself in a bitter battle with Abraham Cahan — the powerful editor of *Forverts* and the author of the seminal novel of immigrant Jewish life and acculturation in America, *The Rise of David Levinsky* — over the serialization in *Forverts* of Bashevis's first major novel written in the United States, *Di familye mushkat,* of which Cahan did not approve. By sticking to his convictions, Bashevis prevailed, but this clash was psychologically not without cost.

The collection concludes with a newly translated chapter from a novel by Bashevis that has never been seen in English before. This novel, serialized in *Forverts* between January 1956 and January 1957, is Bashevis's own unique reworking of yet another well-established genre in Yiddish fiction: the "gangster" novel, which has a long and interesting history in the modern Yiddish literary tradition. In this novel, Bashevis demonstrates once more his easy familiarity with the tradition from which he emerges, and to which he repeatedly returns for models that he subverts or parodies in his own original way. This novel, partly in holograph and

Introduction

partly in published instalments from *Forverts,* forms part of the extensive Singer Yiddish archive that was acquired for the Harry Ransom Humanities Research Center by Robert King when he was dean of liberal arts at the University of Texas at Austin.

This collection of essays, therefore, offers an entirely fresh focus upon the man Yitskhok Bashevis and his oeuvre. It does not deny the valuable insights to be found in earlier collections such as Marcia Allentuck's *The Achievement of Isaac Bashevis Singer* (1969), Irving Malin's *Critical Views of Isaac Bashevis Singer* (1969), David Neal Miller's *Recovering the Canon: Essays on Isaac Bashevis Singer* (1986), Grace Farrell's *Critical Essays on Isaac Bashevis Singer* (1996), and many other fine studies by individual authors. This volume, however, unlike any other, focuses on the Yiddish text as the prooftext and studies the work, its author, and its readership from the perspective of Yiddish culture. All serious literary scholarship treating Isaac Bashevis Singer and his writings must surely henceforth consult and be cognizant of the Yiddish language he wrote in, the Yiddish culture he wrote about, and, above all, his own Yiddish text. The English versions may be "a second original," but they are simply that — a second. The Yiddish locks in the real text, the key text, the masterpiece.

Seth L. Wolitz
University of Texas at Austin

Notes

1. Irving Saposnik, "Translating The Family Moskat," *Yiddish* 1 (Fall 1973): 26–37.

2. His contemporary Khayim Grade, the poet and novelist of Vilna, called me personally at least three times, insisting that I translate his work. Cynthia Ozick wrote a powerful short story on this painful topic: "Envy: or Yiddish in America" (1971).

3. Grace Farrell (ed.), *Critical Essays on Isaac Bashevis Singer* (New York: G. K. Hall, 1996), p. 20.

4. See, for instance, Seth L. Wolitz, "*Der yid fun bovl:* Variants and Meanings," *Yiddish* 11:1–11:2 (1998): 30–47.

5. Personal communication, Joseph Sherman, March 10, 1999.

6. Farrell, *Critical Essays,* p. 2.

7. Ibid., p. 23, n. 23.

8. Ibid., p. 6.

9. Ibid., p. 20.

Seth L. Wolitz

Manuscript page for *Yarme un keyle* (The Spoilers).

יארמע און קיילע

(פארזעצונג)

קאפיטל צװײ

1

יארמע האט געהאט געבראכן די שבועה. װען קיילע האט זיך אויסגעמיטשעטערס האט זי ביטער געװײנט פאר אים. געקושט זײנע פיס און געשװאוירן אז ער ערש זי איר טער מאמע'ן; אז אויב ער װעט איר נישט מוחל זײן, װעט זי זיך זײ אלײן די רעלבן. קיילע האט זיך גערירן אויף די האר. געקלאפט מיטן קאפ אין געװאנט פארריסענ מיט טרערן. גראבט װי צאב. װען יארמע האט זי צום סוף אײריינגעכאפט אין בעט. האט זי אים באו װינן אז ער װײסט נאר נישט װאס איך קענ'סא-נעכטעליער נישט אלײ צװײרוצו און באשרינדיקע 8 מאנסו ביל. יארמע האט זו געענטפערט װער ס'האט זי אױסגעקלערגעט די אלע שאלמוזו אונ קײלע האט אנגעקוו סטן געגעמט פונ אלמאנסטם. געבנס. און פon 8 טרפאצער װאם האט האט גע, האט בײ זי יארמ'ן שטוט 8 שװאָּרצל שפיגל אונ ער האט געוווירינ איך װיא דו גב שאלולון אװא װ/גם איר די פאוירילרויעניע, מאַנשו. געריכעט. װי אויך נאר טרי-טע װאס װײּל זיך באזעיאפעט מיט יעגע װאס בענינעני נאך זײ װימ. דו באל האט גערעכט אזעייוע װילליגװ רױד אנ דעריויילס אזװינע געמאשועלי מעשאלע'ם די נאך יעיעימ מאל אדורית 8 שװערעד דורכ'ן רוקנ- בין. װי אזיױ האט ער געכאבט אויביקירויואיל אז אװ רײניגל ער האט בײ איר די אבגאבאס אריינצוגיווים אונ מוזדע הראואל און זײ לאזן ארעיניי נדר זײן.

יארמע האט עטלעכע מאל זיך געהאט געגוועט מיט דעם לאמעד מאקס. און װי–װואיל מאקס האט אין אנהויבן זיך אראבגעבעטנ נעבן פוילן לאמא אזוי. צו כאפט 8 בל'ק אויף די אל, סע װאננ און סטעטעאויל ער אין דער ט טרפאצ מיט אבטעם גוטע בר-י דער. האט זיך ביסלאכװיז אריוס געוויזַ אז מעט פלענענן זיך אויסגעשלאגט פו תצזעלט און אפ, שער אויר צו מאכ גרווסעני געלטערם. אין בולונ/גע געגארט װי ראיא דע שאװאשארילא אין נאנ דרום'אמעלרי-קע האבנ אױסברעעלט נקבצה'ט אונ מ'האט די! גערמי אװמאטטערין האט אײרזאלפ. מען אויר סאם זא אן פוילן, האט

Warsaw Literary Club card, 1932.

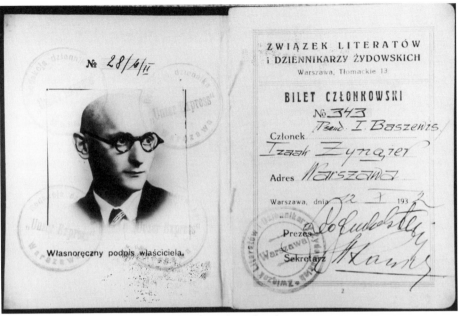

Courtesy YIVO Institute for Jewish Research and Monika Garbowska.

Yiddish P.E.N. Club identification card of 1932.

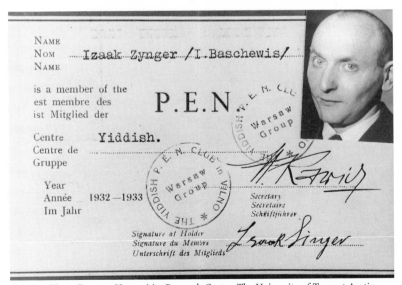

Courtesy Harry Ransom Humanities Research Center, The University of Texas at Austin.

Paris Press card, 1935.

Courtesy YIVO Institute for Jewish Research and Monika Garbowska.

Idea notebook, c. 1960s.

Courtesy Harry Ransom Humanities Research
Center, The University of Texas at Austin.

Jewish quarter in Warsaw, before 1916.

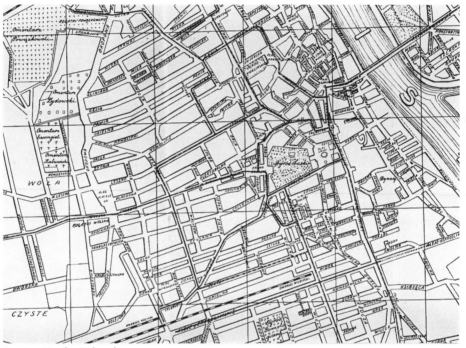

Courtesy Monika Garbowska.

Krochmalna Street, Warsaw, 1934. This street, where Bashevis Singer's family lived in great poverty, was also known for its streetwalkers.

Photo from D. Kobielski, *Warszawa miedzywojenna* (Warsaw between the wars), Warsaw: 1969. Courtesy Monika Garbowska.

The house of the Kotsker rebbe, Kock.

Photo by A. Trzcinski. Courtesy Monika Garbowska.

A local Jew standing next to a peasant seated on his wagon in Bilgoraj, 1942, before the liquidation of the ghetto of this town in which Bashevis Singer was born and grew up.

Courtesy Museum of Bilgoraj and Monika Garbowska.

Jewish cemetery in Frampol (just north of Bilgoray), 1985. Singer places two of his stories in this town.

Singer at YIVO, 1983.

Photo by G. Vanclair. Courtesy YIVO Institute for Jewish Research and Monika Garbowska.

Self-caricatures of Singer, undated.

Courtesy Harry Ransom Humanities Research Center, The University of Texas at Austin.

Singer in New York, undated.

Photo by Seymour Linden. Courtesy Harry Ransom Humanities Research Center, The University of Texas at Austin.

I. B. Singer in Florida, undated.

Courtesy YIVO Institute for Jewish Research and Monika Garbowska.

I

THE YIDDISH
LANGUAGE
AND THE
YIDDISH CULTURAL
EXPERIENCE
IN BASHEVIS'S
WRITINGS

1

A Canticle for Isaac: A *Kaddish* for Bashevis

Irving Saposnik

I was late for his death . . . For several years he had been suffering from an illness that causes loss of memory . . . When it was gone he left this world . . . In silence.

Agata Tuszynska, *Lost Landscapes*

I assumed that when the [funeral] ceremony was over, a convoy of cars would line up to go to the cemetery. Much to my surprise, however, everyone quickly said good-bye and left . . . Had the funeral taken place in Israel, my father's grave would have become a pilgrimage site for Yiddishists, intellectuals, tourists of all kinds. But this godforsaken place would attract no one. There would never be anyone to pay homage to my father in New Jersey.

Israel Zamir, *Journey to My Father*

I

Zamir is right. New Jersey is no place for the Jewish dead. Yet that is where Bashevis lies, forever removed from the Poland of his dreams and the New York of his destiny. Neither Manhattan nor Warsaw, New Jersey offers little Jewish memory, and therefore no fitting memorial. Even Miami would have been a better resting place. Unlike Sholem Aleykhem, whose New York funeral was a massive outpouring of a hundred and fifty thousand, Bashevis died in loneliness and was buried with little ceremony. Even those few who came to see him buried were late for his death.

We were all late for his death, because that was not how his life was supposed to end. The last great Yiddish writer should have gone to his death with greater glory. But Bashevis, even in death, was the *shlemiel* (fool) he often called himself. And so Bashevis lies buried in the wasteland of New Jersey, and with him the Yiddish dream that he more than anyone personified: that Yiddish could re-form itself when it crossed the Atlantic; that it could outwit America *ganef* (thief, trickster);

that Yiddish writers, with more than a little help from their translators, could find an American audience.

More than any Yiddish writer in his time, Bashevis thrived on translation: it was his ship-ticket to success. Without it he would undoubtedly have remained trapped in the Yiddish world of those who envied him: obscure writers for *Forverts*, customers of countless cafeterias, dependent for their meager *parnose* (livelihood) on the largesse of Abe Cahan and a shrinking audience to stay afloat. This might have been his life as well had he not decided to escape, much as he had escaped from Poland in the mid-1930s. How much was craft, and how much luck, we will never know, but it is clear that in time Bashevis was able to transform his Yiddish stories, and his Yiddish identity, into a Jewish-American — or even an American — literature, an achievement beyond even the two Sholems, Aleykhem and Asch, who preceded him. Even as *Forverts* became the repository of his Yiddish originals, he constructed a second, more popular original for his English readers.

By the 1960s, Bashevis was a near-native New Yorker writing for the *New Yorker* and other popular magazines that paid him well and helped him redesign his life and literature. With his initial concerns over whether he or Yiddish had any future in America now part of the past,[1] Bashevis became a Yiddish-Jewish-American writer by design, a model of how an immigrant can adapt to the New World without abandoning the Old. Bashevis built his new identity, in fact, on being a bridge between Old and New Worlds, on being the last Yiddish writer in America able to reconstruct the world of Eastern Europe before its destruction. He offered the authenticity of a witness, the skills of a master storyteller. He was the dream writer of Jewish Americans, a Yiddish author whose fiction offered the immediacy of Yiddish without having to know Yiddish.

From the beginning, Bashevis's success had been both the wonder and the envy of the Yiddish world. Many asked: Why him? Why not Khayim Grade, who wrote better, or Bashevis's brother, who far eclipsed him and would surely have been more successful had he not died young? But Bashevis was more than just a writer; he was an entrepreneur, a skillful marketer of both his image and his imagination. Much like his most famous character Gimpel, he was shrewder than he pretended to be, far more the wily peasant than the impish old man who loved to feed the pigeons in the park. Bashevis often read his American audience better than they read him, and he proceeded to give them what they wanted, all the time concealing both his literary and literal Yiddish originals.

4

A Canticle for Isaac: A *Kaddish* for Bashevis

With both Yiddish originals effectively concealed, the selling of Singer began. Sharp edges were smoothed, ethnic quirks turned into old world charm, *shtetl* superstitions passed for venerable wisdom, and Bashevis crossed over from the mundane obscurity of a Yiddish writer to being the darling of the literary world. Bashevis became perhaps the only Yiddish writer whose Yiddish is an accessory, whose Yiddish is best kept in the background, whose Yiddish is embraced by those for whom its absence makes the heart grow fonder. Like the bagel and the blintz, his translated stories became part of the American diet, tasty but with barely a hint of their original flavor.

Unlike most of the Yiddish writers who preceded him to America, but like most Jewish Americans, Bashevis chose to live in two worlds at once: one, the world of Yiddish, with its few remaining newspapers and journals, its declining population, its diminishing audience; and the other, the world of American letters, with its mass-marketed publications, its entrée into the well-paying lecture circuit, its route to national and international fame and fortune. Like the Jewish and other Americans for whom he increasingly began to write, Bashevis developed a dual existence, a private and public personality, as well as a literature that, like its author, had two parallel but distinct identities. While the Yiddish preceded the translation, the English became the authoritative text. Bashevis's writings followed the demographics of his American audience, from Levantine to Levittown, from Yiddish to *yidishkeyt* (the essence of Eastern European Jewishness), from the promised land of the immigrant generation to the suburban diaspora.[2]

While remaining faithful to his old readers, Bashevis helped his new readers form a Jewish-American culture, a culture based on nostalgia rather than knowledge, on fragments rather than fullness, on a Yiddish original *fartaytsht* and *farbesert* (translated and improved). No longer dependent on knowing Yiddish, Bashevis's new readers could now reclaim the destroyed Yiddish world and likewise recover their ties to a Judaism fast fading into the background. Bashevis, even more than the Jewish American writers born in America, offered an authentic voice that spoke directly to them. Halfway between Henry Roth and Philip Roth, Bashevis was the old and the new in one, a taste of Yiddish for a small appetite.

II

The two works that paved the way for Bashevis's new identity were *The Family Moskat* (1950) and "Gimpel the Fool" (1953). As has been shown elsewhere, Bashevis carefully crafted the translation of *Moskat* with his new audience very much in mind, cutting parts of the original that he felt were unsuitable, rearranging the structure, and eliminating the entire final chapter.[3] The result was an essentially new novel, a novel that Bashevis hoped would serve as his breakthrough to the English reader. While not as commercially successful as he had hoped, *Moskat* was nonetheless the model for subsequent translations, for the symbiotic relationship between the Yiddish original and its English variant. After *Moskat,* translations could never be mere reproductions; instead they served as a commentary on the original, almost a Talmud to the primary text.

While *Moskat* set the standard for all translations from the Yiddish, "Gimpel" was the blueprint, setting forth in context, content, and character the esthetics of both the process of translation and Bashevis's accompanying revised identity. It was also his breakthrough story. "Gimpel" not only established Singer's reputation with his new American audience; it provided him with a character who set the course of his future direction. After "Gimpel," the direction was clear. The marketing of Bashevis was to become an enterprise, in which Gimpel the Simple was to be transformed into Isaac the Wise.

With the publication of "Gimpel" in English, Irving Howe and Saul Bellow not only presented Bashevis to a new group of readers, but also helped him define his agenda. In both Yiddish and English, the key to Gimpel is his self-awareness, the necessary difference between what everyone thinks of him and what he thinks of himself. While the distinction that Bashevis makes between *tam* (simpleton) and *nar* (fool) in the Yiddish defines Gimpel's character immediately, Gimpel remains aware of his actions even in the Bellow translation.[4] Despite being considered a fool by everyone else, Gimpel knows what is happening to him, that he is being tricked by his neighbors, that his children by Elke are not his, that he can reveal the truth at will. But instead Gimpel craftily chooses to construct a calculated façade between the ideal and the real; he chooses to go along with the joke, for he has more to gain by doing so. Far from a fool, Gimpel is in fact misleading his fellow Frampolites by pretending to be more gullible than they are. Gimpel's life is a pose, a disguise behind which he can best relate to a world which constantly threatens his dignity.

Gimpel's naïveté, like much else about him, is a shield against a harsh because uncaring world, a world that is too ready to laugh at his expense, too willing to

A Canticle for Isaac: A *Kaddish* for Bashevis

remind him over and over again that he is a *shlemiel*. But the joke is on them, for Gimpel's *shlemiel*-hood works to his advantage: it becomes his defense mechanism, his protective identity. Gimpel's *shlemiel*-hood allows him to navigate between the real and the ideal, between belief and denial, between this world and the next.

If Gimpel is saint as well as *shlemiel*, as some have claimed,[5] it is because his *shlemiel*-hood is both physical and spiritual. Aware of his choices, Gimpel chooses faith; he chooses to frame his life with a view toward the afterlife, to declare his need to believe: *haynt gloybst du nisht dem vayb, morgn vestu nisht gloybn in got,* "Today you don't believe your wife, tomorrow you won't believe in God."[6] Gimpel's faith is first to believe in the human, to accept the deceptions of this world as but temporary, to understand that *az got git pleytses muz men shlepn dem pak,* "God gives us shoulders so that we can bear our burden" (p. 10). Gimpel believes not because he has to, but because he wants to. He chooses to believe because without belief life would be intolerable.

Bashevis resembles Gimpel in his ability to dissemble successfully. Life for him, too, would be intolerable were he not able to maintain an effective existence in two worlds simultaneously. Like Gimpel, he matches the role to the audience. For the Yiddish reader, he is the master of a malleable language, a juggler of idiomatic phrase and fable, a voice that offers advice and answers questions, a prober into the arcane and twisted beliefs of *shtetl* society. For the English reader, he is more avuncular, a wise old sage, offering up tidbits of learning, sops of philosophy, morsels of an Old World wisdom that sits well with those who crave authority. Like Gimpel, he knows how to hide behind a mask.

Ever the comic, Bashevis had from his youth delighted in amusing and confusing his audience. Even in Europe, Bashevis had a reputation as a sly and skillful prankster, and he continued to use his well-developed skills to confuse his many interviewers and fool his many critics, often offering one-liners and clever quips in place of truth.[7] No less than Gimpel's, Bashevis's life was for the most part a pose, a comic impersonation of what his American audience wanted.

Gimpel most resembles Bashevis at the end of his story when he becomes a storyteller. Like Bashevis, he leaves his home forever and becomes a wanderer, a displaced person, a refugee who goes out into the world in order to assume a new identity. Having lived a life of necessary fiction, Gimpel now turns that fiction into creative expression, stories that transform lies into a form of truth. No longer a

Irving Saposnik

baker, Gimpel now kneads words into ideas and ideas into narrative. Going from place to place, eating at strange tables, both character and author spin yarns, fables, tales that offer them a new identity.

As Gimpel re-creates his experience, his stories revise falsehood and confirm belief. A theme with variations, each story repeats and reinforces the integrity of his experience; each repeated telling is an affirmation that, as Gimpel observes, "there were really no lies. Whatever really doesn't happen is dreamed at night. It happens to one if it doesn't happen to another, tomorrow if not today, or a century hence if not next year."[8]

Each story is likewise a testament to the enduring remembrance of the past. Wherever he may wander, Gimpel is never far removed from his memories of Frampol: *shoyn azoyfil yorn vi kh'bin avek fun frampol, un vi nor kh'tu tzu an oyg—bin ikh vider dort,* "It's so many years that I've been away from Frampol, and yet as soon as I think about it, I'm right back there." So too Bashevis, for whom Warsaw is a constant. Each dreams of his former city, and each transforms his dreams into fiction. Dreams into fiction are the stuff of their stories. By keeping their past ever present, both Gimpel and Bashevis ensure their future.

Over and over again, the story Gimpel tells is his own story. Like his author's, his life serves as a model of survival. His story, in fact, reinforces the biographical impulse that will be part of many of Bashevis's future stories. With Gimpel, Bashevis creates one of the first of his literary alter egos. Gimpel is the prototype for many a Bashevis character to follow, the man/boy in search of God. For both, the all-seeing "I" is at the center of their stories.

As Gimpel moves from pretended fool to storyteller, both he and his stories gain greater certainty. Away from Frampol, with less need of a disguise, Gimpel speaks with increasing authority. Like his author, he proclaims his belief in the power of self-creation, of the necessary ability to endure present deception for the hope of a better tomorrow. Indeed that is what his life has been about, the need to adapt and then carry on. Secure in his disguise, and in his storytelling skills, Gimpel awaits a world in which deception will no longer be required.

Reflecting the truth of his fiction, Bashevis likewise gained greater authority the further he removed himself from Poland. The Poland of his imagination became the authoritative Poland for most of his readers, especially for those who never had firsthand experience of Europe. For many of them, Bashevis was not only a storyteller, but, as Paul Kresh dubbed him, "the magician of 86th Street."[9]

A Canticle for Isaac: A *Kaddish* for Bashevis

III

Gimpel ends his story ready to throw off this life and enter the world of truth: *az der tsayt vet kumen, vel ikh geyn ahin mit freyd,* "When the time comes, I'll enter the next world with joy." Bashevis does not seem to have gone so gently into that good night. In his end of days, with his memory failing, he did little to correct the impression held by even some close friends that he was "closed off, harsh, ruthless, manipulative, cold."[10] In fact, according to those who saw him as he lay dying, he was still as irascible, edgy, and unforgiving as he had been for much of his life.[11] Perhaps in his final days the disguise was beginning to wear thin; perhaps not even a well-constructed mask can last forever.

As Bashevis lived out his final days in a Miami apartment, he was seemingly light-years away from the hovel where Gimpel waits for another *shnorer* (aggressive beggar) to take his place. But Bashevis was closer to Gimpel than many of his readers were aware. The outward signs point to his having made it in America: several city streets named after him, round-the-clock nurse service, a view of the ocean from a luxury apartment on Collins Avenue. More successful than any Yiddish writer in America, Bashevis should be at rest, if not necessarily at peace.

But not even the Nobel Prize seems to have changed his life significantly. A New Yorker by adoption, an Upper West-Sider by choice, Bashevis remained an eternal European, often living his life as if he had never left Warsaw. The byzantine dynamics of the Writers' Club, the petty jealousies and behind-the-scenes intrigues of the Yiddish world, were all part of his life right until the end. Living uptown but working downtown only added to the duality of his existence. Dressed like a European, and carrying his ubiquitous umbrella as if he always expected it to rain, Bashevis never placed himself firmly on the streets of New York. Physically in America, he was still part of the Poland he had supposedly left for good.

Successful at transforming his Yiddish original, he was only partially successful at transforming himself. Outwardly the darling of the literary establishment, popular not only in America but throughout the world, Bashevis was a Yiddish original who never assimilated to his new surroundings. Unlike his stories, he never became Americanized. Those who knew him well saw him for what he really was: *Gimpl tam* of Krochmalna Street.

Those who needed to conjure up a different Bashevis, however, could do so with little difficulty, for he playfully allowed them to re-create him in their own image.

9

Irving Saposnik

He gave them *yidishkeyt* without Yiddish, the *shtetl* in black and white, Eastern Europe at twilight. For them, he was the chronicler of a presumed past, a link to a pre-Holocaust world, before all was burned to ash. Only he could make it live again, for he was there before it disappeared. Only in America could Bashevis have lived the life he lived and have died with so little ceremony. Perhaps America *ganef* won out after all. Alone in Miami, with memory fading and audience reduced, the prizes, Nobel and other, were perhaps worth less than the price. Yiddish into English follows in the footsteps of American Jewry, and Bashevis was all too eager to move in that direction. Had he not been willing, and perhaps eager, to cross the street, he would undoubtedly have been left behind. But he wanted more than to cross over — he wanted to be able to move in two directions at once. For the most part he succeeded, but even he could not walk the tightrope without occasionally stumbling.

For all his peasant practicality, Bashevis was something of a dreamer. Without the dream there would have been no Gimpel; without the dream there would be neither Yiddish original nor English variant. Yiddish in English is unarguably a compromise; as Gimpel might say, an entirely imaginary reconstruction only once removed from the true world. It is perhaps the greatest fiction that Bashevis produced. By creating a "second original," he assured his reputation as a world-renowned writer, but he likewise offered a *Kaddish* (prayer to honor the dead) for Yiddish literature. Escaping first from Poland and then from the Yiddish world, Bashevis freed himself from constraint, but also from community. Removed from its source, Bashevis's "second original" is the imaginary reconstruction that serves most readers. While some may berate the twists of history, the Yiddish dream may very well be realized in another language.

For all his attempts to redesign his life, Bashevis could never have imagined that he would end that life by being buried in New Jersey. But for all Zamir's regret, so Alma chose, and so be it.[12] Bashevis's lasting monument, after all, is not set in stone but etched in words that may have two originals but nonetheless pay eternal tribute to their creator. Even as Bashevis lies alone in New Jersey, his words travel the world.

So Bashevis, as you lie alone in New Jersey, may you rest in greater peace than you had while alive. As you yourself proclaimed at the end of the Yiddish *Moskat*: "Go forth and fear not. On your side is the last victory." And let us say, Amen.

A Canticle for Isaac: A *Kaddish* for Bashevis

Notes

1. Bashevis's apprehensions about Yiddish in general and his own creative abilities in particular are described by Janet Hadda, *Isaac Bashevis Singer: A Life* (New York: Oxford University Press, 1997), p. 105: "In a word, Yiddish in America was obsolete. The reason was twofold, having to do both with the language and with American culture . . . An impoverished Yiddish, infiltrated by Americanisms, was an impediment to creativity." Bashevis likewise placed a similar concern in one of his short stories: "Today I know exactly what I should have done that summer—my work. But then I wrote almost nothing. Who needs Yiddish in America?, I asked myself" ("A Day in Coney Island," in *The Collected Stories of Isaac Bashevis Singer* [New York: Farrar, Straus, Giroux, 1982], p. 372).

2. Bashevis discussed this process as early as 1969 in an interview with Cyrena Pondrom while he was a guest lecturer at the University of Wisconsin, Madison: "It happens often with me, working on the translation and working on the book itself go together, because when it's being translated I see some of the defects and I work on them—so in a way the English translation is sometimes almost a second original . . ." (*Contemporary Literature* 10:1 [Winter 1969]: 1–32). I have suggested elsewhere, and emphasize again, that the process was less casual and more calculating than Bashevis admits.

3. I. Saposnik, "Translating *The Family Moskat:* The Metamorphosis of a Novel," *Yiddish* 1:2 (Fall 1973): 26–37.

4. What the English translation omits is Bashevis's immediate emphasis on Gimpel's self-awareness, which the author establishes at the very beginning of the story. By having Gimpel distinguish between simpleton and fool, Bashevis indicates the dichotomy between the public and the private identity. Bellow's Gimpel takes more time to convince us of his self-control.

5. See especially Ruth Wisse, *The Shlemiel as Modern Hero* (Chicago: University of Chicago Press, 1971).

6. Original Yiddish quotations are taken from *Gimpel tam un andere dertseylungen* (New York: Tsiko, 1963), p. 12.

7. See especially David Roskies, "The Fibs of I. B. Singer," *Forward* (English version), December 18, 1992, p. 9; and "My Uncle Yitzhak: A Memoir of I. B. Singer," *Commentary,* December 1992, pp. 25–32.

8. *Gimpel the Fool and Other Stories* (New York: Noonday Press, 1957), p. 20.

9. Paul Kresh, *Isaac Bashevis Singer: The Magician of 86th Street* (New York: Dial Press, 1979).

10. See Richard Elman, *Namedropping: Mostly Literary Memoirs* (Albany: State University of New York Press, 1998), p. 54.

Irving Saposnik

11. Dvorah Menashe Telushkin, for many years Bashevis's secretary, poignantly describes his final days in her recent memoir, *Master of Dreams* (New York: William Morrow, 1997).

12. According to William Corbett, *New York Literary Lights* (St. Paul, Minn.: Gray Wolf Press, 1998), p. 251: "At his death, Singer had no idea that this was where he would be buried. Alma decided that she wanted to be near her daughter, Inge, from whom she had been estranged after leaving Inge's father."

A Canticle for Isaac: A *Kaddish* for Bashevis

2

Bashevis/Singer and the Jewish Pope

Joseph Sherman

During the almost four centuries between 1602 and 1958, Yiddish literature produced four separate reworkings of the fear-filled folk myth that one day a Jewish
apostate might come to rule the world as pope.[1] The recurrence of this fantasy is
noteworthy, since its roots lie deep in the biblical story of Joseph, with its overtones of Jewish self-eradication through assimilation. From this biblical exemplum it branches out into the urgent messianic longings that inform Jewish writing
through two thousand years of exile.

An informative starting point for exploring the dichotomy between the work
of Bashevis and that of I. B. Singer is a close reading of Bashevis's 1943 pope story,
"Zaydlus der ershter." Not only one of Bashevis's earliest stories written in America, it is also one of the few to exist in book form both in Yiddish and in English translation. Far from seeking a reconciliation of Jews to a secular world, or
from reflecting a passive resignation to a Jewish lot which cannot be amended —
essentially the burden of all three of the other Yiddish versions of the Jewish pope
myth — Bashevis's work militantly dissociates itself not only from the subjectifica-
tion imposed by Orthodoxy, but also from the assimilationism encouraged by the
Haskala. Neither ideological system, in Singer's view, is capable of dealing ade-
quately with the omnipresence of undeserved suffering in the world. In resistance
to the former, he posits protest against what rabbinism is prepared to accept as
the immutable will of God;[2] in antagonism to the latter, he insists that material
aspiration cuts Jews off from spiritual validation for living. Bashevis's work consistently restates his view that although Revelation as the Torah defines it may be
questionable, the moral absolutes of the Ten Commandments are not. While the
premises that God created the world, gave the Jews the Torah, and through the
Torah pointed them to the way of life may not have been true, "once people believed in them there was a way in life for [them]."[3] By contrast, "the worship of
reason [is] as idolatrous as bowing down to a graven image."[4] The ambivalent ma-

terial of the Jewish pope myth offered Bashevis a useful paradigm within which to develop his conception of Jewish identity and its viability in the Western Diaspora.

While all writers reveal themselves primarily through their use of language, Bashevis's case is complicated because the discourse of his Yiddish texts differs markedly from that of the best-selling English translations of them made under the rigorous supervision of his commercial construct, I. B. Singer. To readers who know no Yiddish, Singer may, through the medium of English, address a watered-down version of his unwavering claim that Jews acquire meaning not in the degree to which they ape Gentiles, but in the degree to which they assert moral superiority. Bashevis's Yiddish text, however, emphatically insists upon dissociating itself absolutely from the values of the secular Gentile world, boldly challenging its readership to reject the alien and cling to the authentic.

The opening sentences of Bashevis's pope-myth reworking militantly assert that, throughout the ages, the only Jews who resisted aping the Gentiles were those who loved themselves more than they loved the Covenant of Israel:

> es zenen in ale tsaytn geven layt, vos ikh, der yeytser-hore, hob nisht gekont onreydn nisht tsu retsikhe, nisht tsu nief, nisht tsu royb, ganeyve, ober afile tsu bitl-toyre. der eyntsiker veg, vos m'hot gekont tsukumen tsum koyekh-hadam fun di dozike fayne bries, iz geven durkh eytelkeyt un groyshalterey. (Y 273)[5]

> In all ages there have been folk whom I, the Evil Inclination, have been unable to persuade, not to murder, not to lechery, not to robbery, theft, or even contempt of the Torah. The only way by which one could approach the self-will of these fine creatures was through [their] vanity and egocentricity. (my translation)

Since Zaydl (the diminutive of Zaydlus) is foremost among such egotists, he is marked out for self-destruction, an awareness forced on the reader from the start, because this tale's narrator is the *yeytser-hore*, the Evil Inclination, himself. This narrative device, indicating from the start that Zaydl will lose everything, leads ineluctably to the story's trenchant examination of Zaydl's illusory goals.

Bashevis gives his tempter-narrator all those arguments—grounded in the secular view that the moral aspiration of Jews is merely an effect of their temporal deprivation—used by the *maskilim* (followers of the Haskala) against what they regarded as obscurantism and backwardness. Since, for Bashevis, Jewishness is a way of life confined within absolute categories of Good and Evil, he wholly condemns the attempts of the *maskilim* and their intellectual heirs to reduce Judaism

14

to simply another "religion," a sophistry Bashevis regards as an exercise in moral relativism that deprived Jews of identity and gave them nothing in return.

Discarding the moral imperatives of Judaism, the *yeytser-hore,* playing to the hilt his role as *maskil,* repudiates the Covenantal demand that man subordinate his insignificance to God's greatness and heaps contempt on *shusterlekh un vaser-tregers,* "petty shoemakers and water-carriers," persons who, because they earned their livelihoods in the humblest of trades, are traditionally elevated to sainthood in Jewish folklore (Y 277/E 216–217). He dismisses the entire corpus of Jewish Law as hairsplitting and holds the holy language in which that Law is formulated to have been *mutvilik fargrayzt un farkripelt* (Y 277), "deliberately distorted and corrupted," for the incapacitating purpose of keeping the ignorant in a perpetual state of subjection. Having wholly accepted Christian interpellation of themselves as inferior through centuries of Exile, the tempter goes on to argue, Jews are now incapable of reconstituting King David in the Gemara as anything more than *a kleynshtetldik rebl, vos paskent shayles-nisim . . . alts kedey tsutsunemen fun im dem koved-hamalkhes* (Y 277), "a [petty] provincial rabbi advising women about menstruation [the laws concerning the purity of women] . . . solely for the purpose of depriving him of the majesty of kingship" (E 217), a *koved,* "majesty," they are now rendered forever impotent to reclaim as their own. Citing the Jews' ungrateful treatment of Moses and the Prophets, the *yeytser-hore* sneers that, in regard to worldly *groyskeyt,* "greatness," *der amenivkhor hot faynt* (Y 277), "the Chosen People hate," whereas Gentiles *hobn lib* (Y 277), "love."

Consistent with his materialist position, this demon-tempter rejects as nonsensical Judaism's central ideological belief in the chosenness of Israel, through whose worship alone the knowledge of God's existence is given to the other nations of the earth,[6] and the concomitantly great responsibility thus placed upon them to keep God's laws minutely (Y 278). He repudiates God's close familial relationship with His people, supported everywhere in Scripture (for example, Exodus 4:22–23), in favor of a secular view of an Almighty so indifferent *az der gantser erd un ire bavoyner hobn bay im a ponem vi verem un mikn* (Y 277), "that the whole earth and its inhabitants appear to Him as so many worms and gnats." This demon's logical conclusion is to deny the promise of *shkar v'oynesh* (Y 278), "[Divine] reward and punishment," and he argues that the world operates in a nihilistic void *les din veles dayen,* "without Judgment and without Judge." The demon formulates this denial, so appalling for believing Jews, in *mayse filosof* (Y 278), "after the

15

Joseph Sherman

manner of philosophers," a pejorative description given by the traditionally pious to rationalistic ideas which, Bashevis insists in all his work, lead only to total loss of Jewish identity and irredeemable despair.

As Bashevis repeatedly claims in a great deal of his other work, Christianity, and by extension that other human-centered ideology "Enlightenment," is nothing but idolatry: *oyb zeyer got iz a mentsh, ken bay zey a mentsh zayn a got . . . zey iz alts eyn vos eyner iz—abi r'iz groys, makhn zey im far a gets* (Y 277–278), "if their god is a man, then a man can be a god to them . . . it's all one to them what a person is . . . as long as he's great, they make a god out of him." In this *reductio, got* (God) and *gets* (idol) become interchangeable synonyms, religious faith is reduced to superstition, and its profession is confirmed as an act of worldly expediency. In short, what this *yeytser-hore* offers Zaydl is exactly what tempted Heinrich Heine to apostasy—a belief that he can buy "an entry ticket into European culture." [7] It is the supreme temptation of the heirs of the Haskala, and, as far as Bashevis is concerned, it is a ticket to self-annihilation.

But of course the *yeytser-hore* is not a *maskil;* he is a demon playing a role and, like all Bashevis's Jewish demons, he can function only within Halakhic distinctions between Good and Evil. Obliterate these distinctions, and Jewish demons are obliterated as well.[8] Insistent always that Yiddish is a vehicle for Jewishness and inseparable from it,[9] Bashevis's Yiddish text makes telling use of what Max Weinreich has identified as *lehavdl loshn,*[10] linguistic structures that differentiate absolutely between things Jewish and things Christian. These structures, as this tale deploys them, are loaded with derogatory connotations which Zaydl may ignore, but which Bashevis's Yiddish readers fully recognize. In English translation, this is squarely the place where the achievement of Bashevis is sacrificed to the construction of I. B. Singer, a joint collusion of the ambitious author, his army of awe-struck translators, and the moneymaking interests of his publishers. It is, moreover, also clearly the place where Bashevis's determination to avoid at all costs giving offense to his Gentile and Christian readers led him significantly to weaken, if not wholly to adulterate, one of the most pressing of his artistic concerns.

In Bashevis's Yiddish text—lost in the authorized English version—where Jews *davn* (pray), Christians *blekekhtsn* (prattle) (Y 278); where a Jewish rabbi gives a *droshe* (sermon) (Y 273), Christian priests deliver *predikts* (harangues) (Y 282); a priest himself is a *tume,* "an impure one"; and a Gentile is an *orl* (Y 280), "an uncircumcised one." The *yeytser-hore,* the Evil Inclination and child of Satan, amusingly

Bashevis/Singer and the Jewish Pope

affirms that he only exists because there is a *yeytser-tov,* the Inclination to Righteousness which is the spirit of God, through his instinctive use of Yiddish and *loshn-koydesh* (biblical Hebrew and Hebrew of religious texts) pietisms and pejoratives derived from the Talmud and hence written in "the Holy Tongue." His first mention of God is to the *reboyne-sheloylem* (Y 277), "Master of the Universe"; with stunning irony he promises Zaydl he will become pope *im yirtse-hashem* (Y 279), "if God wills it."

The only motivation the *yeytser-hore* offers Zaydl to abandon Judaism is *oyb du vilst koved oyf der velt* (Y 278), "if you want honor in this world." Nothing could be more explicitly condemnatory of the Jewish impulse toward "Enlightenment." The tempter cynically suggests that Zaydl will reach the pinnacle of worldly glory *az du vest . . . tsunoyfshteln epes a treyf-posl [ritually impure declaration] vegn dem yoyzl un zayn muter, di psule* (Y 279), a piece of derisive Yiddish discourse which entrenches a contempt either lost or deliberately fudged in the approved and sanitized English translation, a piece of which reads, "if you throw together some hodge-podge [*treyf-posl*] about Jesus and his mother the Virgin" (E 219). The Yiddish text, by contrast, is forthright in its ridicule of the central, man-centered, myth of Christianity. True to form, the tempter has earlier contemptuously dismissed Jesus as *a mamzer fun notsres* (Y 278), "a bastard from Nazareth," a forcefully telling abuse in Yiddish. For observant Orthodox Jews, a *mamzer* is the offspring of an adulterous union, the child of a married woman by a man who is not her husband; *treyf-posl,* literally "ritually impure offal," was the term of obloquy applied by the pious to all works of the Haskala, even if — often particularly *because* — these were written in Hebrew,[11] a language strictly regarded as "holy" and therefore to be used exclusively in the service of God, and never in the service of man and his corrupt world. The specific use of the word *psule,* "virgin," conspicuously absent from the Hebrew text of Isaiah 7:14, expressly denies that verse's controversial Christological interpretation, making the conjunction of a *muter* (mother) who is simultaneously also a *psule* (virgin) a self-evident and self-deceiving absurdity.

This black comedy and its far more serious theological import are amplified in further ironic Yiddish wordplay. Apostasy is the process of becoming *a zeyrike* (Y 279), "one of theirs"; to broach the subject with "them," Zaydl should *a shmues ton vegn akhtsn un draytsn* (Y 280), "have a chat about eighteen and thirteen," traditionally ill-omened numbers. His traditional use of these piously Orthodox euphemisms to avoid all mention of the (Christian) profane and forbidden comically

17

Joseph Sherman

enables the Jewish demon-tempter to fake reluctance at soiling his lips with blasphemy while at the same time sharply emphasizing the degree of defilement that such commerce with what Orthodox Judaism regards as Gentile idolatry will bring on Zaydl. Further juggling with the pejorative connotations of Yiddish words underscores Bashevis's view of the materialistic and idolatrous nature of Christianity and the vilely wicked love of worldliness that draws Jews toward it. The demon describes the unthinkable act of conversion with a traditional Yiddish figurative disgust-idiom, *oysbaytn s'rendl* (Y 279), "changing coin," a phrase that for Orthodox Jews appropriately reduces the sublimely spiritual to the grossly material. As Zaydl's disillusionment with this exchange increases, the ironically figurative becomes the bitingly literal—*iz dos torbele mit di gilderne rendlekh, vos iz gehangen oyf [zaydls] haldz hintern tseylem, gevorn alts shiterer* (Y 283), "the bag with the gold coins, which hung round his neck behind the cross, grew steadily more empty." As the money paid him by the Church to become its bought token of its triumph over the Synagogue and on which he subsists—hanging in tellingly close proximity to the physical symbol of the humanist faith he has embraced—dwindles away, *es hot [zaydl] shoyn bang geton vorem er hot ibergebitn dos rendl* (Y 283), "[Zaydl] came to feel regret that he had changed his coin."

Given the Church's centuries-old longing to win over its chief rival, the Synagogue, the Christian attitude to Zaydl's conversion is consistently presented in metaphors of buying and selling. As if to prove the accuracy of the *yeytser-hore*'s rhetorical question, *vos kon zayn a besere shkhoyre far a galekh vi a yidishe neshome?* —"what could be better merchandise for a priest than a Jewish soul?"—the Christians of Yanov hasten to wish Zaydl *goldene glikn* (Y 280), "golden good fortune" on his apostasy, since as the tempter-narrator maliciously affirms, *di galokhim hobn mer in zinen dos gold vi dos opgot* (Y 282), "the priests had their minds fixed more firmly on gold than on their god." Since *opgot* means "idol," however, Bashevis's Yiddish text intentionally effects a devastating double irony and makes a deftly acerbic equation between two indivisible types of idolatry.

The false Christian scholarship through which Zaydl hopes *gikh oyle legdule zayn* (Y 281), "to rise rapidly to greatness," is similarly subjected to a series of verbal derogations which laugh his hopes to scorn. The demon-narrator himself insists upon observing the piously Orthodox practice of making the conventional distinction in Yiddish speech between sacred and profane things mentioned successively. His tart observation that *zaydls khiber hot gezolt vern, lehavdl, a goyisher yod-*

18

Bashevis/Singer and the Jewish Pope

khazoke (Y 281) contains exactly this highly amusing but sharply pointed under-cutting entirely lost in the official English translation: "Zaydl's treatise would be for Christianity what Maimonides' 'The Strong Hand' was for Judaism" (E 221). A more accurate English rendering of the full meaning of this passage in the Yiddish text would be "Zaydl's monograph was supposedly meant to be — forgive the blas-phemous comparison — a Gentile [unbeliever's] version of the *Mishneh Torah*." For Orthodox Jewish believers, such pretensions are sacrilegious and sinful attempts to rewrite Revealed Truth. In seeking material for *dem emes groysn ksav-pilaster* (Y 281), "the truly great libelous tract" that will denounce the precepts of Judaism, Zaydl's researches issue pitifully in a *pashkvil* (Y 281), "pasquinade"; in preparation for what the Yiddish text scathingly dismisses as a *bukh vegn shikuts mishumam* (Y 282), "book about the justification of abomination," Zaydl must seek *bilbulim* (Y 283), "slanders"; in the margins of Jewish holy books he can only write *mare mekoymes* (Y 283), "pseudo-commentaries"; and he does all this to please what are witheringly described as *reshoim* (Y 282), "the wicked," euphemistically and evasively rendered in Singer's official English as "the Church" (E 222).

The demon-narrator's dissociation from the corruption to which he tempts Zaydl is completed by his use of *talmud loshn* — words and phrases derived from the Talmud — which immutably fixes Zaydl's pursuit of worldliness and, metonymi-cally, all Enlightenment in the category of the profane. Reading the Vulgate pre-cipitates Zaydl's descent from a *lamdn,* a Jew learned in Holy Writ, into *a gantser kener in sforim khitsyonim,* "a dab hand at forbidden books." [12] By using the only synonym in Yiddish for pork, the Talmud-derived phrase *dover akher* (Y 278), "proscribed thing," the demon adds the full weight of Jewish Law to the sin of eat-ing it, just as in the very act of mocking the Torah's assertion that humans are *bkhir-hayetsire* (Y 278), "the paragon of creation," the Talmudic discourse that Bashevis puts into his mouth reminds us that in God's creative determination they are in-deed so, implicitly conceding that a mere mortal can never overreach the Almighty power that created him. By reminding Zaydl that even Moses, venerated by be-lieving Jews as Rebbenu, "Our Teacher," who received the Law from God's own hand, was *yilod ishe* (Y 278), "born of woman," he devastatingly undercuts Chris-tian claims that Jesus, also born of woman, was — or could ever have been — an extension of that Divine being who, as Maimonides defined it, has no semblance and is wholly without corporeality.

When he is finally carried from his deathbed down to that *shol-takhtis* (Y 286),

Joseph Sherman

"lowermost hell," so vividly described in the *Kabbala* (the mystical writings of Judaism) he once knew so well, Zaydl receives an unequivocal answer to the chief question of his life, one significantly excised from the official English version: *zenen take di apikorsim gerekht?* (Y 286) — "are the unbelievers then really right?" The term *apikoyres,* "heretic," was rigorously applied by the observant to all *maskilim,* observant or not, who sought to compass the Divine through reason rather than through faith. As a word of Greek derivation and Talmudic usage, it performs the same alienating function as the word *afifyor,* "pope," which Bashevis deliberately chooses in preference to the Germanism *poypst/papst* employed in the other three Yiddish pope-myth reworkings. The cumulative effect of all this exactitude in Yiddish language use is irrevocably to sunder all Zaydl's worldly and assimilationist ambitions from the sole vivifying spiritual experience of being an observant Jew.

In following his folklore source by selecting as his demon-tempter's victim a genius-scholar embodying the highest ideal of Orthodox parents through generations of Exile, Bashevis devastatingly indicts all learning divorced from moral responsibility. Because Judaism recognizes no distinction between orthodoxy and orthopraxis, Zaydl, setting human accomplishment above the Divine Will that makes it possible, begins as he ends, engrossed in vain and rigorously circumscribed self-indulgence. Moreover, to emphasize his dehumanization, Zaydl is grotesquely dissociated from the physical beauty characteristic of the biblical Joseph and his epigones in the other Jewish pope versions:

> *keyn hor zenen im kimat nisht gevaksn, un tsu zibetsn yor iz zayn shaydel geven naket un shpitsik . . . dos ponim iz geven lenglekh, roytlekh un epes vi tsugefroyrn . . . di krume noz hot oysgezen meshune naket . . . unter di ongeroytlte vies hobn gerut a por gele moreshkhoyredike oygn. hent un fis hot der zaydl gehat kleyne un vaybershe.* (Y 274)

> No hair grew on him, and by the age of seventeen his skull was bald and pointed . . . his face was oblong, reddish and somehow frigidly expressionless . . . his crooked nose appeared strangely naked . . . a pair of despondently depressive yellow eyes shifted under the sandy eyelashes. This Zaydl had small feminine hands and feet. (my translation)

Severed from any life-promoting engagement with family or community, Zaydl pursues sterile book-learning: *er hot gebletert, genishtert, arayngezoygn dem shtoyb fun di bleter* (Y 273), "he pored pedantically over leaf after leaf, sucking in the dust

20

Bashevis/Singer and the Jewish Pope

of the pages"; in his home, from which light and air are excluded, *oyf dem mebl [iz] alemol gelegn a shtoyb,* "dust always covered the furniture"; when he walks over his carpeted floors, *di trit zenen geven veykh un fartoybt, vi s'voltn dort arumgegangen nisht mentshn, nor rukhes* (Y 275), "the steps were soft and muffled, as if spirits, not people, were wandering about there." Zaydl's disjunction of erudition from ethics is strikingly conveyed in one notable instance. By the age of seven, we are told, he knew by heart the whole of *Kiddushin* and *Gittin,* those tractates of the Talmud governing marriage and divorce (Y 273/E 212). Apart from the fact that the practical application of these primary laws must be beyond the grasp of any child, Zaydl's conduct as a married adult demonstrates his pathetic incapacity to translate book-learned theory into life-enriching practice. Lovelessly, he enters into an arranged marriage which destroys his wife, for whom he feels neither affection nor responsibility (Y 272/E 214).

This disengagement from life-promoting human contact finds its correspondence in his miserly refusal to share any kind of hospitality (Y 273, 275/E 213, 214). Since he thus willfully chooses to cut himself off from the ideological demands of the Covenant which makes all Israel responsible for one another, it is inevitable that the *yeytser-hore* is able to entrap Zaydl's soul in the course of a debate regarding the nature of faith, the validity of Revelation, and the existence of Truth, since for Zaydl these things are abstract intellectual questions, not concrete lived experiences. Zaydl's hankering for worldly fame blinds him to the logical conclusion of the Evil One's malicious determination to measure spiritual worth in material prices. For if it is true that Christians simplify the nature of the Absolute by conferring divinity upon a man like themselves, Jews surely rightly recognize the ineffable mystery of that Absolute in their willing acceptance of the fact that *vos shtoybiker—alts nenter tsu got* (Y 277), "the closer one is to dust, the nearer one is to God." For Jewish Orthodoxy, however, this dust is not the self-collected sterility in which Zaydl buries himself; it is the dust into which, by blowing the breath of life, God implanted the obligation to fill the interim between cradle and grave with work that, to have any redemptive meaning, must embrace other people. The theology of Judaism insists that an arrogant refusal to accept humankind's humble apportioned lot, coupled with a stubborn determination to comprehend the universe through unaided human intellect, makes an individual willfully blind to the limitations of mortality. The physical blindness which overtakes Zaydl at the end is, on one level, the physical correlative of this self-inflicted spiritual blindness.

21

Joseph Sherman

If he were other than the total antithesis of the true Jewish scholar, Zaydl would see in the *yeytser-hore*'s arguments the strongest reasons for reaffirming Judaism. However, his dominating passion, *gayve,* "pride," makes him willfully repudiate Judaism's understanding of the existential interdependence of God and the People of Israel: as the Talmud teaches, *kudsha brikh hu, yisrael veorayta ehad hu,* "God, Israel, and the Torah are One": "For I am the Lord your God; sanctify yourselves therefore, and be ye holy; for I am holy" (Leviticus 11:44).

To be a holy people imposes enormous responsibility, for if God is invisible, His nature may be made known to other nations only through the behavior of those whom He chose to be the bearers of His name. Any expression of unholiness on the part of Israel reflects adversely on the Divinity of God.[13] Thus Jewish Orthodoxy locates the importance of the dietary laws of *kashrut,* for instance, not in any logic or health benefit, but in the fact that they are God-given commands. They must be obeyed for themselves alone, not for any possible human advantage they might confer. Because of his own determination to deny, Zaydl, always so quick to see faults in the reasoning of others, pathetically fails to recognize his tempter's argument as a sardonic but trenchant assertion — through denial — of God's direct intervention in human affairs. Consequently Zaydl rejoices in receiving *koved* (honor) for the first time in his life, foolishly unaware that this "honor" is bestowed on him by Christians not as an individual, but as a living proof that they, and not the Jews, indeed possess the Truth, for as a learned Jew, has Zaydl not abandoned his faith, betrayed his ancestors, and denied his God? In so doing, therefore, has he not affirmed the misguided stubbornness of the whole Jewish people, who have, for centuries, refused to accept the teachings of Christianity?

Zaydl's apostasy marginalizes him completely, and his reward is total confusion. Psychopathically obsessed with perfection, Zaydl wants to produce a work before whose authority, like that of another revelation, the whole world will bow down. Judging himself a god, he sets standards to which he, as merely a mortal man, can never measure up. His material means and physical strength are dissipated in proportion as his mind rambles, and his degeneration is complete when *yede hofenung tsu vern mefursem bay di umes iz aroysgerungen fun zayn harts* (Y 282), "every hope of becoming famous among the Gentile nations was wrung from his heart." From the day he is suddenly struck with blindness, *hot zaydl gelebt in der finsternish* (Y 283), Zaydl lives in a darkness as much spiritual as physical. So far from gaining absolute glory, he is reduced to abject humiliation (Y 283/E 223).

Bashevis/Singer and the Jewish Pope

Here the narrative takes on an explicitly didactic tone. Ignoring Christian offers of financial help in one last assertion of his divinely given freedom to choose, Zaydl takes up a beggar's place outside a *groys bes-tume*, "great house of impurity," evasively rendered in the official English translation as a "cathedral." As the only freedom left to him, its negative exercise is a recognition of the futility of his quest for "Enlightenment." On the steps of the "impure house" he mumbles only Jewish learning; he has forgotten *goyishe toyres*, "Gentile teachings," as quickly as he learned them. Just as in his days of youthful pride and prosperity he willfully shut out the reality of the world outside, so in his days of beggary and degradation he is both blind and deaf to the life throbbing around him (Y 284–285/E 224–225):

> *di kirkh-gas iz ful geven mit roysh. vogns hobn zikh gekoylert oyf di shteyner. ferd hobn gehirzhet, di shmaysers hobn geshrign mit grobe koyles, un geknakt mit di baytshn. shikses hobn gelakht, gekvitshet. kinder hobn geveynt. goyes hobn zikh gekrigt, zikh gerufn tsenemen, geredt oysgelasene reyd ... di zun hot im gebrent, regns hobn oyf im gegosn, toybn hobn im farumreynikt mit opfal, nor er hot nisht geton keyn akht tsu di droysndike trefenishn.* (Y 284–285)

> The street was full of tumult: wagons rolled by on the cobblestones; horses neighed; coachmen screamed with hoarse voices and cracked their whips; [Gentile] girls laughed and screeched; [children wept; Gentile] women abused one another, uttered obscenities ... The sun burned down on him, the rains soaked him, pigeons soiled him with their droppings, but he was impervious to all external occurrences. (E 224–225, translation modified, omissions added)

This imperviousness to life is precisely what had formerly cut him off from that small measure of perception that Divine Providence grants to humankind. He had sought the meaning of life in places where it was lost in rationalization, only to discover at the end that the wages of barren intellectualization is vain illusion (Y 285/E 225). Only on his deathbed does Zaydl perceive the harsh reality, that the putative glories of the Gentile world are nothing more than savage debauchery:

> *er hot gehert fun gas koyles, geshreyen, a brumenish, a rufenish, a tupenish, a klingn fun glokn, un s'hot im tsumol oysgedukht, glaykh indroysn volt a pebl fun heydn gepravet a khoge, mit trumeytn un poykeray, mit shturkatsn un vilde khayes, mit oysgelasene tents un getsndinerishe korbones.* (Y 285)

> From the streets could be heard voices, screams, [roaring, bawling,] stamping hoofs, ringing bells [and it sometimes] seemed to him [exactly as if outside] some pagan horde was celebrating a [profane] saturnalia with trum-

Joseph Sherman

pets and drums, [with] torches and wild beasts, [with] lascivious dances [and] idolatrous sacrifices. (E 225, translation modified, omissions added)

The only thing Zaydl has learned after all his dead-end travail is simply that man is an effect, not a cause, of Creation and that, the enticements of reason and the world it tries to govern notwithstanding, there is indeed both Judge and Judgment. Zaydl sees with the eyes of the spirit, not with the eyes of the flesh, the Truth of God's Revelation made through the prophet Isaiah (45:6–7): "I am the Lord, and there is none else; I form the light, and create darkness; I make peace, and create evil." As the *yeytser-hore* arrives for the last time, warning him — as Mephistopheles warns Faustus — against any attempt at *tshuve*, "repentance," or at *vidui*, "confession of sins," Zaydl receives him *mit freyd*, "joyously," employing, as one critic has noted, "the Talmudic reasoning of an *a fortiori* argument":[14]

> *oyb a gehenem iz do, iz alts do. un oyb du bist do, iz ER oykh do. itst nem mikh vu du darfst. ikh bin ongebreyt.* (Y 286)

> If there is a Gehenna, there is also a God . . . If Hell exists, everything exists. If you are real, HE is real. Now take me where you must. I am ready. (E 226)

The *leytsim*, "mocking imps," who await Zaydl at the gates of Gehenna contemptuously contrast the roles of *yeshive bokher* and *afifyor* to point out the gulf that separates the worship of One God from the adoration of idols, vindicating, in blackly comic terms, the Jewish definition of human nature.

Bashevis's Yiddish version of the Jewish pope myth aggressively denies and unwaveringly condemns as idolatry the temptations of worldliness (Y 279/E 219). Zaydl's glad acceptance of the torments of hell is Bashevis's uncompromising assertion that the powers of Evil cannot destroy Israel as long as Israel is faithful to its Covenant. All this is manifestly plain in the story's powerful Yiddish text. If its message is not wholly lost in the authorized English version, it is certainly considerably watered down, and, perhaps even more disappointingly, it is tenuously universalized. What is, in its original Yiddish version, a radically conservative defense of the inviolability of the theology of Orthodox Judaism, a moral and spiritual code impregnable against the false claims of Christianity, becomes in its official English translation a more enfeebled ecumenical statement about the advantages of maintaining one's personal integrity. An impassioned defense of Judaism in wholly Jewish terms is translated into a genteel rebuke of scholarly vanity. Clearly, Singer's publishers were concerned that his sales should not suffer through a popular perception that he was too "ethnic" or too "sectarian," or that he might, perish the thought, boldly assert the truth of his own faith over and above the claims of others. With this marketing strategy Singer was evidently fully prepared to cooperate. Hence he was wholly content to dilute the strong medicine he prescribed for Jews who could read Yiddish into a mild placebo for Gentiles (and Americanized Jews) who could not. As this central tale clearly demonstrates, he was fully prepared to set up two separate canons of work and, through both his own efforts and a cynical reliance on the inevitable demise of Yiddish, to ensure that his Yiddish canon, rarely and skimpily made available in book form, would quietly vanish from sight.

Seen in these terms, the self-deluded Zaydl becomes a startling metonym for Bashevis Singer himself. Read retrospectively, the Yiddish version of this story offers a provocative metaphorical insight into the role Bashevis came to play in the America in which he repeatedly pretended to be "lost." Thirty-five years after this story was first published—in America—Bashevis, in the persona of I. B. Singer, became the first, and only, Yiddish writer to be honored with the Nobel Prize. The arrogance of his would-be Jewish pope—to become Zaydlus *der ershter,* "the first"—can be read as a self-reflecting irony on the Faustian bargain his creator had every intention of making himself. Bashevis may not have been *der ershter,* "the first," Yiddish writer to covet the glories that attend acceptance into the canon of Western literature; as I. B. Singer he was certainly *der eyntsiker,* "the one and only," to enjoy them. Doubtless he was convinced the price was worth paying; how far he recognized the actual cost of this price, we can only surmise.

Notes

1. The four versions, in order of publication, are "Der yidisher poypst," in *Mayse-bukh* (Basel, 1602); Ayzik-Meyer Dik, *R. Shimen Barbun der rabiner fun maynts oder der dray-fakher troym* (Vilna: Rom, 1874); "Zaydlus der ershter," in Yitskhok Bashevis, *Der sotn in goray un andere dertseylungen* (New York: Farlag Matones, 1943); and "Der yidisher poypst: historishe dertseylung," in Yehiel Yeshaya Trunk, *Kvaln un beymer* (New York: Unzer Tsayt, 1958).

2. A typical rejection of this kind of passivity, repeated in numerous other interviews in English, is the following:

I myself try to think that I have made peace with human blindness and God's permanent silence, but they give me no rest. I feel a deep resentment against the Almighty.

Joseph Sherman

My religion goes hand in hand with a profound feeling of protest . . . My feeling of religion is a feeling of rebellion. I even play with the idea of creating (for myself) a religion of protest. I often say to myself that God wants us to protest. He has had enough of those who praise Him all the time and bless Him for all his cruelties to man and animals . . . I may be false and contradictory in many ways, but I am a true protester. If I could, I would picket the Almighty with a sign, "Unfair to Life." (Richard Burgin, "Isaac Bashevis Singer's Universe" [the second of a two-part series], *New York Times Magazine,* December 3, 1978, 52)

3. Richard Burgin, "A Conversation with Isaac Bashevis Singer," *Michigan Quarterly Review* 17:1 (Winter 1978): 124.

4. Isaac Bashevis Singer, "If You Could Ask One Question about Life, What Would the Answer Be? Yes . . . ," *Esquire,* December 1974, 95-96.

5. Yitskhok Bashevis, "Zaydlus der ershter," first published in *Svive* 1 (1943), under the subtitle "Fun a serie dertseylungen oyfn nomen fun 'Dos gedenkbukh fun yeytser-hore.'" It was republished in book form the same year in Yitskhok Bashevis, *Der sotn in goray un andere dertseylungen* (New York: Farlag Matones, 1943), with a foreword by Arn Tsaytlin, pp. 273-286. This edition was photomechanically reprinted by the Yiddish Department of the Hebrew University of Jerusalem in 1972. All page references to the Yiddish text of this story are to this last edition and are cited parenthetically after the letter "Y." The English translation, approved by Singer, was made by Joel Blocker and Elizabeth Pollet for Singer's third anthology in English, *Short Friday and Other Stories* (New York: Farrar, Straus, Giroux, 1963; reprinted New York: Fawcett Crest, 1964). My quotations from this translation (with page references cited parenthetically in my text after the letter "E") are from Isaac Bashevis Singer, *Short Friday and Other Stories* (New York: Farrar, Straus, Giroux, 1980), pp. 212-226. This edition is hereinafter cited as *Short Friday.* Where the Yiddish text differs in significant respects from the official English version, I have made my own translation and noted the discrepancies and omissions.

6. See Moshe Sharon, *Judaism, Christianity and Islam: Interaction and Conflict* (Johannesburg: Sacks Publishing House, 1989), p. 33.

7. Todd M. Endelman (ed.), *Jewish Apostasy in the Modern World* (New York and London: Holmes and Meier, 1987), pp. 9, 109.

8. One of the most vivid examples of this positioning of the demon-narrator can be found in Singer's story "Mayse tishevits," in *Der shpigl un andere dertseylungen* (Jerusalem: Magnes Press, 1975; reprinted 1979 [all quotations in the text are from the 1979 reprint]), pp. 12-22. The official English translation of this story appears as "The Last Demon" in *Short Friday,* pp. 145-158.

9. See, for instance, Singer's scathing review of the first issue of the newly revived *Soviet-*

Bashevis/Singer and the Jewish Pope

ish Heymland, July–August 1961, in *Commentary* 33:2 (March 1962): 267–269, where he trenchantly argues this point, so clearly demonstrated by Max Weinreich.

10. Max Weinreich, *History of the Yiddish Language,* translated by Shlomo Noble, with the assistance of Joshua A. Fishman (Chicago and London: University of Chicago Press, 1980), pp. 193ff.

11. Ibid., p. 278.

12. This term originally designated the Apocrypha, books outside the authorized canon of the Scriptures, but it gradually became a blanket condemnation of all books forbidden to God-fearing Jews.

13. Sharon, *Judaism,* p. 36.

14. Shalom Rosenberg, cited by David Levine Lerner, "The Enduring Legend of the Jewish Pope," *Judaism* 40:2 (Spring 1991): 168.

Joseph Sherman

3

History, Messianism, and Apocalypse in Bashevis's Work

Avrom Noversztern

I

It is doubtful whether any of the exclusive group of Yiddish readers who started reading *Der sotn in goray* (Satan in Goray) by Yitskhok Bashevis in the January 1933 issue of the Warsaw journal *Globus* realized that these were the opening chapters of what would prove to be one of the most remarkable works of modern Yiddish literature, one that departed significantly from contemporary literary norms. There was nothing stylistically remarkable in the first sentences, and the subject matter itself might have induced a sensation of *déjà vu* in the reader:

> *in shnas takh, in der tsayt, ven bogdan khmelnitski mit zayne makhnes hobn balagert di shtot zamoshtsh un zi nisht gekont baykumen tsulib der shtarker festung, vos hot zi arumgeringlt, hobn di totern gemakht groyse shkhites in to-mashev, bilgoray, khrubyeshov, krashnik, turbin, shebreshin un oykh in goray der hek, vos ligt tsvishn berg. m'hot dortn yidishe kinder bagrobn lebediker-heyt, geshundn di hoyt, geshokhtn, getsvungen vayber tsu znus in di oygn fun zeyere mener un dernokh oyfgetrent zeyere baykher un farneyt in zey kets.* (Y 15)

In the year 1648, during the time when Bogdan Chmielnicki and his followers besieged the city of Zamosc but could not take it, because it was strongly fortified, the Tartars carried out large massacres in Tomaszow, Bilgoray, Hrubieszow, Krasnik, Turbin, Szczebrzeszyn — and in Goray too, the town that lay in the midst of the hills at the end of the world. They buried Jewish children alive, flayed, slaughtered, violated women before the eyes of their husbands and afterward ripped open their bellies and sewed cats inside.[1]

The subject matter, the Chmielnicki massacres of 1648–1649, was hardly new to Yiddish literature.[2] More than ten years before the publication of *Der sotn in goray*, the massacre of Jews in Eastern Europe in the seventeenth century had served as

28

the background for Sholem Asch's novel *Kidush hashem* (Martyrdom), which became one of the greatest successes of the most prolific and widely read prose writer of his generation. Traumatized by the bloody pogroms in the Ukraine during his own time, Sholem Asch wrote *Kidush hashem* in the United States in 1919, and this novel was reprinted over and over again in New York and Warsaw. Encountering the opening of *Satan in Goray*, therefore, a reader familiar with Yiddish culture could not avoid comparing the work of the famous author Asch with that of his young and little-known colleague.[3]

It can be assumed that a significant number of *Globus* readers would also have recognized the well-known source from which Bashevis drew his descriptions—Nathan Nata Hannover's chronicle *Yeven Metsulah* (Abyss of Despair), which originally appeared in Hebrew in 1653 and was republished many times both in Hebrew and in a Yiddish translation.[4] *Yeven Metsulah* was for generations perhaps the most popular work on the history of Jews in Eastern Europe. Tragically enough, this chronicle of the most savage of pogroms never lost any of its immediacy: its readers could always compare its descriptions of the terrible events of the past to the atrocities continually perpetrated during their own time. For example, in 1930 a new edition of this book was published in modern Yiddish, and in his introduction the translator, Wolf Latzky-Bertholdi, recalled that he was working on it in 1920 at the very time that a wave of pogroms again swept through the Ukraine. Several years later, *Yeven Metsulah* was published in a critical edition in Yiddish, with a wide-ranging historical introduction by Jacob Shatzky (Vilna, 1938). For the Yiddish reader, consequently, the Chmielnicki massacres of 1648–1649 mentioned in the opening of *Satan in Goray* were not a vague, remote historical event. The writer who was revisiting this topic was perforce obliged to grapple with a living literary tradition and a long-lasting cultural memory.

The opening of *Satan in Goray* could also have aroused the expectation that the reader was about to delve into a historical novel. The genre of historical novels had become widely accepted in contemporary Yiddish literature as a result of writers' conscious efforts to bestow on Yiddish writing the status of a national literature.[5] The typical features of the genre are clear throughout the opening passage: the author makes frequent mention of the names of places, both well known and little known to the contemporary reader. A glance at the index of persecuted communities in the 1938 critical edition of *Yeven Metsulah* reveals that all but one of the towns named in the opening paragraph of *Satan in Goray* are also named in the

Avrom Noversztern

old chronicle. Right from his opening paragraph, therefore, Bashevis is being as factually accurate as possible and is apparently proclaiming that *Satan in Goray* intends to revive the past in all its exact details. However, because the facts in themselves are not strange and distant, readers were made aware that the dry, factual style in which they were imparted was, in itself, an innovation. The style neutralizes the emotional baggage of descriptions that are steeped in the ethos of Jewish martyrology. The same aloof detachment also plays a clear intraliterary role: from the novel's very beginning it is clear that the young author, Yitskhok Bashevis, was consciously dissociating himself from the sentimentality so characteristic of Sholem Asch's popular novel, which was known also to have made considerable use of *Yeven Metsulah* as a source. Sholem Asch took as an epigraph to his novel a passage heavy with emotional overtones:

> *mir shemen zikh ales aroystsushraybn, vos di kozakn un tatarn hobn geton mit di yidn, kedey mir zoln nisht farshemen dem min mentsh, vos iz geboyrn in gots geshtalt (fun an alt seyfer).*
>
> We are ashamed to write down everything that the Cossacks and Tartars did to the Jews, lest we disgrace humankind, who is born in the image of God (from an old chronicle).

His own use of the very same historical reservoir enables the young Bashevis to make an implicit declaration that his treatment of the material is to be different from that of his predecessor. In contrast to Sholem Asch's loaded epigraph, Bashevis himself is not "ashamed," as it were, to tell "everything," including details of the most repulsive atrocities. His novel makes no mention of God's name, nor is there any appeal to heaven. At this stage, since the author does not proclaim open compassion for the feelings of the suffering victims at the most terrible moments of their lives, as would have been expected according to the norms of contemporary Yiddish literature, the reader may wonder whether he is going to display empathy for his characters as his work proceeds. At the start of *Satan in Goray* there is clear reason to suspect that the author intends to keep a considerable distance from the victims of the events he recounts.[6]

Further reading of the same long opening paragraph reveals to the reader the beginning of another qualitative difference between Yitskhok Bashevis and Sholem Asch. The great catastrophe serves the young writer only as a starting point for a work that is apparently going to describe the return to life after the destruction.

History, Messianism, and Apocalypse in Bashevis's Work

The flow of the narrative is not impeded with lengthy descriptions of the massacres, so that the title of the first chapter, "The Year 1648 in Goray," does not describe its contents accurately: this chapter focuses on the survivors returning to their homes and laboring to rebuild their lives. The author speeds things up: he has had enough of chronicle-style sentences describing the catastrophe, because his main interest lies not in the horror but rather in the multifaceted existence that develops in its aftermath. Examining how the narrator connects the catastrophe with the attempt to renew Jewish life after it, we discern subtle signs of widely disparate viewpoints. Each of these viewpoints attempts to answer the question: What actually happened to the Jews of Poland after the Chmielnicki massacres? Clearly the author of *Satan in Goray* does not consider it his responsibility to suggest an orderly historiographical scheme. On the contrary, the differences between various approaches to renewal are deliberately blurred and indistinct.

One viewpoint that accords with the central historical facts as well as the position expressed in the last part of *Yeven Metsulah* is, broadly, that the "golden age" of Polish Jewry ended with the Cossack massacres of 1648–1649. After this butchery, the glorious Jewish community of Poland started to deteriorate. Traces of this attitude in Bashevis's novel are evident in the flashback that the author inserts after the first three chapters describing the consequences of the catastrophe and the beginning of the messianic ferment. The fourth chapter, entitled in the Yiddish original "Goray before the Chmielnicki Massacres" ("The Old Goray and the New" in the English translation), is devoted to a depiction of the *shtetl* as a traditional Jewish community, calmly going about its quotidian business and observances.

A writer like Bashevis is unlikely to paint a picture of a "lost paradise," and it is therefore interesting to examine how he depicts the world that was destroyed. He does not embrace Sholem Asch's characteristic sentimentality; his people do not live idyllic lives. His spotlight does not fall on glory and sanctity: Jews studied Torah—but they also quarreled among themselves about trifles; they married—but they also divorced. And yet two main elements sunder the era before the Cossack massacres from the era that came afterward, and there can be no doubt that these elements attest to a narrator whose philosophy is indubitably conservative: order and authority were the fundamentals of the old world that was destroyed. This loss is the most conspicuous feature of the postdestruction era.

The story opens with the local rabbi, Benish Ashkenazi, returning to Goray after the destruction. However, the respected rabbi, whose authority is preemi-

Avrom Noversztern

nent, does not succeed in restoring the old order, and the first part of *Satan in Goray* ends with his sudden death. It is beyond even his power to check the erosion in the community after the false lure of Sabbateanism (the messianic movement involving the false Messiah, Sabbatai Zevi, which came to a head in 1666). After his death his community is left like a flock without a shepherd. From this historiographical perspective, a process of constantly worsening crisis is described, and the *shtetl* of Goray, the home of a typical traditional Jewish community, steadily deteriorates.

Thus Bashevis opens his novel at the very point at which Sholem Asch concluded his own in *Kidush hashem,* but the tone of the young writer is completely different from that of his celebrated predecessor. Not only does his sober approach reject all dramatization of the horror, but in emphasizing the community crisis that follows he seems to deny his predecessor's optimistic conclusion. Asch's novel ends with a scene that became deeply engraved in the consciousness of Yiddish readers and critics: after the destruction, the hero, Shloymele, the only survivor of his family, reaches the city of Lublin and sees the Jews there trying to rebuild their lives. On his way, he chances to enter an empty shop, and when he asks the salesman what he is doing, because the shop is empty, the answer is, *Ikh farkoyf bitokhn,* "I sell faith."

Any reader who compares the implicit historical patterns that inform these two novels must wonder at a certain paradox. The plot of *Kidush hashem* is constructed around various stages in the fate of a Jewish community, starting with its promising beginnings and ending in its destruction. *Satan in Goray,* in contrast, shapes a completely different historical process. No doubts at all are expressed about the survival of the Jewish community in Goray. In the fourth chapter, which describes its way of life before the Chmielnicki massacres, the community is called "The Old Jewish Town" (E 34). This is a community whose historical roots are planted deep in time and whose initial foundation is beyond the author's purview. Even the horrors that befall it — the Chmielnicki massacres from without and the Sabbatean ferment from within — never succeed in actually undermining its existence. The novel's end closes the circle by showing how, when the crisis is over, life returns to normal. Therefore, although the dispassionate author of *Satan in Goray* has no need of Sholem Asch's lofty language, he reveals himself as one who has faith in the vitality of the traditional community not one whit less sincere than the faith that *Kidush hashem* trumpets so ostentatiously.

History, Messianism, and Apocalypse in Bashevis's Work

The opening of *Satan in Goray* describes a return to life, but the author monitors the process with a sober eye. He does not consider the behavior he describes as spiritual heroism, as unusual deeds worthy of encouragement and esteem, but as additional proof of the blind flow of life. In the long paragraph that opens the novel, there is a clear indication of antiheroic common sense: *ober der shteyger fun der velt iz, dos mit der tsayt kert zikh alts vider um tsum gevezenem,* "But it is the way of the world that in time everything reverts to what it has been." His descriptions of the survivors' readjustment complement the final sentence in Sholem Asch's novel, but in *Satan in Goray* the author delineates the process without the use of flowery expressions steeped in sentimentality. Behind the historical model that describes the growing crisis among Eastern European Jews in the wake of the Chmielnicki massacres a somewhat different perception can be discerned: in all cases and under all circumstances, primeval forces exist that operate blindly to restore life after every catastrophe.

Despite Bashevis's veiled reservations about Sholem Asch, in *Satan in Goray* he undertakes to revivify the literary enterprise begun by Asch. In the introduction to a volume of his writings that includes *Kidush hashem* and *Di kishef-makherin fun kastilien* (The Witch of Castille), Sholem Asch observes: "Two elements of Jewish history were always of interest to me: Jewish martyrdom and the messianic yearning that usually followed it."[7] However, if we disregard for a moment Asch's youthful play *Shabse Tsvi* (Sabbatai Zevi, 1908), it was evident to every Yiddish reader until the early 1930s that Asch did not turn his artistic attention to messianic movements in any of their different variations. In *Satan in Goray* the young Bashevis followed the same historical-spiritual route earlier explored by his older colleague, but devoted his creative energy to that stage in history that his predecessor had not addressed. In making this point, I do not imply any conscious linkage between the two writers. Such a link shows only how strongly the multifaceted connections between the concepts of "destruction" on the one hand and "redemption" on the other resounded in the world of Yiddish literature between the two world wars.

II

With *Satan in Goray* Bashevis joined the impressive list of major twentieth-century Yiddish and Hebrew writers who placed messianism and apocalypse at the center of their work. This list ranges from Khayim Nakhman Bialik and Yitskhok Leybush Peretz to Arn Tsaytlin, a close friend of Bashevis and his senior partner in editing the journal *Globus,* in which *Satan in Goray* was first published. This is the context in which to study Bashevis's first novel. It should also be the starting point for understanding many of its artistic devices, which require some explanatory comments.

The first point to note is that the main vehicle for messianism and apocalypse in Yiddish literature is poetry, as in the work of Kh. N. Bialik, Moyshe-Leyb Halpern, H. Leivick, Arn Leyeles, Perets Markish, and Uri Tzvi Greenberg. Drama was the preferred genre of Arn Tsaytlin and Moyshe Kulbak. Prose was the medium least employed, and Moyshe Kulbak's *Meshiekh ben Efrayim* (1923) is the only significant work in this medium.[8] Bashevis was the first to shape his own version of this widely deployed subject matter in a full-scale prose novel. When we add to this recognition the fact that the subtitle of *Satan in Goray* is *A mayse fun fartsaytns* (A Tale of Bygone Days) — a pointer that further arouses the reader's expectation of engaging with a historical novel — we have the key to understanding Bashevis's unique approach to an often deployed theme that ignited the imagination of his generation. The main question to ask in this context is: What are the manifold relations between messianism and apocalypse as a literary theme on the one hand and the historical perspective used by the narrator of *Satan in Goray* on the other?

Second, there is a clear forward movement in the novel's plot. After the first hesitant steps toward rebuilding a Jewish life after the great catastrophe, the intoxication of messianic delusion arrives to create another kind of chaos, and the novel ultimately ends with a return to the normative ways of Halakhic Judaism. With this ending, a severe judgment is passed on the nature and fate of the messianic movements. They are revealed as transient fantasies, destroying not creating. Received historical perspective on the Sabbatean failure naturally supported the author's stringent and unequivocal verdict at the end of his novel. But an examination of the relative parts played in the novel by "destruction" and "redemption" makes clear that the author does not play fair. Sabbatai Zevi's messianic fervor makes itself felt like a distant echo from afar. By contrast, the author shows the internal destruction in the community from close at hand and describes it with great force. Obviously a lack of balance of this kind reflects both Bashevis's artistic intentions and his fundamental system of values. His intention is to lead the reader totally to discredit the messianic ideal in the end. What literary means could the writer

History, Messianism, and Apocalypse in Bashevis's Work

use to make this point? For example, what is the significance of his choosing to describe the messianic ferment taking place in, of all places, the remote *shtetl* of Goray? The setting he uses is a major artistic device.

Third, an examination of the ways in which *Satan in Goray* describes the messianic ferment is likely to awaken some reservations about the opinions among Bashevis's critics that became accepted at a very early stage.[9] S. Niger, in his short review of the novel's first edition, based his critical approach on the duality between *kedushe,* "holiness," and *tume,* "desecration," and he emphasized this most strongly in writing about the New York edition of 1943.[10] Niger's approach is fairly representative of the kind of Yiddish criticism that loved to point out various moral and ideological values in works under review, but it is doubtful whether such an approach could do full justice to Bashevis's novel. When one examines the novel's progression, what stands out most obviously is the author's tendency to blur the struggle between contradictory spiritual forces that tear Goray apart. It is no coincidence that Rabbi Benish Ashkenazi, the Halakhic and moral authority, leaves the stage at the end of the first part of the novel, so that in its second part, and until the conclusion, Halakhic Judaism has no real representative in the *shtetl* capable of struggling with the Sabbatean illusion. It is only toward the end, when Sabbatai Zevi's conversion to Islam becomes known, that the plot openly becomes an unequivocal struggle. The titles of Chapters 10 and 11 in Part 2, "Di bney-heymonuso un di misnagdim" (The Faithful and Their Opponents) and "Di kedushe un di tume" (The Sacred and the Profane), speak for themselves. But for the rest, the plot of *Satan in Goray* shapes a pattern in which one spiritual power fills the vacuum that remains when the other quits it.

Finally, the messianic fantasy holds four main characters in its power. These characters constitute a triangle of which Rechele and her visions form the apex. At the sides stand the representatives of two opposing forces that together are designed to express the duality of the Sabbatean experience: the introverted asceticism of Itche Mates on the one hand and the extrovert *joie de vivre* of Gedaliya on the other. In addition, there is Mordecai Joseph, a son of the *shtetl* who passes through the most traumatic spiritual changes, moving from being a fervent supporter of the Sabbatean faith to the bitter disillusionment he eventually comes to share with Itche Mates.

It is obvious therefore that to stress only the elements of licentiousness and

Avrom Noversztern

sexual anarchy is not fully to understand the text, since lewd sexuality is portrayed as the attribute of only one main character, Gedaliya. Another narrow approach presents the plot as a struggle between the powers of Good — Halakhic Judaism — and the powers of Evil — the Sabbateans. Supporting this approach is the result of reading the text superficially, latching exclusively onto only a few of the author's remarks that accord with the values of traditional Jewish community. There are indeed intimations of Evil in Gedaliya's behavior, especially in the later stages when he fights the Sabbatean movement's rearguard after its beliefs have come to naught and its leaders have converted to Islam. But that does not fully explain the whole of Gedaliya's complex nature, and these concepts do even less justice to the spiritual world of the other characters. It is clearly difficult to label Mordecai Joseph and Itche Mates as "Evil." The interplay among the characters in the novel is one of the keys to understanding its complexity.

The plot shows the characters fluctuating between a world identified by a spiritual and social order on one side and anarchy and anomie on the other; the normative is pitted against the unusual and the abnormal; sexual licentiousness is counterpoised against abstinence; individual imagination strives toward spirituality while experiencing a sensual love of life that breaks all boundaries. The messianic ferment is presented in *Satan in Goray* as a factor that releases hidden impulses that should not by mere definition be labeled simply as negative. If indeed a guilty verdict is eventually pronounced on all these phenomena, its source is the conservative values that the sophisticated author of *Satan in Goray* fully endorses.

Throughout the entire text of *Satan in Goray,* Bashevis makes a deliberate effort to minimize the ultimate spiritual relevance of messianism and apocalypse as it came to be depicted in contemporary Yiddish literature. Just as the approach to this theme is inseparably connected to the growth of modernism, so Bashevis's first novel reveals the young author's reservations both about messianic and apocalyptic motifs and about modernism. His attitude is definitely (neo)conservative, even though, when it was first translated into English, the critics deemed the novel to be a unique manifestation of modernism.[11]

A comparison with other works in contemporary Yiddish literature proves the antimodernist bias in *Satan in Goray.* The basic feature of the apocalyptic mood in Yiddish literature is its totality: it places the fate of the generation and of all humanity in the balance, for clemency or for doom, for destruction or redemption.

History, Messianism, and Apocalypse in Bashevis's Work

As Reb Shloyme in Peretz's drama *Di goldene keyt* (The Golden Chain) remarks, *tsvishn toyt un lebn / vaklt zikh a velt! / a velt zinkt in more-shkhoyre arayn, a velt!:* "Between death and life / a world oscillates / a world sinks in gloom, / a world!" In the 1920s Uri Tzvi Greenberg expressed this feeling of totality in his Hebrew poetry when he constantly used the phrase "At the crossroads of the world, the crossroads of time." Consequently one of the first signs in *Satan in Goray* of its author's reservations about the apocalyptic atmosphere prevailing in Yiddish literature is the fact that the story is set in the remote *shtetl* of Goray. The setting is not "at the crossroads" but on the margins of the historical highway, a place that may react to earth-shattering events but can never give birth to them. Whoever acts within Goray is in fact acted upon.

Had the borders of the work's entire setting corresponded simply to the borders of the *shtetl,* the novel's author could have situated the apocalyptic experience only within Goray, thereby shaping it into a work of magical realism that obeys only its own internal laws and no other and apparently has nothing in common with the external world. But as the story unfolds, the space in *Satan in Goray* is divided into two entirely different spheres. The "here" is Goray, while Sabbatai Zevi is "over there" in a distant and fantastic region. The history and fate of the false Messiah, his rise and fall, are inserted into the novel as "fantastic rumors" that arrive from afar; there is never a direct connection between the two spheres. Only in one place in the text—when the author describes Rechele's traumatic experiences during her childhood and adolescence in Lublin—does he break through Goray's boundaries. Apart from this one passage, he hardly leaves the town, and the *shtetl* is his entire world.

This highlights one facet of the tension between the categorization of *Satan in Goray* as a historical novel and the messianic and apocalyptic theme that forms its core. The "rumors" that reach Goray seem like the fantasy of an Eastern fable, as indeed they would appear to the residents of a Jewish *shtetl* in Poland in the seventeenth century. They are heard for the first time from a nameless Sephardic rabbinical emissary who arrives in Goray:

> —*nisim venifloes tut der geakhperter in yerusholayim . . . in meyron iz gezen gevorn a fayerdiker zayl fun der erd biz tsum himl . . . es zenen af im oysgekritst geven mit shvartse oysyes der shem-havaye un shabse-tsvi . . . di vayber, vos zogn vor fun tropns boyml, hobn gezen af shabse-tsvis kop di kroyn fun dovid*

Avrom Noversztern

hameylekh . . . a sakh apikorsim leykenen un viln zikh nisht umkern bay der shvel fun genem . . . vey iz tsu zey! . . . zey veln farfaln vern in shol-takhtis! . . . (Y 43)

Wonders and miracles are performed in Jerusalem . . . in Miron a fiery column has been seen stretching from earth to heaven . . . The full name of God and of Sabbatai Zevi were scratched on it in black . . . The women who divine by consulting drops of oil have seen the crown of King David on Sabbatai Zevi's head . . . Many disbelievers deny this and refuse to turn back at the very threshold of Gehenna . . . Woe unto them! They will sink and be lost in the nethermost circle of Sheol! (E 42)

In this report to the people in the synagogue, the fantastical nature of the apocalyptic tidings is recounted with an overlay of certain distinctive linguistic features of *taytsh* (the Yiddish of old prayer books for women), the translation into stylized Yiddish of sources from the holy tongue. These features can be discerned in both vocabulary and syntax. But to the modern reader, this attempt to reconstruct speech from the seventeenth century sounds like an echo from the dim past. It is a style that distances the modern reader from the power of the apocalyptic vision. The narrator's mediation is also patent when he uses a direct scenic technique, as when he describes Rechele's fantasies:

arum ir hot oyfgeblitst a sharlakh royte shayn, vi flamen voltn arumgekhapt dos hoyz, un zi hot farnumen a ruf:
—rekhele, rekhele! . . .
—red, dayn dinstmoyd iz ongebreyt!—hot geentfert rekhele di voylkenerin, vos hot gelernt tanakh un hot gedenkt in der mayse fun dem yungn shmuel un eli dem koyen. (Y 125)

A bright red glow surrounded her; flames seemed to overwhelm the house, and a voice called:
—Rechele, Rechele!
—Speak, for thy servant hearkeneth,—replied Rechele, who had studied the Bible and remembered the tale of the young Samuel and Eli, the priest. (E 153)

Here also the author inserts words and phrases from the language of the *taytsh*. At the same time he reveals his own presence. By reminding the reader of Rechele's literary sources, he shatters the illusion that the reader is witnessing an experience that is wholly personal, original, and direct. The language he chooses to describe her visions shows traces of texts that she has frequently studied. This old-fashioned

History, Messianism, and Apocalypse in Bashevis's Work

style, with its aura of past generations, cannot convey the full strength of a truly new apocalyptic revelation.

The setting of the action is one of the principal means whereby the narrator detaches himself from the focal point of the messianic events. In *Satan in Goray* there is a lively movement of people who arrive from outside the "remote place." The Sephardic rabbinical emissary who spreads the tidings about Sabbatai Zevi to the masses is the first of these. Itche Mates, the bookseller, also arrives in Goray from far away, carrying secret letters from the sect in his bag and imparting the great news in confidence (Part 1, Chapters 9ff.). Gedaliya, too, who in the future will replace him as the leader of the sect in Goray, is not a native of the town, but comes there from neighboring Zamosc (Part 2, Chapter 3). A list of the novel's characters reveals that the number of those who arrive in Goray from elsewhere or who spent a significant portion of their lives outside the confines of that *shtetl* — Rechele, for instance — is greater than the number of its native-born. Even the last wish of the local rabbi, Benish Ashkenazi (at the end of Part 1), is to be carried to Lublin, because he does not want to be buried in Goray, where the forces of Evil now prevail, although he has spent most of his life there.

The narrator himself, however, hardly ever leaves the boundaries of Goray and does not follow his characters on their journeys. This enables the narrator to remain faithful to one of the basic models for construction of space in Yiddish prose. An outsider, swathed in the glory of mystical magic, reaches a Jewish *shtetl* and changes its usual way of life. He becomes a focus for whispering, backbiting, and rumors. Sometimes he projects an erotic energy that adds to the strangeness and the intriguing uncertainty. His identity is never certain and unambiguous. In classic Yiddish prose this model reflected the ideology of the Enlightenment. Conservative Jewish society, the Enlightenment believed, could change, and this change is made possible when the spirits of modernization penetrate it from outside and break through its "fortified wall." In time, the ideological motivation for this usage of setting disappeared, but the complexity of the relationships between those "inside" and those "outside" remains in Yiddish prose. We find it, for instance, in the enigmatic *daytsh* (German) and his seductive daughter in Peretz's poem *Monish* (1888) and in the mysterious magician in his "Der kuntsn-makher" (The Conjurer, 1904); a generation later, in Dovid Bergelson's impressionistic novella *Opgang* (Descent), we witness the "late return" of the "lost son" who returns from a distance to his native soil. This brief list of works, taken from the literary output

Avrom Noversztern

of two generations of Yiddish writers, is evidence of how a single basic model is reworked in different literary contexts.

Not only the "Sabbatean revolution" is imported into Goray from outside. The bitter disappointment it causes takes place far from the narrator's sight. Mordecai Joseph and Itche Mates go out into the "wide world" in order to spread the news about Sabbatai Zevi, the Messiah, and Rechele, his prophetess. There is something grotesque in the fact that one of these two "missionaries" is the lame Mordecai Joseph:

> *ale yorn hot reb mordkhe yoysef der mekubl un bal-muser oysgekukt dem tog, ven es vet im gegebn vern reshus zikh avektsulozn iber der velt.* (Y 129)
>
> All his life Reb Mordecai Joseph, the cabalist and student of mysteries, had anticipated the day when his mission would be to go into the world. (E 158)

The narrator, however, is not present during the longed-for journey, when his characters have fulfilled their desires and left the *shtetl,* charged with the conviction that they are carrying a mission to the wide world. Neither is he present at the decisive moment in their travels when, somewhere in a foreign land, they discover that Sabbatai Zevi has reneged on Judaism, becoming overnight a false Messiah, a deceiver who has shattered the high hopes reposed in him. There is no doubt that for the two emissaries hearing this news is a decisive moment in their lives, collapsing their passionate faith. This dramatic reversal occurs far away in a foreign location, however, so the narrator does not even mention it. He is silent on the subject of those harrowing moments of soul-searching, and his readers are not shown either the inner torments or the fierce disputations of the betrayed. Mordecai Joseph and Itche Mates reappear only at the door of the synagogue in Goray, in mourning and shame, to tell the bitter tidings. Bashevis does not permit any single ideological struggle or value to dominate his work. The narrator's eye is focused as far from the stirring messianic events as from his characters' crucial spiritual transformation.

III

Satan in Goray projects an image of a narrator who is "provincial," whose world and value system are limited to the cultural horizons of an anonymous resident of a remote *shtetl.* The "missing" elements are provided in a manner typical of a traditional closed community—through "rumors." The narrator's personality also

History, Messianism, and Apocalypse in Bashevis's Work

offers an excuse for the little he tells about another, more central area — the inner life of his characters. The narrator treats this in the same way as did the real people of Goray in the seventeenth century: since they were not supposed to be interested in the inner life of other members of their community, the narrator, presenting himself as one of them, could also limit himself to describing his main characters from the outside, without penetrating their inner world.

There is no doubt that the narrator of *Satan in Goray* paid a heavy price for reducing his perspective so drastically. One must assume that acceptance of the Sabbatean faith was accompanied by a dramatic personal inner struggle by every-one who was part of the sect: to leave the ways of Halakha and be swept away into belief in Sabbatai Zevi, to have an hourly expectation that redemption was really imminent only then to experience piercing disillusionment. The arguments between those who believed in Sabbatai Zevi and those who denied that he was the Messiah were acrimonious, and even among his most faithful followers doubts arose after his conversion to Islam. On the other hand, there was the tormented repentance of some of those who had believed in him. All these dramatic and dy-namic changes must have been accompanied by emotional storms and inner crises, within a fairly short space of time. Yet Bashevis chooses to describe this spiritual turbulence from outside, without entering into the inner life of the believers.

The style of *Satan in Goray,* creating as it does the impression that the reader confronts a premodernist narrator, seems to distance the novel from other cen-tral texts with messianic and apocalyptic motifs in Yiddish literature. In most of those texts, the rich inner world lies at their very center, presenting the author as a tormented individual, full of contradictions. *A nakht* (A Night) by Moyshe-Leyb Halpern is perhaps the most outstanding example of this. By comparison with these works, *Satan in Goray* shows unmistakable antimodernist tendencies.

This interconnection between the novel's narrative technique and its histori-cal content offers one of the chief reasons for considering Bashevis's first novel the best in his long literary career. By setting his tale in a distant historical period, he has ready to hand an artistic motivation for the limitations he imposes on his nar-rator. Instead of giving shape to the inner spiritual complexity of his characters, torn between opposing urges, he shapes an array of personages, each of whom is an extreme and distinct expression of one aspect of the messianic ferment. The interrelationships among them create the complex pattern of the novel.

Itche Mates on one side and Gedaliya on the other lie at opposite poles, and the

Avrom Noversztern

clash between them is clear and sharp. It is the conflict of a man of spirit against a man of flesh, of a man of faith utterly unfit for this world against a man of action who can adapt himself to any situation and make the most of it, of a suffering ascetic against a hedonist rake, of an introvert against an extrovert. These contrasts are everywhere present in the text and are evident from the moment each of them first appears. Itche Mates is short and sloppily dressed (Y 64/E 70). Gedaliya is tall and elegant with a respected social position (Y 114/E 139). Yet it is significant that neither of them achieves the status of being the novel's protagonist. This distinction falls to Rechele, the mediator between them. She is the only one whose whole life story, from birth to burial, is recounted by the narrator,[12] and she is also the only one whom the author accompanies outside the boundaries of Goray.

Rechele's place in the narrative is one of the chief features that renders *Satan in Goray* so ambivalent among other thematically related messianic and apocalyptic works in Yiddish literature. Rechele's full inner world, her feelings, and even her position as a woman move her into the role played by the main character in the other works of this corpus. In *Satan in Goray* Rechele is the harbinger of the apocalyptic vision, the role played in Peretz's dramas by Reb Shloyme in *Di goldene keyt* (The Golden Chain) and by the jester in *Bay nakht afn altn mark* (Nighttime in the Old Marketplace) and by the poet himself in such texts as Halpern's *A nakht* and *Di kupe* (The Heap) by Perets Markish. Like them, Rechele enjoys a special status, but for radically different reasons. To those around her she appears an abnormal figure, with unambiguously pathological characteristics. In other works of this genre clear hints are given about the lack of psychological stability of the main characters, all of whom tend toward disturbed mental states bordering on insanity. Yet they are presented positively, in the Romantic spirit that adored characters with pathological sensitivity. In Rechele's case, by contrast, her sickness is imbued with negative, morbid associations, reflecting the norms of the society in which she lives. Her physical and mental illnesses, real and imaginary, are among the facts that the narrator does not question (Y 72/E 82; Y 85/E 101; Y 92/E 108; Y 111/E 134). By refraining from entering Rechele's inner world, contenting himself with external observation only, the narrator adopts the values of her milieu without reservation. Hence the possibility that she might be a "witch" is deduced from the unusual contrasts in her appearance:

> *bay rekhelen zenen di lange flekhtn tselozt, vi bay a makhsheyfe, ful mit federn un shtroy. eyn halb ponem iz royt, vi optselegn, dos andere halbe—blas.* (Y 67)

History, Messianism, and Apocalypse in Bashevis's Work

Rechele's long braids were undone, like a witch's, full of feathers and straw. One half of her face was red, as though she had been lying on it, the other half was white. (E 75)

It is possible to offer many explanations of the origins of Rechele's "pathology,"[13] but these are far less interesting than an understanding of the literary role this pathology plays. This is not a case study of a psychiatric condition dictated by real life, nor an instance of psychological determinism. Rechele's characteristics are the product of a conscious artistic choice that compels us to understand her role in the fabric of the work of art.

More than any other figure in the novel, Rechele is divorced from her surroundings. She is the prisoner of inner mental dictates, of a manic-depressive cycle in which her moods swing from one extreme to the other. At one extreme she has death wishes (Y 74/E 84); at the other she experiences ecstatic messianic visions that are made public. An examination of the developing dynamics in these scenes reveals how a pattern is created that is different from anything known before in messianic and apocalyptic works in Yiddish literature. Those earlier texts construct two basic models of the relations between the visionary individual and those to whom he speaks. The first model can be seen in those works set against the background of traditional Jewish community — Peretz's plays are the outstanding example. These present an unusual, isolated, elevated individual who proclaims his apocalyptic vision to the general public, who are supposed then to flock after him, but who very soon abandon the visionary and return to the traditional way of life they have followed for generations. The second model is shaped within several modernistic Yiddish poems: these concentrate entirely on the individual's psyche, leaving no significant role for the external world.

Satan in Goray creates a third, quite different model. Since the plot of this historical novel is located entirely within traditional Jewish society, in a small *shtetl* in the past, the possibility never occurs to the narrator that the apocalyptic vision will remain the sole domain of the individual. Such a vision must have a public dimension, and the public must be a partner to it. Thus, for example, the chapter *Rekhele zogt nevies,* "Rechele Prophesies" (Part 2, Chapter 8), opens with the inner revelation that Rechele experiences in her own confined quarters. But since the revelation must become public knowledge, the very next morning Rechele walks to the synagogue to announce the news to the community that swarms to hear her. *Satan in Goray* is therefore one of the few messianic and apocalyptic works

43

Avrom Noversztern

in Yiddish literature that envisions the possibility of forging a close connection between the visionary individual and the public that follows him/her.

Bashevis's novel portrays mass scenes of a whole community in the clutch of messianic ecstasy, but the author never shuts his vigilant eye. He observes the exaltation as it dominates everyone, but he gives priority to its dissonant chords. A scene of possessed dancing is obviously the most appropriate at which to fuse contradictory elements into one ecstatic whole, and Bashevis could have obtained a close understanding of its hidden potential from such Yiddish drama and theatrical performances as Y. L. Peretz's *Bay nakht afn altn mark* and S. Anski's *Der dibuk* (The Dybbuk). This is how he depicts the grotesque consequences of the words of the anonymous Sephardic emissary about the approaching redemption:

> *reb mordkhe-yoysef hot a zets getun mit zayn kulye. di tseflikte zhupitse hot zikh tsekneplt, di koltenes zenen zikh tsefloygn, vi in vint, un er hot fun hislayves genumen shlukhtsn mit a khorhldik kol:*
> *—yidn, vos shvaygt ets, yidn! geule boo laoylem!... yeshue boo laoylem!...*
> *er hot mit der linker hant a shlog getun in kop arayn, un mit eyn mol genumen tantsn. dos shvere dembene krikholts untern orem hot geklapt ibern bret vi in a poyk, di farkriplte fis, in groyse shtivl, hobn zikh vi farflokhtn, un er hot kaykhndik gerufn on oyfher an eyn un eyntsik vort, vos keyner hot nisht farshtanen.* (Y 43–44)

Reb Mordecai Joseph banged the table with his crutch. His stained coat came unbuttoned, his unkempt locks flew about wildly, and he began in his passion to stutter and gasp.

—Jews, why are you silent? Redemption hath come to the world! . . . Salvation hath come to the world!

He beat his forehead with his left hand and all at once began to dance. His oaken crutch drummed, his large foot dangled and, gasping, he cried one and the same phrase over and over again, a phrase which no one was able to make out. (E 43)

The contrasting elements in this presentation are designed to produce a deliberate disharmony. The narrator emphasizes the fact that this ecstatic mystical call emerges from the body of a disabled and sick man, and his description strongly suggests that this is not simply physical disability. Mordecai Joseph's explicit summons touches the innermost heart of Jewish belief, but the author adds secondary "tasteless" details of his sloppy clothes and his demeanor that totally lack any glamour. This scene recalls the impressive appearance of Reb Shloyme in the first act of *Di goldene keyt,* but this implicit comparison also reminds us that Mordecai

History, Messianism, and Apocalypse in Bashevis's Work

Joseph's literary lineage is closer to Mendele Moykher Sforim's Fishke the Lame than to Peretz's lofty Hasidic rabbi. There is no beauty of any kind in Bashevis's scene: this is not a dance of rapture but an accumulation of reckless and ridiculous movements. It is not a song but a squawk—no musical instrument sounds, only crutches that drum on the floor. To crown it all, this event, at once ecstatic and grotesque, passes in a moment, terminating when Mordecai Joseph faints—a mundane sign of his weakness and his sickliness.

This scene is the first time the Sabbatean belief erupting in the *shtetl* is described, and at this stage it is not at all clear that the community is going to embrace the faith in the new Messiah. The only word that Mordecai Joseph repeats over and over again is incomprehensible to those around him, and they do not join him in his grotesque dance. This is made more evident in the novel's next description of an ecstatic dance. This time it is part of a much more usual event—the betrothal party of Rechele and Itche Mates:

> *reb itshe-mates merkt gornisht, tantst vayter mit der fatsheyle in der hant, plontert mit di fis vi in shikres. dos ponem iz tseglit fun hislayves, dos zaydene malbesh iz fitsh-nas; shnirelekh shveys rinen fun der bord, glitshn zikh iber dem ofenen horikn harts. der gartl iz fun im aropgefaln, eyn pole shlept zikh nokh afn fargosenem dil, der kop iz farrisn aroyf, glaykh er volt di gantse tsayt epes gezen ibern niderikn farroykhertn balkn. reb mordkhe-yoysef kon zikh mer nisht aynhaltn, heybt on shver tsu krekhtsn, git a zets mit zayn kulye un nemt mit eyn mol gikh hotsken, shlukhtsn un yomern:*
> *—yidn, lomir tantsn!... lomir nisht farshpetikn! di gantse pamalye-shel-mayle vart af undz!...* (Y 85–86)

Reb Itche Mates noticed nothing; the kerchief still in his hand he danced on, his feet stumbled over each other like a drunken man's. His face glowed with mystic enthusiasm, his silk coat was wringing wet; beads of sweat ran down his beard and glided over his open chest. His sash had fallen off, one of his kaftan tails trailed on the drenched floor, his head was turned up and tilted, as though he constantly stared at something beyond the ceiling. Unable to restrain himself any longer, Reb Mordecai Joseph groaned, pounded the floor with his crutch, and suddenly began to hop about, sobbing and yammering:
—Dance, men! Let's not delay! The divine company await us! (E 101–102)

During the dance, Itche Mates the Sabbatean removes himself from the real world. The narrator by contrast insists on piling on ever more physical and sensory details. The extreme tangibility of his descriptions constitutes a counterweight

Avrom Noversztern

to the ephemeral messianic vision. While the character he is describing "noticed nothing," the narrator seems to notice everything, down to the tiniest concrete detail. As is the way with mystics, Itche Mates's vision floats and ascends on a vertical axis, but the author makes sure to remind us, with a grain of cynicism, about the low, sooty ceiling that stops its progress. Itche Mates is also shown to be on the verge of drunkenness. Unlike his single word in the previous scene, Mordecai Joseph's cry here has a clearly mystical character. For him, the dance itself is supposed to connect the lower and the higher realms, even though his disconnected words do not answer the question as to whether this ecstatic dance will bring redemption nearer or serve as a sign that it is coming. Mordecai Joseph's words erupt with enormous emotional energy, but they are not heard as a clear and certain call. They come out with "sobbing and yammering."

At the end of this episode, the reader has probably "forgotten" that the setting is an engagement party, just as the bridegroom himself has "forgotten" the bride, Rechele. She is not a part of the ecstatic scene at all. On the contrary, she is having one of the attacks caused by her illness:

> eyder nokh me loyft tsu tsu ir, falt zi avek hintervaylekhts un nemt aroyslozn opgehakte kvitshn, vi shlukertsn. di ofene oygn vern fargleyzt un ful mit vaysl. hent un fis krimen zikh oys un a shoym nemt ir loyfn fun oysgedreytn moyl, vi bay a nikhpenitse. (Y 85)

> Before anyone could reach her, she had fallen and she lay choking with sobs. Her eyes glazed, her arms and legs contorted, foam ran from her twisted mouth. She shuddered, twisted, and a vapor rose from her as from an epileptic. (E 101)

A seizure on the one side and mystic exaltation on the other join hands at an event that is described in all its grotesque weirdness. Moreover, when the vision breaks from the individual into the public sphere, not everyone wants to lay claim to it. In this scene, no sober opponent's voice is heard pouring doubt on the validity of the messianic fever. The narrator reserves that role strictly for himself: only his vigilant eyes are permitted to discern all the possible manifestations of disharmony between body and soul.

The rhetorical stratagems used to characterize Rechele are brought to a climax in the novel's last two chapters, written in the style of a chapbook that tells the story of the exorcism of a dybbuk. In these two chapters, the voice that is heard is different from the one heard throughout the rest of the text. Clearly it is meant

History, Messianism, and Apocalypse in Bashevis's Work

to read like the Yiddish translation of a Hebrew chapbook written to teach a cautionary moral lesson. Bashevis transfers to the voice of piety the responsibility for describing Rechele's fate. The tendency of the narrator of *Satan in Goray* to limit his information on Rechele to externals is even more pronounced when the narration is handed over to the pious author of the putative chapbook. Obviously it is out of the question for a pious Jewish man to penetrate a woman's inner world, but this is the least of it. Her personality is erased entirely when the dybbuk enters her:

> *den ir geshtalt iz geven graylekh farendert un ir ponem iz geven vi krayd un di leftsn oysgekrimt vi fun farkhapenish loy oleynu un di aplen fun ire oygn zenen geven ibergekert sheloy-kederekh-hateve: un dos kol iz nisht geven ir kol: den ir kol iz geven dos kol fun an ishe un der dibek hot gerufn mit dem kol fun a mantsbil un mit fil geveyn un yomernish dos a dershrekenish hot arumgekhapt un di hertser zenen tsegangen un di kniyen hobn geshtroykhlt.* (Y 175–176)

> For her shape was completely changed and her face was as chalk and her lips were twisted as with a seizure (God save us) and the pupils of her eyes were turned back after an unnatural fashion: And the voice that cried from her was not her voice: For her voice was a woman's voice and the dybbuk cried with the voice of a man with such weeping and wailing that terror seized all that were there and their hearts dissolved with fear and their knees trembled. (E 222)

The traditional chapbook solves in its own way the duality of body and soul in the characterization of Rechele. The woman's true voice falls silent and is no longer heard in public. For the author of the chapbook, Rechele is nothing more than a woman's body hosting a dybbuk.

From the pious storyteller's perspective, Rechele cannot possibly be considered a "prophetess." The core of his tale is the expulsion of the dybbuk, for which Rechele pays with her life. But at this point even Rechele's status as a main character in Bashevis's stylized version of a chapbook is called into question. Instead the plot of the chapbook starts and ends with Gedaliya. The ending is also the only part of the novel that offers some deviation from what is normally expected from a chapbook of this type:

> *un gedalye hot zikh loy-oleynu geshmadt un iz gevorn bay di akum a bishof un a tsoyrer hayehudim: un andere hobn gezogt dos gedalye iz geven der samekh-mem un ale zayne maysim zenen geven eytl farblendenish.* (Y 189)

47

And Gedaliya became an apostate (God save us) and rose to the position of a bishop among the idolaters and a troubler of Jews. And some folk say that Gedaliya was none other than Samael himself and that all his deeds were naught but seduction. (E 238)

The path of sin and punishment is shown to be different for men and for women: where there is death for the woman, the man lives on as a highly successful apostate.

This ending is completely at variance from that in the text that probably served Bashevis as a source. In his book *Bilder fun der yidisher literaturgeshikhte* (Images from Jewish Literary History; Vilna, 1928), Max Weinreich analyzed an anonymous chapbook from the seventeenth century, and several details in the last chapters of *Satan in Goray* are similar to those described by Weinreich.[14] But the seventeenth-century booklet ends with the dybbuk being expelled from the woman's body and her eventual marriage—a truly "happy ending." Bashevis chooses a conclusion that is fundamentally pessimistic: death for one and conversion to Christianity for the other. The traditional Jewish community is restored: the language and values of the stylized chapbook that ends *Satan in Goray* point unequivocally in that direction. But not all those who were swept away in the false Sabbatean ecstasy return to the bosom of the community. There is indeed a hidden tension in the ending of Bashevis's novel. The language could not be more pious, but the novel's main characters do not have fates that conform comfortably to the accepted pious norm.

When the Sabbatean delirium has died out, traditional forces in the Jewish community have gained the upper hand, but their victory is by no means total. The fading of the messianic delusion is described in the last chapters of *Satan in Goray* in many subtle subtextual ways. The narrator of the chapbook, for instance, uses the radical technique of silence. He passes cursorily over the whole dramatic process of the Sabbatean ferment in Goray, reserving his main focus for the dybbuk that entered Rechele's body as a punishment for her sins and the means of expelling it. Such a chapbook, after all, is supposed to be written within the framework of traditional Jewish society and to justify Orthodox Judaism's conceptions of reward and punishment both in this world and in the world to come. From this perspective, the messianic and apocalyptic episode plays no meaningful role. Sabbateanism is not mentioned as being the explicit sin of Rechele and Gedaliya; nor is the possibility even considered that the story of Sabbatai Zevi, the false Messiah, might serve as an example and a warning for generations to come. Traditional

48

Jewish belief in the coming of the Messiah is mentioned only in the colophon, together with a dire warning not to anticipate or attempt to hasten his coming:

un fun der mayse kon men oplernen: dos got borekh-hu zol keyner dertsernen:
der toyt vet dan vern farmitn: un lilis vet vern farshnitn: tsum goles vet kumen
an end: un der sotn vet vern farlendt:
un yankev vet oyfrikhtn zayn getselt:
un dos likht fun der shkhine
mekht onfiln gor di velt.
omeyn selah (Y 189)

And from this tale one may derive the following moral lesson: Let no one provoke God, Blessed be He, to anger: Death will then be averted: And Lilith will be clean cut off: An end will come of the Exile: And Satan will be annihilated:
And Jacob will restore his tents:
And the light of the Divine Presence
will have the power to radiate through the world.
Amen. Selah. (E 239; the last four lines, which are not included in the English translation, were translated by Joseph Sherman)

The supposed author of this chapbook cannot do other than end his story with formulaic clichés. The circle is, to some extent, closed. The conventional phrases that conclude *Satan in Goray* include a hope for the coming of the Messiah and thus offer a conclusion perfectly commensurate with the world of traditional Jewish values and an appropriate rounding off of the central theme of the whole work. But it is worded without any power or creative imagination. The fire of messianic vision is completely extinguished at the end of *Satan in Goray.*

IV

If *Satan in Goray,* which was written before the Holocaust, expressed such strong reservations about the messianic and apocalyptic fervor that permeated substantial parts of contemporary Yiddish literature, it could have been expected that Bashevis would maintain this position after the Holocaust. Evidence for this can be found in his short story "Mayse tishevits" (1959), translated into English as "The Last Demon," [15] which has a rather problematic status.

From the point of view of theme, this story cannot by any means be considered as a representative text, because there are not many like it in the extensive corpus of Bashevis's prose. Certainly this story, written in the form of a demon's mono-

49

logue, is not "representative" in the general context of post-Holocaust Yiddish prose, which refrained from creating such characters. But from its very beginning, this story touches on basic problems of contemporary Yiddish literature. One of the covert tensions in "Mayse tishevits" is the strain between the messianic yearning that is the substructure of the plot and the apocalyptic atmosphere that envelops the very act of the monologue's utterance. It is hardly surprising that a writer should evoke an apocalyptic atmosphere at the end of the 1950s, a decade after the Holocaust and during the era of the atom bomb. The crucial question, however, is how this atmosphere is to be deployed by Bashevis, a writer who throughout his entire creative life made use of apocalypse only in order to discredit it.

> *ikh a shed, zog eydes, az s'zenen mer nishto keyn sheydim. tsu vos sheydim, ven der mentsh aleyn iz itst a shed? tsu vos onredn tsu shlekhts ven der ongeredter iz zay vi greyt? ikh bin efsher der letster tsvishn di nisht-gute, ikh halt mikh uf af a boydem in tishevits, tsi kheyune fun a mayse-bikhl af yidish-taytsh vos hot zikh do farvalgert fun farn khurbm. di mayse aleyn iz kubebe mit katshke-milkh, ober yidishe oysyes hobn a haft.* (Y 12)

> I, a demon, bear witness that there are no more demons left. Why demons, when man himself is a demon? Why persuade to evil someone who is already convinced? I am the last of the persuaders. I board in an attic in Tishevits and draw my sustenance from a Yiddish storybook, a leftover from the days before the great catastrophe. The stories in the book are pablum and duck milk, but the Hebrew letters have a weight of their own. (E 179)

The demon who introduces himself at the opening of this story—the speaker of this post-Holocaust monologue—is a stark metonym for the problematic status of the Yiddish writer.[16] They both see themselves as the last remnant of a world that is no more, continuing to exist under radically altered circumstances in a universe that for them has become an apocalyptic wilderness. Totally isolated in his attic, the demon is the last representative of a race of "Jewish demons." In the past, in a time before the Holocaust, he had a brother demon who was his companion in the attic, a harmless joker like himself. But he disappeared without leaving any trace, and the speaker in "Mayse tishevits" does not even bother to tell what happened to him. Like a Yiddish author who writes literature that draws its inspiration from memories of the past, from memories, this narrator-demon draws his sustenance not from "life" but from "literature," from novels that have been miraculously preserved from the pre-Holocaust era. Therefore he has no need to leave the narrow confines of the attic. He is satisfied as long as he has a *mayse-bikhl af yidish-taytsh,*

History, Messianism, and Apocalypse in Bashevis's Work

a Yiddish chapbook. The literary text has become his entire world. The physical doorway would only lead him outside into the streets of a *shtetl* that is no longer home to Jews, an empty world for him.

The demon, like the Yiddish writer after the Holocaust, has been forced to relinquish the essence of his nature and the mission on which that existence is predicated. He has no desire whatever to tempt or to influence anyone, because his target audience no longer exists. Exactly like the post-Holocaust Yiddish writer, the demon weaves into his monologue another clearly apocalyptic motif—the sense of arrested time: "I speak in the present tense as for me time stands still" (E 179). As with Y. L. Peretz in *Bay nakht afn altn mark,* time no longer flows, but for Bashevis's demon the apocalyptic significance of his circumstances is far more extreme than that presented in Peretz's seminal play. Both these texts center on the unrestrained rule of impurity, but the impurity in "Mayse tishevits" prevails over a world that, in the view of the monologist, is completely empty. Peretz raises the dead at night, in the market square, and breathes life into them, even if only for a moment. But the demon in the attic receives no sign at all of any life around him.

What is the secret of the vitality of the demon who is nourished by "a Yiddish chapbook"? Here, once again, Bashevis settles accounts with all modern Jewish literature. His fundamental opinion, that Yiddish literature embodies the internal contradictions of Jewish secularism, was widely known at the time his story appeared, perhaps so well known as to be annoying, and it was articulated in innumerable articles he published. It was neither original nor particularly profound, since it was in harmony with the winds of "repentance" that blew from the 1930s onward among the main representatives of the Yiddish intelligentsia. But the monologist in "Mayse tishevits" provides a new face and a new sweep of vision for the banal arguments repeated in Bashevis's articles. Opinions that had been previously voiced by a modern Yiddish writer are now expressed by a Yiddish-speaking demon, and there is a seeming paradox in the fact that it is actually he, a demon, who has adopted the basic terminology of traditional Judaism:

> *kh'leyen dem koydervelsh fun bukh. s'shraybekhts iz fun undzer nusekh: kugl mit khazer-shmalts, shmad geviklt in yire der muser-haskl iz: lehadam. ober di oysyes zenem fort yidishe. dem alef-beys hobn zey nisht gekont tsetrentslen. derfun zeyg ikh. derin tu ikh mikh klamern.* (Y 21–22)

I keep on reading gibberish. The style of the book is in our manner: Sabbath pudding cooked in pig's fat: blasphemy rolled in piety. The moral of

Avrom Noversztern

the book is: neither judge nor judgement. But nevertheless the letters are Jewish. The alphabet they could not squander. I suck on the letters and feed myself. (E 186)

In contrast to the attitudes of many Yiddish writers, who viewed themselves as legitimate heirs of traditional Judaism and even ascribed an aura of sanctity to the Yiddish language itself, a diametrically opposed attitude is trenchantly displayed here. The original thrust of Yiddish as the vehicle for a modern literature was opposed to traditional Jewish values. Hence when Yiddish authors tried to give their writings a more "Jewish" character, they produced a profane combination, a "Sabbath pudding cooked in pig's fat," forbidden on the spiritual table of devout Jews. The content of modern Yiddish literature is unquestionably beyond the pale of Jewish tradition. Nevertheless, the literature is written in Hebrew letters. These letters are the last remnant of holiness to survive in the demon's world after the Holocaust. As the last representative of the forces of *klippah* (Evil), the demon-narrator of this monologue knows that his very existence in this world is dependent on those sparks of sanctity that are concealed in the letters of the Hebrew alphabet.

One facet of the charm of "Mayse tishevits" is the possibility of discovering in it different aspects of the analogy between the devil and the post-Holocaust Yiddish writer. For instance, in contrast to a writer, who should continue to *create* — otherwise he ceases to be a writer — the demon *consumes* the holy letters and in so doing becomes the manifest representative of the forces of destruction and oblivion. Then, at the conclusion of the story, other facets are revealed: the persona who throughout the text has been a kind of folksy storyteller is in the end transformed into a popular poet, a versifier: "I count the words, make rhymes and tortuously interpret and reinterpret each dot" (E 186). The trauma of the Holocaust affects everyone, overtly or covertly. After such destruction there is apparently no possibility of creating original Yiddish literature, so the demon cannot be expected to compose innovative poetry. Hence his rhymes are a grotesque and bitter metamorphosis of a well-known children's ditty whose aim was to assist pupils to remember the names of the Hebrew letters and the order of the alphabet. The demon is fully aware of the limited significance of his work and openly admits it; in his view he produces only rhymes and nothing more. But the topsy-turvy transformation of the familiar rhymes with which he concludes "Mayse tishevits" is much more than this. Not only is the threatening mood they evoke very distant from their origi-

History, Messianism, and Apocalypse in Bashevis's Work

nal spirit,[17] but they connect beginnings with endings, memory with forgetfulness, and they refer not to children in a *kheyder* but to adult Jews in the post-Holocaust world: "A Jew forgets . . ." In this line, in the middle of the alphabet, the rhymes end. Where there is forgetfulness, there is no possibility of creativity of any kind, not even on the smallest scale.

The demon's severe judgment given at the beginning of "Mayse tishevits" against the spiritual significance of modern Jewish literature remains, but his terms are somewhat softened in the concluding paragraph of the story. They point not only to modern Jewish literature, but also to a spiritual entity with a much wider validity, because the concept *a yidish vort* (the Jewish word) implies both writing and speech, the holy tongue as well as Yiddish:

> *yo, vi lang z'iz do a yidish vort, hob ikh an onhaltenish. vi lang di milbn hobn nisht ufgegesn s'letste bletl, iz nokn do mit vos zikh tsu shpiln. vos s'vet zayn shpeter, vil ikn farn moyl nisht brengen.*
> *On a yidish oys—*
> *Iz a shed a yid—oys . . .* (Y 22)

> Yes, as long as a single volume remains, I have something to sustain me. As long as the moths have not destroyed the last page, there is something to play with. What will happen when the last letter is no more, I'd rather not bring to my lips.
> When the last [Hebrew] letter is gone,
> I, the last [Jewish] demon, am done. (E 187)

In the stark context of the immediate post-Holocaust apocalyptic reality, the ending of "Mayse tishevits" is therefore far removed from the lofty words uttered during those years in Yiddishist circles about the "eternality" of Yiddish literature even after the Jewish world, the soil in which it grew, had been annihilated. But on the other hand it does not take the stance that everything is "vanity of vanities." A total void is expected, and accordingly the story ends with two lines of double negation. *Oys* (no more) is the very last word of the story, but the demon refuses to tackle all its implications. He refuses to adopt a stance of total nihilistic negation. For the moment, he implies, it is better to cling to the word's vital force.

In the context of this argument the importance of "Mayse tishevits" is that it does not conclude on the clear apocalyptic note that is sounded in the story's outer frame. Its plot is woven from various strands, taken both from messianic motifs in modern Yiddish literature and from traditional Jewish concepts and beliefs. The demon tells how he was sent on his mission, to lead the Jews in the *shtetl* of Tishevits astray, in the "good old days" before the Holocaust. First he meets with the local demon and, being newly arrived from the wide world, he reports its latest news to his older colleague who had been sitting idly in the Tishevits attic for an unendurably long time. He tells him that demons themselves are now unemployed, because modern Jewish writers, the heirs of the Haskala, have themselves become emissaries of Evil and have achieved considerable success in diverting masses of the Jewish people from the straight and narrow. The demon shows himself knowledgeable about the spiritual roots of modern Jewish literature, so attention should be paid to his single characterization of its spiritual world:

> —haskole. in di tsvey hundert yor vos du sekest do hot der yeytser-hore far-kokht a frishe kashe. s'zenen ufgekumen shrayber bay yidn, af loshn-koydesh, af ivre-taytsh, un zey hobn ibergenumen undzer melokhe. mir darfn zikh raysn dem haldz mit yedn khamereyzl bazunder, ober yene drukn zeyere shmontses in a sakh kopyes un tseshikn bekhol-tfutses-Yisroel. zey kenen ale undzere shtik: shpot iz shpot un frumkeyt iz frumkeyt. zenen metaher dem sheretsh bekan-teamim. viln nisht andersh nor oysleyzn di velt. (Y 14)

> —Enlightenment! In the two hundred years you've been sitting on your tail here, Satan has cooked up a new dish of kasha. The Jews have now developed writers, Hebrew ones, Yiddish ones, and they have taken over our trade. We grow hoarse talking to every adolescent, but they print their kitsch by the thousands and distribute it to Jews everywhere. They know all our tricks — mockery, piety. They have a hundred reasons why a rat must be kosher. All they want to do is to redeem the world. (E 180–181)

As this demon presents it, the great sin of modern Jewish literature is as clear as daylight: it inflames messianic yearnings. When the demon tries to tempt the town's rabbi away from the path of righteousness, he uses the same approach. He harps on the sense of pride that the rabbi probably carries deep in his heart, urging him to consider the possibility that perhaps he himself will be the one to bring the Messiah:

> m'hot af dir faribl in der pamalye-shel-mayle. az me git pleytses, darf men trogn. onev gramt zikh mit zonev. zey visn az reb avrom-zalmen iz geven meshiekh ben yoysef un du bist ongebreyt aroptsubrengen meshiekh ben dovid. ober shlof nisht. gurt on di lendn. di velt zinkt in mem-tes sharey-tume. ober du bist boykea-rekiim. in ale heykholes hert men eyn geshrey: der tishevitser! (Y 18)

The higher-ups are annoyed with you. Broad shoulders must bear their share of the load. To put it in rhyme: the humble can stumble. Hearken to this: Abraham Zalman was the Messiah, son of Joseph, and you are or-dained to prepare the way for the Messiah, son of David, but stop sleeping. Get ready for battle. The world sinks to the forty-ninth gate of uncleanli-ness, but you have broken through to the seventh firmament. Only one cry is heard in the mansions, the man from Tishevits! (E 184)

The rabbi is almost led astray by the demon's tempting words; they are imbued with all the traditional values of the pious Jewish world. But at the last minute he realizes that behind these seductive words the devil is hiding, and he manages to resist the temptation. This victory of the rabbi in "Mayse tishevits" thus gives Bashevis's story an ending contrary to the conclusion of the well-known tale of Joseph della Reina, who failed to resist the temptation of pride, also mentioned in the demon's monologue.

This also explains why the *shtetl* of Tishevits was chosen out of hundreds of similar places scattered throughout Poland: there could not be a better setting for a temptation to hasten the coming of the Messiah. In the actual *shtetl* of Tishevits there was indeed a local tradition that it was the burial place of Abraham Zalman, the Messiah ben Joseph, who was killed during the Chmielnicki massacres of 1648–1649.[18] This tradition existed in Tishevits until the time of the Holocaust, and the local inhabitants could point out the grave of Reb Abraham Zalman. Not only did Bashevis know this tradition at first hand, having spent his childhood nearby, but he could also appreciate its artistic potential. He touched on it in one of the open-ing chapters of *Satan in Goray* (Y 29/E 22), and in an article he wrote in 1943 he offered it as an example of the folk sources Yiddish writers need to give substance to their work.[19] In this way the demon who comes to tempt the local rabbi em-ploys folklore surrounding the Messiah ben Joseph that connects redemption with death. In a post-Holocaust story, this connection cannot be fortuitous.

Not merely the long-held local tradition is incorporated into the text of this story in order to lend more substance to the fabric of its messianic motifs. The plot of "Mayse tishevits" stands in direct antithesis to one of modern Yiddish litera-ture's most seminal texts, Y. L. Peretz's poem *Monish* (1888), which was the first to insert messianic motifs into a tale of temptation and falling into sin. Peretz's main character is a young prodigy, not the rabbi of a small town, but there is a distinct similarity in their status. The local elders are certain that Monish will be a Torah sage. His name even reaches Mount Ararat, where Asmodeus, king of demons, re-sides. One of his subordinates comes to inform Asmodeus that this young man,

Avrom Noversztern

who is growing up in a remote *shtetl*, is likely in the course of time to become the Messiah and, if that should happen, Asmodeus will reign no more. A plan to tempt Monish is then devised, and, in the end, all hopes pinned to the young prodigy are indeed dashed. An alien, foreign character arrives in the *shtetl* from elsewhere—a *daytsh*, an enlightened Jew, perhaps even a non-Jewish German; the term itself is ambivalent. He is a merchant from Danzig who brings with him his lovely daughter, ambivalently named Marie, and she entraps Monish in the mesh of sin. Peretz's poem ends with the unequivocal triumph of the king of demons, celebrating his victory at a mass banquet with his entourage.

In Peretz's *Monish,* published at the dawn of modern Yiddish literature, the messianic motif plays only a secondary role. It is possible to see in the messianic hopes that are pinned on the central character of the poem the kind of traditional, idiomatic phrases of exaggerated appreciation for a young and learned student. Bashevis, who wrote "Mayse tishevits" from the perspective of three literary generations later, deploys these materials quite differently. He could show that messianic pretentiousness indeed lay at the heart of modern Yiddish literature and that its writers could only be regarded as the devil's loyal servants.

Bashevis's story builds on the same literary model as Peretz's poem, only to reverse it completely at the end. In Bashevis's story the demon also arrives from far away. Tension is engendered as well between the "wide world" and the *shtetl*—the same tension that is generated on several different levels in *Satan in Goray.* The demon who has just arrived in Tishevits can tell his old friend of the sinful doings in the depraved cities of Odessa and Lublin, the provincial capital city nearest to the remote *shtetl* where Jews, too, do not resist temptation. Meanwhile Tishevits remains in many respects still an oasis of traditional observance, faithfully preserving its Jewish way of life. But from there Bashevis's story develops in entirely the opposite direction from Peretz's poem. Unlike many other instances in Bashevis's work, the center of this text's conflict is assigned to an individual who resists temptation, even when that temptation seems to be clothed in traditional Jewish garb. The demon's attempt to lead the local rabbi astray makes use of many Jewish apocalyptic symbols, stressing how time presses:

> —alts hengt af mishkoyles, tishevitser! du konst ibervegn di vogshol.
> —vos zol ikh ton?
> —horkh mikh, alts vos ikh vel dikh heysn. afile ven kh'zol dir bafeln tsu zayn an oyver al das, tu mayn gebot.

History, Messianism, and Apocalypse in Bashevis's Work

—ver bistu? vos iz dayn nomen?—elyohu hatishbi. kh'halt greyt dem shoyfer
shel meshiekh. fun dir, tishevitser, hengt op tsi s'zol kumen di geule, oder me
zol zinken in khoyshekh shel mitsraym nokh tarpat alofim yor. (Y 19)

—Everything hangs in the balance, man of Tishevits; you can tip the scales.
—What should I do?
—Mark well all that I tell you. Even if I command you to break the law, do
as I bid.
—Who are you? What is your name?
—Elijah the Tishbite. I have the ram's horn of the Messiah ready. Whether
the redemption comes, or we wander in the darkness of Egypt another 2,689
years is up to you. (E 184)

A dramatic atmosphere, charged and waiting for decisive cosmic events, a great
struggle between the forces of Good and Evil—all the motifs that characterize
apocalyptic works in Yiddish literature appear in this demon's words of temptation, including the magnification of one individual's strength to supernatural dimensions. There is no doubt that the Tishevits rabbi is indeed one of the outstanding representatives of the anti-Promethean stance that is a feature of all Bashevis's
works, a point made by the Yiddish critic Shloyme Bikl, and one that Irving Howe
loved to quote.[20] For a moment the rabbi almost succumbs to the words of temptation, but in the end his desire to carry on studying Torah wins out, and he does
not see any need or sense any compulsion to engage in a messianic endeavor.

The reader of "Mayse tishevits" feels that there are hidden connections between
the plot's apocalyptic motifs, the unusual fact that, unlike those in Bashevis's other
stories, the hero here resists temptation, and the text's setting in a post-Holocaust
context. In his monologue, the demon is very much aware of the special circumstances in which he is speaking:

s'iz oys yeytser-hore, oys yeytser-tov. oys avoynes, oys nisyoynes. dos dor iz
shoyn zibn mol kule-khayev, nor meshiekh kumt nisht. tsu vemen zol er ku-
men? az meshiekh iz nisht gekumen tsu yidn, zenen yidn avek tsu meshiekhn.
vey, me darf mer nisht keyn sheydim! me hot undz oykh fartilikt. ikh bin ge-
blibn eyner, a polet. kh'meg shoyn geyn vu kh'vil, nor tsu vemen zol geyn a
shed fun mayn sgal? tsu di rotskhim? . . . (Y 21)

There is no longer an Angel of Good or an Angel of Evil. No more sins, no
more temptations! The generation is already guilty seven times over, but
Messiah does not come. To whom should he come? Messiah did not come
for the Jews, so the Jews went to Messiah. There is no further need for demons. We have also been annihilated. I am the last, a refugee. I can go any-

where I please, but where should a demon like me go? To the murderers? (E 186)

Although Bashevis, as is well known, deliberately did not write directly about the Holocaust itself, it nevertheless permeated many of his writings, including "Mayse tishevits." In this monologue story Bashevis gives a subtle answer to Theodor Adorno's well-known assertion; in Bashevis's opinion it is certainly possible to write literature after Auschwitz—but that literature will be like a demon's monologue. Precisely because of that intimate knowledge of the apocalyptic tradition in modern Yiddish literature against which he struggled for many years, Bashevis was able to view the Holocaust in a different way from writers in other literatures. He regarded the Holocaust in no way as an apocalyptic event, but as an entirely human occurrence, with its roots deep in history. The rabbi from Tishevits who was murdered to sanctify the Holy Name is certainly not a modern reincarnation of the Messiah ben Joseph.

"Mayse tishevits" takes a most original stance at the crossroads of history, messianism, and apocalypse. In the eyes of a Yiddish writer, the Holocaust brought to a tragic end a period of increased apocalyptic expectation articulated in Yiddish literature. In *Monish* Peretz showed with ironic sobriety how erotic desires aroused in his hero thwart traditional messianic expectations. Within eighty years the circle was closed. Yitskhok Bashevis shows in "Mayse tishevits" that modern history, in the form of the Holocaust, is what thwarts, with cruel finality, the messianic and apocalyptic expectations of his time. All that remains for the Yiddish author is words—at least for the time being.

Notes

1. In this case, the first version has been quoted. All subsequent quotations are from the second edition (New York: Farlag Matones, 1943; reprinted Jerusalem: Hebrew University Press, 1972). The first edition came out in Warsaw (PEN-Klub, 1935), and in preparing it Bashevis did some slight stylistic editing of the text that does not change the plot, nor add to or detract from any episodes. The main aim of the changes was to bring the text closer to the style of Old Yiddish. Other changes, also minor, were introduced for the New York edition. In the original publication in *Globus*, the chapters did not have titles; these were added in the Warsaw edition.

The English text is taken from *Satan in Goray* (New York: Noonday Press, 1955), translated by Jacob Sloan. In this instance, as well as in some others, a few changes have been

History, Messianism, and Apocalypse in Bashevis's Work

made to conform more closely with the original version. A new English translation of the colophon of *Satan in Goray* (Y 189) was graciously provided by Joseph Sherman.

When two page numbers are given in the text, the first is for the Yiddish original (Y) and the second is for the English translation (E).

2. For a review of this topic, see Ch. Shmeruk, "Yiddish Literature and Collective Memory: The Case of the Chmielnicki Massacres," *Polin* 5 (1990): 187–197. This is a preliminary survey that does not engage in literary analysis of the texts.

3. A. Rubinstein makes a short remark that compares the atmosphere of the two works in his article "Beyn Goray le-Bilgoray," in *Min hakatedra: Sugiyot bakhevra hayehudit uvetarbuta* (Bar-Ilan: Bar-Ilan University Press, 1981). See also the article by Dovid-Hirsh Roskies, "Yitzkhok Bashevis un zayne sheydim," *Di goldene keyt* 134 (1992): 158. Khave Rosenfarb has made an extensive comparison between the two authors, but she does not contrast *Kidush hashem* with *Der sotn in goray:* "Yitskhok Bashevis un Sholem Ash: a pruv fun a farglaykh," *Di goldene keyt* 133 (1992): 75–104. For a comparison between *Der sotn in goray* and *Der novi* (The Prophet) by Sholem Asch on the occasion of the publication of the English translations of both novels, see Judd L. Teller, "Unhistorical Novels," *Commentary* 21 (1956): 393–396. The original edition of the Sholem Asch novel is Sholem Asch, *Kidesh Hashem: un andere ertsehlungen* (New York: Forverts, 1919), translated into English by Rufus Learsi as *Kiddush Ha-Shem: An Epic of 1648* (Philadelphia: Jewish Publication Society, 1926).

4. Seth L. Wolitz pointed to this source in his article "Satan in Goray as Parable," *Prooftexts* 9 (1989): 17.

5. We still lack a survey on the development of the historical novel in Yiddish literature. An illuminating instance describing the welcome that the genre received, from the perspective of national ideology, is the article by Y. Schiper, "Afn veg tsu di urbilder fun der yidisher neshome: Vegn di nayste yidishe historishe romanen," *Varshever shriftn* (Warsaw, 1926–1927): 2–9 (separate pagination). Bashevis himself wrote briefly about the genre in his review of a novel by Yosef Opatoshu, "Pundeko retivto," *Globus* 15 (September 1933): 86. He complained about the limited place that Yiddish literature had until then given to historical material, and he welcomed the constantly growing interest in it as a sign that the Yiddish writer was not subject to the terror of leftist ideologies that consider all reference to the past as an indication of "a reactionary viewpoint." In this context, it should be pointed out that the first two chapters of Max Weinreich's novel *Shturemvint: Bilder fun der yidisher geshikhte in zibetsetn yorhundert* (Vilna: Tamar Farlag, 1927) cover the Chmielnicki massacres and Sabbatai Zevi. See the article by Dovid-Hirsh Roskies, "Max Vaynraykh: af di shpurn fun a lebedikn over," *Yivo-bleter* n.s. 3 (1997): 308–318.

6. Ruth Wisse refers to the antisentimental tendency in this passage in her introduction to the new edition of *Satan in Goray* (New York: Farrar, Straus, Giroux, 1995), p. xxxiv.

Avrom Noversztern

7. From the introduction to Sholem Asch's *Gezamlte shriftn,* vol. 12 (Warsaw: B. Kletskin, 1926).

8. Avrom Noversztern, "Moyshe Kulbaks *Meshiekh ben Efrayim:* A yidish modernistish verk in zayn literarishn gerem," *Di goldene keyt* 126 (1989): 181–203; 127 (1989): 151–170.

9. For a survey of the criticism of *Satan in Goray,* see Wolitz, "Satan in Goray as Parable," pp. 13–25; Avrom Ayzen, "Yitskhok Bashevis, *Der sotn in goray,*" *Yivo-bleter* 12 (1937): 386–395. Among the articles that appeared after Wolitz's study, mention should be made of Ruth Wisse's introduction to the new English edition of the novel (see note 6 above); Janet Hadda, *Isaac Bashevis Singer: A Life* (New York: Oxford University Press, 1997), pp. 71–77; and Bilha Rubinstein, "Meshyakh lo ba vehasatan meraked barekhovot," *Chulyot* 5 (1999): 237–247.

10. S. Niger, *Yidishe shrayber fun tsvantsikstn yorhundert,* vol. 2 (New York: Congress of Jewish Culture, 1973), pp. 299–308.

11. One of Irving Howe's articles on Bashevis was entitled "Demonic Fiction of a Yiddish Modernist." Bashevis himself responded to such a claim in a way that was both playful and reserved. See, for instance, one of the interviews with him in *Critical Views of Isaac Bashevis Singer,* ed. Irving Malin (New York: New York University Press, 1969), pp. 10–11. Bashevis's relation to modernism, a term used both with and without quotation marks, is common in Anglo-American criticism. See, for example, Charles Isenberg, "Satan in Goray and Ironic Restitution," *Yiddish* 6 (1985): 101.

12. This point is made by Wisse, introduction to *Satan in Goray,* p. xxi.

13. Hadda, *Singer,* pp. 71–73.

14. For a detailed description of the source itself, see Sarah Zfatman, "Maaseh shel ruakh bekak Korets—Shlav khadash behitpatkhuto shel zhaner amami," *Mekhkarey yerushalayim befolklor yehudi* 2 (1982): 17–65. The possibility that this text, through the mediation of Max Weinreich's research, served as Bashevis's source of inspiration has been raised by Hadda, *Singer,* p. 75, and by Roskies, "Maks Vaynraykh," pp. 309–312.

15. It first appeared in *Forverts,* March 29, 1959. It was later included in his volume *Gimpl tam un andere dertseylungen* (Gimpel the Fool and Other Stories) (New York: Tsiko, 1963), pp. 237–245; and *Der shpigl un andere dertseylungen* (The Mirror and Other Stories) (Jerusalem: Hebrew University Press, 1975), pp. 12–22: this edition is quoted here. The English translation is by Martha Glicklich and Cecil Hemley in Isaac Bashevis Singer, *The Collected Stories* (New York: Farrar, Straus, Giroux, 1982).

16. Ken Frieden, "I. B. Singer's Monologues of Demons," *Prooftexts* 5 (1985): 266–267.

17. David G. Roskies, *Against the Apocalypse: Responses to Catastrophe in Modern Jewish Culture* (Cambridge, Mass.: Harvard University Press, 1984), pp. 194–195.

History, Messianism, and Apocalypse in Bashevis's Work

18. David G. Roskies, *A Bridge of Longing: The Lost Art of Yiddish Storytelling* (Cambridge, Mass.: Harvard University Press, 1995), p. 300.

19. Yitskhok Bashevis, "Arum der yidisher literatur in Poylin," *Di tsukunft* 48 (August 1943): 468–475. Translated into English by Robert Wolf, "Concerning Yiddish Literature in Poland (1943)," *Prooftexts* 15:2 (1995): 113–127. Bashevis remarks, in the English translation, "In Tysowce, the Messiah son of Joseph had lived and been martyred" (p. 121).

20. Shloyme Bikl, *Shrayber fun mayn dor,* vol. 1 (New York: Matones, 1958), p. 358. Irving Howe, "I. B. Singer," in *Critical Views of Isaac Bashevis Singer,* ed. Irving Malin (New York: New York University Press, 1969), pp. 118–119.

Avrom Noversztern

4

Sociolinguistic Views of Isaac Bashevis Singer

Mark L. Louden

In this essay I will analyze a number of observations that I. B. Singer made in essays written from 1943 to 1978 on the sociolinguistic status of the Yiddish language; hence the intentional *tsveytaytshikeyt* (ambiguity) of the title. In his role, especially after receiving the Nobel Prize for Literature in 1978, as arguably the most familiar speaker and writer of Yiddish to Jewish and non-Jewish audiences, Bashevis's thoughts on various aspects of the language are of interest, regardless of whether or not they were consonant with the views of other Yiddish-speaking intellectuals (often they were not).

I will begin by briefly describing what sociolinguistics is and then proceed to review some of the facts of the sociolinguistic history of Yiddish in America. Then we will explore Bashevis's stand on a number of issues pertaining to Yiddish, including its status in America, its historical origins, its status in the Soviet Union, its relationship with Modern Hebrew, and finally, appropriately, its future. I will proceed chronologically, discussing his writings in order of their publication and situate them to some extent in the context of his life experience at the time. To contextualize Bashevis's sociolinguistic views somewhat, I will also pay special attention to the views of two sociolinguists *avant la lettre*, Einar Haugen, a linguist whose particular research interests included the situation of European immigrant languages in North America, and Max Weinreich, the dean of Yiddish linguists, known especially for his classic work on the historical development of Yiddish.

What Is Sociolinguistics?

Let us begin by considering what is meant by the term *sociolinguistics*. Generally stated, sociolinguistics is that subfield of linguistic science which addresses questions pertaining to a language within the context of its speakers, either individually or as a social group. Given the fact that language is so fundamental to human interaction, and one of the primary ways we define ourselves as individuals or as members of groups, one might find the term *sociolinguistics* somewhat redundant. Indeed, the most familiar sociolinguist in the North America today, William Labov of the University of Pennsylvania, has made just that point.[1] The term is not redundant, however, due to the fact that one may with equal validity view language as a structured system independent of its actualization in the speech of its users. The grammar of a language, for instance, may be accurately described with no direct reference to the individuals who would draw on it to produce utterances. For example, the statement "For Yiddish and English, definite and indefinite articles precede rather than follow the nouns they modify" is correct and need not refer to any particular speaker of Yiddish or English using the language at any particular point in time. This language-internal perspective is often described as *formalist linguistics* and in the United States is most commonly associated with the work of Noam Chomsky at the Massachusetts Institute of Technology.

Interestingly, the emergence of sociolinguistics as a distinct linguistic subfield has strong ties to Yiddish linguistics. William Labov's dissertation, "The Social Stratification of English in New York City," which is considered the first modern sociolinguistic study, was completed at Columbia University in 1966 under the supervision of none other than Uriel Weinreich, Max's equally brilliant son. Furthermore, an important contemporary of Weinreich and Labov was Joshua Fishman, recently retired from Yeshiva University and the acknowledged pioneer of the subfield of sociolinguistics known as the *sociology of language,* which examines, for example, demographic patterns of preservation and decline in the use of languages, especially minority and immigrant languages.

An important received wisdom which has emerged within sociolinguistics has been that every speaker has very specific and strongly held notions about what language is and how it works, many of which, however, are at odds with the objective reality studied by scientists of language. The study of language attitudes, including stereotypes, nevertheless is important because, regardless of how "accurate" or "inaccurate" they may be, they are part of the real life of language. And it goes without saying that the attitudes of those whose professional activity is centered around language, such as writers, are of singular interest. Before proceeding to consider Bashevis's thoughts on Yiddish, in America and in general, we should consider a few facts about the history and sociolinguistic situation of Yiddish in America.

Mark L. Louden

Yiddish in America

The earliest evidence of Yiddish being spoken and written in North America is to be found in personal correspondence as far back as the middle of the eighteenth century.[2] It appears that most of these Yiddish speakers originated in Western and Central Europe, that is, in the Western Yiddish dialect area, which was largely coterritorial with German, and displayed no particular interest in the maintenance of Yiddish beyond the first generation. This is evidenced by the fact that until the last quarter of the nineteenth century there was effectively no institutional support for Yiddish in American public life (through schools, print media, theater, etc.).[3] It is quite likely that these early American Ashkenazic Jews shared the strongly assimilationist attitudes of their upper-middle-class counterparts in Germany at the time, attitudes which did not dispose them positively toward Yiddish and much of Eastern European Jewish life.

The situation of Yiddish in America changed dramatically around 1880 with the beginning of the large influx of Jews from Eastern Europe, virtually all of whom were native speakers of Yiddish. The arrival of these Yiddish speakers thus also heralded the beginning of the active use of Yiddish in America supported by precisely those public institutions, especially the press, which were lacking earlier. As Benjamin Harshav puts it, the establishment of Yiddish in America during this time was a "significant third 'moment'" in the history of the language, after, first, its emergence in medieval Central Europe and, second, its subsequent growth in Slavic territories to the east.[4] Part of the significance of this expansion of Yiddish beyond Europe lies in the complex relationship that developed between the Old World and the New over the "proper" use of Yiddish and indeed the very nature of the language itself. The fact that Yiddish was entering its Golden Age in Europe at precisely this time, from the end of the nineteenth to the beginning of the twentieth centuries, underscores the importance of the discourse between and among European and American speakers of Yiddish concerning the language.

Yiddish in America was viewed negatively by many European Yiddishists in much the same way that other colonial varieties of European languages such as French, German, Spanish, and Portuguese were (and, to a large extent, still are) regarded by speakers who remained in Europe. Typical criticisms focus on the nonstandard features of many of these colonial varieties, as well as their relative openness to the incorporation of new vocabulary borrowed from other languages

Sociolinguistic Views of Isaac Bashevis Singer

with which they come into contact (for example, English in North America). This latter phenomenon of lexical borrowing is one of the most universally stigmatized processes of natural linguistic development in the view of language purists, who describe it in terms such as "corruption," "bastardization," and "mongrelization" (see also the following section). In the case of Yiddish, the comments of Khayim Zhitlovski reflected the attitudes of many European Yiddishists toward the use of the language by some in America:

> When one thinks of Yiddish in America, one must not forget that we have here two brands of Yiddish. One brand is the wild-growing Yiddish-English jargon, the potato-chicken-kitchen language; the other brand is the cultivated language of Yiddish culture all over the world.[5]

Emblematic of what was viewed as the abasement of Yiddish in America was the language of *Forverts* under the editorship of Abraham Cahan, who was utterly receptive to the lexical influence of English on written Yiddish, in line with the way the language was being naturally spoken by his American readership.[6] When we consider Bashevis's views on American Yiddish below, it will be important to remember that Cahan, as editor of *Forverts*, was Bashevis's employer for several years after his arrival in New York in 1935.

The disdainful attitude of some observers toward American Yiddish was, however, part of an older and broader debate within Europe itself between what Benjamin Harshav terms the "purists" who wanted to assert the autonomy of Yiddish from other languages, on the one hand, and the "Europeanizers," on the other, who wanted to take advantage of the inherent "openness" of Yiddish to "foreign" (e.g., German and Slavic) linguistic elements, especially vocabulary, for enriched expressive potential.[7] In brief, the incorporation of linguistic borrowings into Yiddish, be they from Hebrew, German, Russian, or English, especially in the early part of the twentieth century, was alternately viewed as a sign of the weakness or the strength of the language, depending on the perspective of the observer. Against this sociolinguistic background we may now consider some of Bashevis's expressed views on Yiddish in America.

Bashevis on Yiddish in America

In 1943 Bashevis published two rather gloomy articles on Yiddish literature.[8] What both these essays have in common is the view that the Golden Age of Yiddish lit-

Mark L. Louden

erature has passed and that any hope of transplanting *yidishkeyt* onto foreign soil such as that of the United States is futile. For Bashevis, Yiddish is only an appropriate vehicle for the expression of life in the Old Country, specifically the *shtetl*, and utterly unsuited for the circumstances of Jewish experience outside of Eastern Europe. Consider the following excerpt (in translation) from the second essay referred to above:

> There is a considerable difference between an undeveloped language and an obsolete one. The word pool of a primitive African tribe might seem immeasurably poor when compared to that of a European language, and yet be vital and perfectly expressive of that group or tribe's particular world view. The situation is completely different when a language moves backwards in time while its speakers and intelligentsia move forward. This disproportion stems from the speakers' expressing most things in another language, turning to the original only in certain situations. Many words thus lose their earlier, specific meanings and assume idiomatic connotations. Others are completely forgotten. New words fail to appear, or appear only in particular categories and in disharmony with the original lexicon. With time the language shows the indelible mark of history. It belongs, one might say, to another era.
>
> It is sad to note that this has gradually become the case with Yiddish, especially in America. Many Jews who speak Yiddish on this or that occasion cannot make use of the language in other situations. Doctors, lawyers, engineers, agronomists, technicians and factory workers who still speak Yiddish to their fathers and grandfathers cannot use it when speaking or writing about physiology or anatomy, in the courtroom or in the laboratory, on the farm or in the factory. They cannot express the relevant concepts in Yiddish, nor is it necessary that they do so.[9]

A few remarks on Bashevis's notions of linguistic "primitiveness" versus "obsolescence" are warranted here. In the quotation above, he is perpetuating the old but fundamentally misguided notion that languages, like the cultures of their speakers, may be arranged on a developmental continuum of relative backwardness versus advancement. He imagines some African language that may lack words for, say, "typewriter" and "telephone," a presumed indicator of both linguistic and cultural impoverishment. The simplest refutation of the idea that certain languages remain undeveloped is the success of translation (e.g., the Bible) into (especially) the languages of "primitive" societies. On the other hand, Bashevis does acknowledge the utility of all languages within certain conditions: for example, this African

Sociolinguistic Views of Isaac Bashevis Singer

language is perfectly adequate for the daily needs of Africans in Africa, though presumably inadequate if the circumstances of its speakers were to change. Yiddish, he implies, is not an "undeveloped" language (presumably because of the "civilization" of European Ashkenazim), but nonetheless becomes "obsolete" when its speakers have been transplanted outside of Europe. That a language may become obsolete is recognized (though regretted) by linguists (cf. the rapid decline of indigenous languages in the Americas). At the same time, language death is not to be attributed to any structural (including lexical) inadequacy within the language itself, but to the changing circumstances of its users.

That Bashevis should be so pessimistic about Yiddish's present and future in 1943 is entirely understandable given his life circumstances at the time. He had only been in America since 1935 and was therefore far from acculturated, socially or linguistically; his professional life as a writer for *Forverts* was less than fulfilling; and, as Janet Hadda aptly discusses in her important biography of Bashevis,[10] he was struggling with his emotions toward his older brother, Israel Joshua. And, perhaps most important, the Shoah that was to claim the lives of his mother and younger brother Moyshe was well under way. He was understandably distraught at standing by while the world which had nourished him intellectually was being destroyed. His characterization of Yiddish as alien in the United States parallels what he himself must have felt at this time.

Words, like people, sometimes endure a severe disorientation when they emigrate, and often they remain forever helpless and not quite themselves. This is precisely what happened to Yiddish in America. Most of the small town immigrants brought with them a smattering of Jewish learning, a poor vocabulary, and a tremendous desire to become Americanized. What they did to Yiddish here had — from a linguistic point of view — a negative effect. They vulgarized the language, mixing in hundreds of English and anglicized words and expressions, and creating a gibberish which no self-respecting Yiddish writer could use in good conscience. Literature is created when a language is ripe, crystallized, when the linguistic lava — so to speak — has begun to cool and harden, not when it is still bubbling and flowing and changing shape every minute. There is a split, a division in the mindset of Yiddish prose writers who try to write about America. The graceful words have *too much* tradition; the new ones are somewhat strange and tawdry, and ungainly to boot. Americanisms reek of foreignness, of cheap glitter, of impermanence. The result is that the better Yiddish writers in America

Mark L. Louden

avoid treating American life, and they are subjectively (aesthetically) right to do so. Their linguistic foundations are completely undermined here.[11]

Bashevis's very obvious disdain for a Yiddish which shows the effects of contact with English in the United States is consonant with the linguistic purism of recent immigrants, especially highly educated ones, in other contact situations that are common in countries of immigration, such as the United States and Canada (see also the discussion in the previous section). This kind of purism is, of course, familiar in nonimmigrant contexts as well; the most familiar example of this is the movement in France to purge its national language of vocabulary borrowed from other languages, especially English. Furthermore, it might strike some as ironic that one should adopt such a puristic stance toward, of all languages, Yiddish, itself a "fusion language,"[12] composed of Hebrew-Aramaic, Romance, Germanic, and Slavic components. Nevertheless, Yiddish has not been immune to the feeling among many of its speakers that there are "better" and "worse" forms of the language. The tension between "purists" critical of trends of popular usage and "realists" (cf. the "Europeanist" Yiddishists referred to above) who acknowledge them was clearly evident, as Joshua Fishman points out,[13] in the debates between Yiddish writers such as Bashevis and editors of popular print media, the most prominent example of the latter being Bashevis's boss and nemesis at *Forverts,* Abe Cahan. Cahan, as noted earlier, was particularly tolerant of what became known as *potato-yidish,* Yiddish interspersed with English lexical items, a form of the language typical of everyday immigrant speech, but a source of consternation for purists such as Bashevis.

Not surprisingly, the equation of language contact with a form of miscegenation is not in line with the thinking of linguists. The receptiveness of languages to borrowed words, in particular the introduction of loanwords, is viewed neutrally as the inevitable result of cultural contact. Nevertheless, the positive valuation attached to "purity" in language evidenced by Bashevis above has been widespread. Consider the remarks of Einar Haugen below, one of the first linguists to consider the status of immigrant languages and patterns of bilingualism in the United States:

Many have been the scornful expressions used by observers about the "mongrelian" languages, as the popular publicist Brander Matthews once

Sociolinguistic Views of Isaac Bashevis Singer

called them . . . This opinion has been shared to a high degree by the more educated members of each immigrant group, who have lashed their less fastidious countrymen for their treatment of the native tongue. Each critic has usually been familiar with his own group only, and has assumed that some personal or national perversity was the underlying cause. Observers fresh from overseas have been the most vehement in their critique, for to them the phenomenon has often seemed particularly conspicuous. It is noticeable that some years of sojourn among their fellow bilinguals have usually softened many of these judgments, and led even the most puristic to temper their speech to the winds of mongrelianism.[14]

Bashevis on Yiddish and the "Ghetto Myth"

Not surprisingly, as Bashevis became more comfortable with his situation in the United States, professionally and emotionally, he, too, tempered his speech "to the winds of mongrelianism" and began to express greater optimism about the future of Yiddish. He never really altered his basic belief that the Golden Age of Yiddish had passed, though, and expressed the view that Yiddish was essentially the product of and belonged to a homogeneously Jewish world. As illustrated in another quotation from the 1943 essay "Problemen fun der yidisher proze in Amerike," he rejects the idea that Yiddish could be a vehicle for "cosmopolitan" (that is, assimilated or no longer truly Jewish) experience and even takes a jab at that most cosmopolitan of Yiddish institutions, the Litvak YIVO (Yiddish Scientific Institute for Jewish Research, which was founded in Vilna by Max Weinrich and continues in New York).[15]

> Yiddish literature is a product of the ghetto with all its virtues and faults, and it can never leave the ghetto. This is the key to the riddle. The idea that Yiddish literature—and indeed Yiddish culture—can be cosmopolitan, an equal among equals, was from the beginning built upon misconceptions. The Jews who wanted to be one hundred percent cosmopolitan switched to other cultures and grew accustomed to foreign languages. Those drawn to Yiddish words, to Yiddish letters, were bound by a thousand threads to the whole spiritual baggage of the Diaspora . . . The Diaspora—the Jewish communities and their leaders, rabbis, ritual slaughterers, trustees and scholars; the pious shopkeeper and the artisan, the fervent housewife, the yeshiva boy and the childbride—this is and shall remain the subject of Yiddish literature and the determinant of its content and form. However, nothing here can alter the fact that this way of life is vanishing, if it has not already vanished

Mark L. Louden

without a trace. This is a truth which will displease many of our dedicated Yiddishists and cultural activists, but it is true just the same . . . The neologisms created by the philologists at YIVO are needed by no one and no one will use them. The reader of Yiddish, insofar as he still exists, turns to Yiddish books mainly for their Jewish content, not for their ill-conceived and pathetically rendered "worldliness." [16]

It is worth considering a cosmopolitan Yiddishist's response to the "ghetto myth" of Yiddish origins. Though Max Weinreich's observations concerning the reality of Ashkenazic history offer an appropriate corrective to the idealized isolationism of Bashevis, Weinreich was reacting more to the unsophisticated view of chauvinist German philologists that Yiddish was nothing more than bad German mangled by ignoramuses on the social periphery. Indeed, the exclusionist undertones in the non-Jewish characterization of the origins of Yiddish bear strong similarity to those of white American accounts of the history of African-American Vernacular English (Black English, Ebonics), the linguistic system of another historically oppressed and at times ghettoized people. In the excerpts below, Weinreich sketches his basic understanding of Yiddish as a fusion language. Crucial to Weinreich's thesis is the idea that rather than being "corrupted" by contact with non-Jews and their languages, the Ashkenazim and their language, Yiddish, were enriched. It follows logically that this pattern of what he terms the "insulation without isolation" of diaspora Jewish sociolinguistic history should continue in the next way station, the United States.

There is just no point in the assumption that such a potent and consistent culture system as that of Ashkenaz was created and sustained by the existence of separate living quarters, compulsory or otherwise . . . [T]he basic causes for the rise and the continuing existence of Ashkenaz must be sought not in curbs imposed from outside or in certain institutions but in the vitality of the society which, in spite of seemingly overwhelming odds, managed to keep its head above water . . . Ashkenazic reality is to be sought between the two poles of absolute identity with and absolute remoteness from the coterritorial non-Jewish communities. To compress it into a formula, what the Jews aimed at was not isolation from the Christians but insulation from Christianity . . . The culture patterns prevalent among Ashkenazic Jews . . . are mid-course formations as those found wherever cultures meet along frontiers, in border zones, or in territories with mixed populations.

The most striking result of this encounter of cultures is the Yiddish language. When the Jews entered Loter, their vernaculars were western Laaz

Sociolinguistic Views of Isaac Bashevis Singer

and southern Laaz, the Jewish correlates of Old French and Old Italian, while Hebrew-Aramaic was the sacred tongue. But the non-Jewish population of Loter spoke regional variants of German, and it is this German determinant which brought into the new fusion language of Ashkenaz its quantitatively strongest component. Is this not irrefutable proof of a high degree of contact? On the other hand, the Ashkenazim did not simply become German speakers but fused their acquisitions from German with what they had brought with them in their Hebrew-Aramaic and Laaz determinants. The same applies to the Slavic determinant which made itself felt after the middle of the thirteenth century. Doesn't this, in turn, testify to a remarkable degree of independence? [17]

In response to the charge made by critics such as Bashevis that Yiddish had become an obsolescent language due to Jewish emigration from or annihilation in Eastern Europe, Weinreich argues that Yiddish's historical receptiveness to changes in the social and cultural conditions of its speakers augurs well for its ability to be adapted yet again in the American context:

> This new literary language, as intimated, is the result of fusion with regard to the underlying dialectal substructure. In a social sense, it also reflects an intense process of fusion. On the basis of the *English-Yiddish Yiddish-English Dictionary* by Uriel Weinreich, which YIVO brought out in 1967, these conclusions could even be quantified, but the general qualitative statement is well beyond doubt. Contemporary Yiddish has acquired the preciseness and flexibility of the Western languages, not in the least under their influence. Yet, the imagery has remained to a large degree that of the traditional Ashkenazic folk life. For some time it seemed . . . that the secular sector was about to part ways linguistically with the traditional strata since both were driving in opposite directions. No such premonitions are felt now, due to the cohesive forces in the Ashkenazic community which were reinforced by the experiences common to all European Jews in the years of the German war against the Jews. So again, while actual cultivation of Yiddish language and literature is still by and large limited to the secular sector, the traditionalists share in this development in growing measure. So far, Ashkenazic cohesiveness and all-inclusiveness have stood the test in the field of Yiddish, as well. [18]

Important to note here is Weinreich's optimism that Yiddish can serve as the vehicle both for the transmission of (idealized?) traditional culture so central to Bashevis's literary output (if not always his own life experiences) and for more modern (i.e., "cosmopolitan") Jewish life.

71

Mark L. Louden

Bashevis on Yiddish in the Soviet Union

As mentioned above, Bashevis's pessimism about the future of Yiddish eventually lessened somewhat, and he came to espouse the idea that, contra Max Weinreich's view, though Yiddish remained firmly rooted in an Eastern European past, its life ought to be prolonged as a link with this past. For Bashevis, Yiddish was an essential part of historic and modern Jewish identity. On the other hand, Yiddish without Jewishness was for him meaningless. This is illustrated in his harsh assessment of *yidishkeyt* in the Soviet Union excerpted from a 1962 article. One should note here also a bit more sophistication in his brief recapitulation of the history of Yiddish compared to what he had written in 1943:

> Philologists tell us that the Diaspora Jews did not have a single, common language of their own, but many languages, borrowed from the Gentile peoples among whom they lived. The Jews adapted these languages to their own ethos, adding many Hebrew and Aramaic words, creating the dialects of the ghetto. Slavic, French, and Spanish all made their contributions to the evolution of these dialects . . . And finally, Yiddish was spoken by millions of East European Jews. All these languages had one thing in common—they were forged as an instrument of Jewishness. Hebrew was too holy for everyday use and was to be spoken only at the advent of the Messiah.
>
> Thus, since the Yiddish of East European Jews has been, above all, an instrument of their Jewishness, it becomes flat and barren when used for the denial of Jewishness. One might say that the language cannot tolerate atheism. Purged of the religious sentiment which gave it cohesion, Yiddish is reduced to a conglomerate of disparate elements, and only then justifies the accusations of its adversaries that it is gibberish, jargon . . . The Yiddishists of Soviet Russia have never recognized this truth.[19]

Of course, in light of Bashevis's own somewhat idiosyncratic "religious sentiment," one wonders if perhaps his dislike of Soviet Yiddishism was not more directly the product of his hostility toward the political left.

Bashevis on Yiddish and Modern Hebrew

As central as Jewishness (*yidishkeyt*) was to Yiddish for Bashevis, so too was Yiddish a necessary part of contemporary Jewish identity. This view is reflected in his assessment in 1967 of the relevance of Yiddish in the face of competition from Hebrew. Though Yiddish was still the language of the now nonexistent *shtetl*, ignorance of one's past was for Bashevis akin to a psychological disorder.

Sociolinguistic Views of Isaac Bashevis Singer

Many young Hebraists forget that the creators of the neo-Hebrew literature were also the classicists of Yiddish literature. Some of the Hebraists who repudiated and hated Yiddish still thought, spoke, dreamed, and often wrote in Yiddish. Indeed, they used Yiddish to deprecate Yiddish. For many *maskilim* Yiddish became the symbol of backwardness, provincialism, superstition, spiritual petrification, in short, the symbol of the *shtetl*. But where did the *maskilim,* Zionists, Jewish socialists, *halutzim* [pioneers], and even the present "Canaanites" [Zionists who wished to return to a pre-Yahwistic paganism] come from if not from the *shtetl*? And was not the *shtetl* also the original home of most Jews now in America, England, France and Soviet Russia?

Not everybody will agree with me that the spiritual crisis which Jews in Israel are now undergoing is largely due to their forgetting Yiddish. But I still believe this to be true. Amnesia is a dangerous malaise for the human spirit. For the people of Israel, whose entire survival is based on remembering, amnesia is fatal. It is not chauvinism or boastfulness when I assert that Ashkenazic Jewry carried on its shoulders Jewish progress in the last five or six centuries. In trying to forget or ignore the language of these Jews, their creativity, their problems, hopes, traits, peculiarities, we are succumbing to a national psychosis, to complexes that can lead to national dementia. Yiddish is our memory, the bridge between our yesterday and our today, between the diaspora and Israel. This holds both for the language and for its genuine literary productions. The *Sabra* who prides himself on not knowing Yiddish negates the Jewish past; he speaks and behaves like a Hebraic convert. He has excommunicated himself and destroyed his roots.[20]

Thus we have a sense of Bashevis's stand on the vexing question of Hebrew versus Yiddish in modern Jewish identity. It is ironic that his views here place him closer to two otherwise rather antagonistic factions, "cosmopolitan" Yiddishists and the "traditionalist" ultra-orthodox Hasidim, neither of which Bashevis would overtly have identified himself with.

Bashevis on the Future of Yiddish

Thus we have seen patterns of constancy and change in Bashevis's expressed sociolinguistic attitudes toward Yiddish. Though he never really gave up the idea that Yiddish was essentially suited (and limited) to the expression of the Jewish experience in Eastern Europe, he came to see the increasing need to continue to convey the richness and depth of that experience to future generations. For him, Yiddish went from being a language rendered moribund by the destruction of its sociolinguistic world to the timeless means through which modern readers may preserve the beauty and wisdom of that world. In this way, for Bashevis, Yiddish finally transcends the *shtetl* or ghetto and becomes, as he movingly states in his 1978 Nobel acceptance speech, a truly universal language:

There are some who call Yiddish a dead language, but so was Hebrew called for two thousand years. It has been revived in our time in a most remarkable, almost miraculous way. Aramaic was certainly a dead language for centuries, but then it brought to light the Zohar, a work of mysticism of sublime value. It is also a fact that the classics of Yiddish literature are also the classics of modern Hebrew literature. Yiddish has not yet said its last word. It contains treasures that have not been revealed to the eyes of the world. It was the tongue of martyrs and saints, of dreamers and Kabbalists — rich in humor and in memories that mankind may never forget. In a figurative way, Yiddish is the wise and humble language of us all, the idiom of frightened and hopeful humanity.[21]

Notes

1. "This type of research [which focuses upon language in use within the speech community] has sometimes been labelled as 'sociolinguistics,' although it is a somewhat misleading use of an oddly redundant term" (William Labov, *Sociolinguistic Patterns* [Philadelphia: University of Pennsylvania Press, 1972], p. 183).

2. See J. H. Neumann, "Notes on American Yiddish," *Journal of English and Germanic Philology* 37 (1938): 403–421, especially pages 407–410, on the history of Yiddish in America.

3. Ibid., 408.

4. Benjamin Harshav, *The Meaning of Yiddish* (Berkeley: University of California Press, 1990), p. 30.

5. Quoted in George Wolfe, "Notes on American Yiddish," *American Mercury* 29 (1933): 473–479.

6. In Cahan's defense, Harshav (*Meaning*, p. 66) states that "[i]n a profound sense, Cahan was not just an opportunist: he understood the open nature of the Yiddish language, as did his readers. The purist writers launched a losing battle against him until both succumbed to complete Americanization, embraced by the sons of their readers." In any case, the admixture of English-derived vocabulary in written American Yiddish was probably overstated. Neumann, in his study of three New York Yiddish daily newspapers, the *Morgn zhurnal,* Cahan's *Forverts,* and *Der tog,* found an average of only about 10–15 percent lexical borrowings from English, depending on the section ("Notes," pp. 410–411).

7. See Harshav, *Meaning,* pp. 61–73.

8. I. B. Singer, "Arum der yidisher literatur in Poyln," *Di tsukunft* 48 (1943): 468–475,

reprinted in English translation in *Prooftexts* 15 (1995): 113–127; I. B. Singer, "Problemen fun der yidisher proze in Amerike," *Svive* 2 (1943): 2–13, reprinted in English translation in *Prooftexts* 9 (1989): 5–12.

9. Singer, "Problemen" (1989), pp. 5–6.

10. Janet Hadda, *Isaac Bashevis Singer: A Life* (New York: Oxford University Press, 1997).

11. Singer, "Problemen" (1989), p. 9; emphasis added.

12. The expression was introduced by Max Weinreich in his *History of the Yiddish Language* (Chicago: University of Chicago Press, 1980). Compare also Harshav's description of the "openness of Yiddish" (*Meaning*, p. 61).

13. Joshua A. Fishman, *Yiddish: Turning to Life* (Amsterdam: John Benjamins Press, 1991), pp. 102 and 158, n. 17.

14. Einar Haugen, *The Norwegian Language in America* (Philadelphia: University of Pennsylvania Press, 1953), p. 12.

15. In light of the earlier discussion of the purist/Europeanist debate within Yiddish letters, it is important to acknowledge that the linguist and YIVO founder Max Weinreich, who was inclined to sympathize with the "purists" referred to above in the interest of asserting the independence of Yiddish from other European languages, at the same time acknowledged the natural appropriateness (within certain limits) of incorporating "foreign" (e.g., English) vocabulary into Yiddish; see Max Weinreich, "Vegn englishe elementn in undzer kulturshprakh," *Yidishe shprakh* 1 (1941): 33–46.

16. Singer, "Problemen," pp. 10–11.

17. Max Weinreich, "The Reality of Jewishness versus the Ghetto Myth: The Sociolinguistic Roots of Yiddish," in Joshua A. Fishman, ed., *Never Say Die! A Thousand Years of Yiddish in Jewish Life and Letters* (The Hague: Mouton, 1981), pp. 109–110.

18. Ibid., pp. 116–117.

19. I. B. Singer, "A New Use for Yiddish," *Commentary* 3 (1962): 267.

20. I. B. Singer, "The Future of Yiddish and Yiddish Literature," *Jewish Book Annual* 25 (1967/1968): 70, 72.

21. I. B. Singer, *Nobel Lecture* (New York: Farrar, Straus and Giroux, 1978), p. 8.

Mark L. Louden

II

THEMATIC
APPROACHES
TO THE STUDY
OF BASHEVIS'S
FICTION

5

Bilom in Bashevis's *Der knekht* (The Slave)

A khaye hot oykh a neshome (An animal also has a soul)

Leonard Prager

Walking about Jewish neighborhoods today, in almost any country in the West or anywhere in Israel, one sees many dogs of every breed and pedigree. This makes it difficult to realize that some of us in childhood heard parents and grandparents repeat the now wholly comic saying, *oyb a yid hot a hunt, oder der yid iz nisht keyn yid oder der hunt iz nisht keyn hunt,* "If a Jew has a dog, either the Jew is not a Jew or the dog is not a dog." But to our Eastern European forebears, there was nothing funny about dogs.[1]

In 1945 Yudl Mark published a list of thousands of Yiddish folk-similes in common oral use collected by young students in one corner of Lithuania in the mid-1920s and mid-1930s.[2] Psakhye Frimer and Mendl Mark expanded this list,[3] and the latter analyzed their objects of comparison and the folk attitudes they reflect, asking:

> *vosere farglaykh-obyektn kumen tsum oftstn dem yidish-reyder oyfn tsung (bavustzinik tsi umbavustzinik) baym veln zikh oysdrikn pinktlekher, bild-lekher oder vitsiker?*[4]
>
> What objects of comparison roll off the tongue of Yiddish-speakers—consciously or unconsciously—most often in their effort to be more exact, vivid, or witty?

The most common objects of comparison, he found, were the dog, cat, and pig, and *oyfn ershtn plats loyt der tsol farglaykhn kumt der hunt (arayngerekhnt key-lev, tsoyg, un klavte),* "and in first place in the number of similes comes the dog (including bitch)."[5] Mark went on to explain:

> *der hunt iz do veyniker fun alts der "getrayer fraynd," vos iz ibergegebn dem balebos un iz greyt im tsu dinen. er iz gikher der beyzer soyne, vos balangt tsu der goyisher velt, bafalt on a farvos, hot faynt di yidishe kapote un makht dos lebn nokh mer mizerabl.*[6]

The dog here is least of all the "faithful friend" devoted to his master and ready to serve him; he is rather the evil enemy who belongs to the Gentile world. He attacks capriciously, hates the Jewish gaberdine, and increases misery.

Mendl Mark's simile studies are corroborated by proverb collections and common expressions. Ignats Bernshteyn's classic study includes the categorical and implacable assertion *a hunt blaybt a hunt,* "a dog remains a dog," and *es iz nit do keyn guter hunt,* "there is no such thing as a good dog."[7] A very wicked person is called in Yiddish *a keylev shebeklovim,* literally "a dog of dogs."

The most compelling evidence of this hostile view of "man's best friend" among *shtetl* Jews during the nineteenth and the beginning of the twentieth centuries is found in Yiddish literature. However, there it coexists with its negation. Nowhere is this negation more far-reaching than in Yitskhok Bashevis's novel *Der knekht* (The Slave).[8] A telling scene in the middle of the novel defines these contrasting attitudes:

> *dem poretses hint vos zaynen kapabl tsu tseraysn a mentsh oyf shtiker un vos gershn hot far zey getsitert bizn letstn tog, hobn epes oyf a soydesdikn veg geshlosn sholem mit im, yankevn, gedreyt mit di ekn ven er hot zikh dernentert tsum toyer.* (Y 177)

> The landowner's dogs, that were capable of tearing a person to shreds and that terrified Gershon to his dying day, appeared in some way to have made a secret truce with Yankev — when he approached the gate they wagged their tails.

Here we have a vignette of the typical *shtetl* dog-versus-Jew antipathy, but countering this stereotype the dogs here are credited with a capacity to discriminate, and they somehow accept Yankev — he has lived with animals and "understands" them. Yankev's empathy with the world of nature and in particular his relationship with the dog whom he curiously names Bilom (English: Balaam) parallel Bashevis's personal vegetarianism and horror at animal abuse, manifest throughout his works and often expressed in his public statements.[9] Why did Bashevis choose to have the chief character of his novel call a dog by the biblical name Bilom, and what role does this creature play in a novel whose core is the love between a man and a woman from seemingly irreconcilable worlds? *Der knekht* proves to be a web of antinomies which are ultimately brought into a pattern of reconciliation. Bilom (Balaam) plays a significant role in this pattern.

Bilom in Bashevis's *Der knekht*

The Autonomy of Animal Life

Der knekht opens with a bird cry, which in retrospect sounds like a clarion call. The first animal encounters in *Der knekht* are anthropomorphically framed: the bird signals to its *mishpokhe,* "family," the approach of day, the cow turns its head to look with curiosity at the human—*hintervaylekhts* means "cunningly" as well as "backward"—and the human addresses the cow by name and engages in sociable chatter. On arising, Yankev recites *Moyde ani,* a prayer which, because it does not mention God's name, can be said before cleaning oneself, and washes his hands:

> *in der rege hot a ku zikh oyfgeshtelt. zi hot umgekert dem bahorntn kop un geton a kuk hintervaylekhts, vi naygerik tsu zen vi azoy der mentsh hoybt on dem frimorgn. di groyse oygn, ful mit shvartsapl, hobn opgeshlogn dem purpur fun zun-oyfgang.*
> *—gut morgn, kvyatula!—hot yankev tsu ir geredt.—zikh gut oysgeshlofn, ha?* (Y 9)

At that moment a cow stood up. She turned her horned head and gave a cunning glance backward, as though curious to observe how this man started the morning. Her huge eyes, almost all pupil, reflected the purple of the sunrise.

> —Good morning, Kwiatula!—Yankev said to her.—Have you slept well, then?

Genesis tells us that on the fifth day God gave humans dominion over all the animals, but at the outset of *Der knekht* we read:

> *a gayer iz gefloygn iber dem kholel, oysterlish pamelekh, ful mit nakhtisher ru, mit der fartrakhtkeyt fun a bashefenish vos iz iber ale mentshlekhe badrengenishn. yankevn iz forgekumen az der gayer flit shoyn azoy on iberrays zint der velt-bashafung.* (Y 10)

A hawk flew with studied slowness across the skies, sated with nocturnal rest, rapt in the musings of a creature which is above all human constraints. Yankev had the feeling that the hawk had been flying in this manner without interruption since the Creation.

In his captivity, Yankev, the former yeshiva student turned herdsman, has learned to "read" nature: *yankev iz gevorn aza meyvn oyf flantsn az er hot dershmekt yedes bliml, yedes grezl* (Y 12), "Yankev had become such an authority on plants that he knew the smell of every variety of flower and grass." In developing his chief character in a manner strikingly different from the conventional Jewish norm, perhaps Bashevis recalled Knut Hamsun's lyrical and romantic novel *Viktoria,* which he himself translated into Yiddish at the age of twenty-five.

In *Viktoria,* the hero, the miller's son in love with the landowner's daughter, is wholly at home in nature. In the first pages of Hamsun's novel we find the hero as a passionate lover of nature, etching on stone and talking to himself, all details strikingly analogous to elements in *Der knekht.* Although this comparison offers a subject for study in itself, here it is worth noting the potential influence on *Der knekht* of the following passages in Bashevis's own Yiddish translation of *Viktoria:*

> *er hot zikh umgekukt tsu zayne feygl in vald, er hot zey ale gekent, gevust vu s'zenen do zeyere nestn, hot farshtanen zeyere koyles — un hot zey opgeentfert mit farsheydene rufn. er hot zey shoyn nisht eyn mol gebrengt kleyne mel-keykelekh fun foters mil.* (Knut Hamsun, *Viktoria,* Yiddish translation by Y. Bashevis [Vilna: B. Kletskin, 1929], pp. 5-6)

> He looked out for his birds in the wood. He knew them all, of course, knew where their nests were, understood their cries and answered them with a variety of calls. More than once he had given them pellets of dough kneaded from the flour in his father's mill. (Knut Hamsun, *Victoria: A Love Story,* newly translated from the Norwegian by Oliver Stallybrass [London, 1974], pp. 3-4)

> *ale boymer baym veg zenen geven zayne gute bakante. in friling hot er fun zey getsapt zhivitse un in vinter iz er geven far zey a kleyner foter, hot fun zey opgeshoklt dem shney un tsurik oyfgeshtelt di tsvaygn. afile oybn, in dem far-lozenem granit-brukh, iz im keyn shum shteyn nisht fremd geven. in a sakh shteyner hot er oysgehakt oysyes un tseykhns . . .* (*Viktoria,* p. 5)

> All these trees bordering the path were good friends of his. In the spring he had drained their sap; in the winter he had been almost like a father to them, releasing them from the snow which weighed their branches down. Even up in the abandoned granite quarry no stone was a stranger to him; he had cut letters and symbols on them all . . . (*Victoria,* pp. 4-5)

> *. . . er iz gevoynt geven do arumtsukrikhn un tsu redn mit zikh aleyn . . .* (*Viktoria,* p. 6)

> He often wandered around here, talking aloud to himself. (*Victoria,* p. 5)

In an earlier (and stranger) Hamsun novel translated by Bashevis — *Pan: fun leytenant tomas glans ksovim* (Pan: From Lieutenant Thomas Glahn's Papers) (Vilna: B. Kletskin, 1928) — the protagonist reminisces about his life two years

Bilom in Bashevis's *Der knekht*

earlier in the North as a hunter, where he lived with a dog he named Aesop—a Greek name which doubtless stimulated our Jewish writer to find an equally striking Hebraic one for his dog—in a forest cabin next to a "magical" and "friendly" boulder, attuned to the life of flora and fauna about him. Here is one passage from Bashevis's translation, which, perhaps somewhat crudely (one really needs to know the original Norwegian), makes explicit the kind of coupling of Eros and nature which characterizes *Der knekht:*

> *ober itst in der nakht-sho zenen plutsling aroysgekumen in vald groyse, vayse blumen. zeyere bekherlekh zenen ofn, zey otemen. tsoytike nakht-babelekh zetsn zikh avek tsvishn zeyere bleter un makhn tsitern dos gantse geviks. kh'gey fun eyn blum tsu der anderer. zey zenen baroysht. zey zenen geshlekhtlekh baroysht, un kh'ze zeyer baroyshung. (Pan, p. 43)*

James W. McFarlane renders this passage as follows:

> But now, in the night hours of the forest, great white flowers have suddenly opened out, their chalices spread wide, and they breathe. And furry hawkmoths bury themselves in their petals and set the whole plant quivering. I go from flower to flower; they are in ecstasy, and I see their intoxication. (Knut Hamsun, *Pan,* translated by James W. McFarlane [London, 1974], p. 52)

Like the other herdsmen among whom he lives, Yankev has to keep a dog as protection against wild beasts. At the outset he does not like his sharp-toothed black dog, and his repulsion is both visceral and theological. He cannot bear to be licked by the dog and recalls how the Talmud paints dogs and how certain kabbalists, especially the Ari (Rabbi Isaac Luria), saw them as devils:

> *yankev hot gemust haltn a hunt. di hint hobn bashitst di beheymes un oykh di pastukher fun vilde bestyes. in onhoyb hot yankev nisht gern gehat dem shvartsn keylev mit di sharfe tseyn un mit der shpitsiker morde. er hot nisht gelitn nisht zayn biln un nisht zayn lekn. zaynen den nisht di reshoem geglikhn tsu hint? yankev hot gedenkt vos di gemore zogt vegn hint un vi azoy der ari un andere mekubolem farglaykhn di hint tsu di klipes. (Y 15–16)*

> Yankev was obliged to keep a dog. The dogs protected both the cattle and the herdsmen from wild animals. At first Yankev had disliked the black dog with its sharp teeth and pointed muzzle. He could tolerate neither its barking nor its licking. Were not the wicked akin to dogs? Yankev remembered what the Gemara said about dogs and how the Ari [Rabbi Isaac Luria], along with other kabbalists, compared dogs to the satanic hosts.

Leonard Prager

Curiously, the Ari in particular greatly praised the *Perek shiro* (in Yiddish, *Peyrek shire*), that remarkable tract in which each element or creature in Nature praises God daily according to its character.[10] Women would come upon this devotion in the opening pages of their *Sidur Korban Minkho* (in Yiddish, *Korbn-minkhe-sider*), which a scholar like Yankev would not have used.[11] Here indeed the dog is not omitted, but he appears in the last two lines of the last section. And what *klovim oymrim,* "dogs say," is *bo-u nishtakhave ve-nikhroo lifney-adoynoy oyseynu,* "come and let us bow down and fall upon our knees before our Creator." The dog's dependency here makes him a model for humanity, which should also totally trust in God. Yankev, however, comes to appreciate his dog in an unprogrammatic manner, endowing him with an identity by giving him a name and discovering in the canine character not cravenness but simple faithfulness:

> *ober mit der tsayt hot yankev ongehoybn zikh tsugevoynen tsu dem keylev. er hot im afile gegebn a nomen: bilom. bilom hot yankevn aroysgevizn getrayshaft. ven yankev hot zikh oysgeshtrekt unter dem boym, hot bilom zikh avekgezetst, oysgetsogyn di lapes, iber im gevakht.* (Y 16)

> Gradually, however, Yankev began to grow accustomed to the dog. He even gave him a name: Balaam. Balaam was loyal to Yankev. When Yankev stretched out under a tree, Balaam sat down, stretched out his paws, and kept watch over him.

Why Bilom (Balaam)?

Why does Yankev name his dog Bilom? Is this a nonce choice by the author or does it carry significance? It is not a usual name for a dog, but then some dogs—both in life and in literature—have unusual names. Writing of Shmuel Yosef Agnon's *Tmol shilshom* (Formerly) (Tel Aviv: Shokn, 1945), which he calls "probably the best modern Hebrew novel," Ezra Spicehandler also claims that "the story within the story, that of Balak the dog, is one of the profoundest animal symbolic fables in world literature."[12] The French translators of the novel chose to give it the title *Le Chien Balak* (The Dog Balak), and the dog is unquestionably central to the novel at every level. Agnon's dog has, among numerous other interpretations, been seen as symbolizing Zionist secularism as against traditional Judaism and as a positive as well as an evil force.[13] In *Der knekht,* the dog Bilom—named for the Gentile seer/soothsayer summoned by the Moabite king Balak to curse Israel who blesses

Bilom in Bashevis's *Der knekht*

her instead — is linked with Vanda and represents instinctual freedom as opposed to the ceaseless self-examining and inhibited behavior of Yankev. Is Bashevis's Bilom some kind of associative response to Agnon's Balak and equally symbolic?

The biblical Balak is unequivocally an enemy of Israel. The biblical Balaam — there are fifty-seven mentions of him in the Hebrew Bible and two in the New Testament — is to this day a puzzle to scholars. Both the biblical and postbiblical views of him are contradictory. In one passage he is Yahweh's obedient servant (Numbers 22:1–21, 31–41; 23:1–24:24), and in the very same Balaam cycle he is satirized as a "blind seer" (Numbers 22:22–30). The majority image of him is of a *rashah*, "a wicked person." One scholar of the Balaam traditions concludes that

> few traditions in the Hebrew Bible manifest so great a degree of internal conflict as do the Balaam traditions. The simple task of designating who Balaam was and what he did in Israelite history appears to have been one of the most delicate and complex issues Israelite tradents ever had to face.[14]

Balaam's paradoxical status may be the key to Bashevis's use of his name. Can one of the most vilified creatures in Yiddish folk consciousness, the dog, be the bearer of consciousness, have a "soul"?

In some Jewish sources, Balaam is credited as being the only Gentile prophet, even greater than Moses in one view.[15] This challenge to Jewish exclusivity in the realm of prophecy is echoed in *Der knekht* by a variety of blurrings or diminutions of the Jew versus Gentile divide. Vanda and her father cease to be total outsiders, at least on a symbolic level. Consider, for example, Yankev's musings on Jan Bzhik:

> *nu, s'iz alts soydes, groyse soydes . . . ale mentshn zaynen bashafn betseylem elokim. ver veyst? aza yan bzhik kon amol zitsn in gan-eydn mit di andere khside-umes-hooylem.* (Y 86)

> Well, these are all secrets, great secrets . . . all human beings are created in the image of God. Who knows? A person like Jan Bzhik might some day be seated among the Righteous Gentiles in Paradise.

More radically, the story of Bilom challenges the human versus animal divide. By the novel's end Yankev asks, *heyst es az a hunt oykh hot hashores hanefesh?* (Y 253), "Does this mean that a dog also has an immortal soul?"

The multiplicity of meanings which a reader may uncover may, of course, never have been intended by an author. The actual history of the name-giving might be

Leonard Prager

quite elementary, even banal. In referring to a very evil person one says in Yiddish: *bilom iz geven a hunt antkegn im,* "Balaam was a dog compared to him." This translates into "he is worse than a dog." Bashevis may have recalled the first four words of this saying, namely, "Balaam was a dog," and called Yankev's dog Bilom on that basis alone.[16] A. A. Robak notes that *oyf aza vos redt nor antkegn yidn ober geyt nit vayter in zayn propagande, zogt men "a bilom,"* "a person who defames Jews but goes no further than to talk is called a Balaam." Robak reasoned that *di asonants shpilt do a shtikl role in der gedanken-farbindung—bilom un biln,* "assonance plays a part in the association between 'bilom' [Balaam] and 'biln' [barking]." It is possible that Bashevis, too, sensed the sound connection in Yiddish between the words for "Balaam" and "barking."[17] In the case of Bilom, however, close readers will persist in seeking more literary relationships. Balaam, we remember, is famous for his ass, the only animal in the Bible empowered with human speech.

Bilom's Symbolic Roles

The symbolic weight of the few scenes in which the dog Bilom appears makes him unforgettable. At an early point in the relationship between Yankev and Vanda we read:

> *der hunt vos iz geshtanen nebn yankevn, iz ir akegngelofn, gedreyt mit dem ek, geshprungen oyf ir mit beyde fodershte lapes. zi hot zikh tsu im tsugeboygn un er hot gelekt ir ponem.*
> *—Bilom, genug!—hot zi bafoyln gutmutik. tsu yankevn hot zi zikh ongerufn:*
> *—er iz tsugelozener vi du.*
> *—a hunt hot nisht keyn flikhtn.*
> *—a khaye hot oykh a neshome . . .* (Y 22–23)

The dog that had been standing near Yankev ran up to her, wagged his tail, leaped up to her with both his front paws. She bent down to him and he licked her face.
—Balaam, enough! she commanded gently. Turning to Yankev, she said:
—He is more affectionate than you.
—A dog has no religious obligations.
—An animal also has a soul.

Bilom's licking of Vanda prompts her to rebuke Yankev with the assertion that the dog shows more affection to her than he does. In defense, the grave former yeshiva instructor replies that dogs have no religious obligations to perform, to which Vanda unhesitatingly responds: *a khaye hot oykh a neshome,* "an animal also has a soul."

Living isolated in the mountains, Yankev develops a close relationship with the dog. Before he starts etching the 613 positive commandments on a rock to buttress his threatened beliefs and to provide himself with an insurance against forgetting the duties of an observant Jew, *bilom der hunt hot genumen dreyen mitn ek un untergeshprungen, a shteyger zayn hintishe zel volt banumen vos zayn har greyt zikh do tsu ton . . .* (Y 39), "Balaam the dog began wagging his tail and jumping up, as though his canine soul understood what his master was about to do here." The notion of a canine soul, first invoked by Vanda, has here — albeit playfully — become plausible. This may be regarded as part of Yankev's education in the mysteries of nature, effected largely through his relationship with the more instinctual, demonstrative Vanda. By the novel's end the dog Balaam's moral nature will become a near certainty to Yankev.

Vanda dies in childbirth, and dragoons come to imprison Yankev as he sits mourning over her dead body. Their child is abandoned. In this historical novel set in the period following the terrible *gzirot takh-ve-tat,* the Chmielnicki pogroms of 1648, a Jew who lived with a Gentile woman was in breach of both Jewish and state law. Yankev, having escaped from the dragoons, lies on the ground in the woods totally exhausted, yearning for the release of death and dreaming feverishly. He imagines he is with his beloved and that her separate personae of Sore and Vanda have merged into one composite as Sore-Vanda; Yosefov and the Gentile mountain village, too, *zaynen gevorn eyns* (Y 244), "became one." Now follows a passage of paramount importance in defining the moral role, in the thematic development of the novel, of the dog Bilom, a passage which, oddly enough, is omitted from the official published English translation, *The Slave:*

> *yankev hot geefent di vies un far im iz geshtanen a hunt. yankev hot im der-kont. s'iz geven bilom, yan bzhiks hunt vos hot oyf im, yankevn, zumer gevakht bay der shtol oyfn barg. vi kumt aher bilom? — hot yankev zikh gefregt. — vi hot er gevust dem veg? yankev hot im tsugerufn, ober er iz nisht tsugekumen. er iz geshtanen fun der vaytns un gedreyt mitn ek. yankev hot im gevorfn a shishke, ober er hot nisht gebilt. shtum, oder vos? . . . yankev hot banumen az der hunt vart oyf im. er hot zikh oyfgehoybn un genumen im nokhgeyn. er iz gegangen un gedrimelt. er iz gegangen un s'hot zikh im gekholemt. s'hot nisht lang gedoyert vi er iz tsugekumen tsum breg vald . . . yankev hot aropgekukt un derblikt in der tif di vaysl . . .* (Y 246)

Leonard Prager

Yankev opened his eyes and before him stood a dog. Yankev recognized him. It was Balaam, Jan Bzhik's dog which during the summer had stood guard over him by the barn on the mountain. How could Balaam have come here? — Yankev asked himself. How did he know the way? Yankev called him but he did not come. He stood at a distance and wagged his tail. Yankev threw him an acorn, but he did not bark. Was he mute, or what? . . . Yankev understood that the dog was waiting for him. He got up and began following him. He walked and dozed, walked and dreamed. Before long he reached the edge of the wood . . . Yankev looked down and in the distance he saw the Vistula . . .

Yankev is guided to the wood's edge, where he sees the safety of the Vistula, but Balaam, clearly a benign manifestation of succor sent by unseen powers, has disappeared. Only now that he has been led to security by the dream-vision of the faithful dog does Yankev recall that Balaam is dead, viciously killed by Stefan, Zagayek's villainous son, as malicious revenge for Vanda's refusal to sleep with him. Perhaps Bashevis was persuaded to omit this crucial metonymic dream sequence because for the publishers of the novel in English it appeared to repeat — rather than to reinforce — the earlier interpolated refugee's tale of another supernatural dog that led a Jew fleeing from Chmielnicki's murderers to safety:

di nakht iz geven varem vi batog. geredt hot men, vi ale mol, fun khurbm. der mansbil, moyshe-ber, hot dertseylt vi azoy er iz antlofn fun khmelnitskis haydamakes. dos kol zayns iz geven shorkhedik, nogedik.
—yo, kh'bin gelofn. der mentsh loyft den? di fis loyfn fun zikh aleyn. kh'hob gevolt blaybn mit zey, mayn mishpokhe, ober az s'nemt dikh on der pakhed, veystu nisht vos du tust. azoy vi kh'bin itst gevorn a vanderer, azoy hob ikh mikh amol nisht aroysgerirt fun der heym . . . gevust hob ikh az nisht vayt fun shtot zaynen faran tsvey derfer: di liptses un di maydanes. in di liptses hob ikh gehat a goy vos iz geven greyt tsu geyn far mir in fayer arayn . . . di maydanes vider hobn gehat a shlekhtn shem . . . zey hobn geholfn di haydamakes ra- birn. nu, shtey ikh oyfn shaydveg un veys nisht vu tsu geyn, rekhts oder links. mit a mol vakst oys a hunt. er iz aroys vi fun der erd. er dreyt oys tsu mir di morde un shoklt mit dem vaydl. mir dukht zikh vi di shtume khaye vil zogn: gey mir nokh. nu, un er nemt take geyn pamelekh un zikh umkukn fun hinter- vaylekhts. bekitser, kh'bin im nokhgegangen un er hot mir tsugefirt glaykh tsu di liptses. az kh'hob shoyn derzen di liptses, hob ikh gevolt ton dem hunt a glet oder efsher im tsuvarfn a shtikl broyt, ober s'iz oys hunt. er iz tsegangen mamesh far mayne oygn. demolt hob ikh gevust az s'iz nisht geven keyn hunt, nor a sheliekh fun himl.

Bilom in Bashevis's *Der knekht*

—der goy hot aykh take oysbahaltn?

*—kh'bin opgezesn bay im vokhn lang in shayer. er hot mir gebrakht fun
aldos guts.* (Y 193–194)

The night was as warm as the day. As always, the talk was of the Destruction.
The man, Moyshe-Ber, related how he fled from Chmielnicki's brigands. He
spoke with a rasping, haunting voice.

—Yes, I ran. Was it I who ran? My feet carried me of their own will. I
wanted to stay with them, with my family, but when fear seizes you, you
don't know what you're doing. Just as I've now become a wanderer, in the
past I never budged from home . . . I knew that there were two villages not
far from town: Lipcy and Maidan. Among the people of Lipcy there was a
Gentile who was prepared to go through fire for me. The people of Maidan,
on the other hand, had a bad reputation . . . They helped the brigands to
plunder. Well, there I stood at the crossroads and didn't know which way to
turn, right or left. Suddenly a dog appeared. He seemed to spring straight
out of the earth. He turned his muzzle toward me and wagged his tail. It
seemed to me that the dumb animal wanted to say: follow me. And, indeed,
he began to move slowly, looking back every now and then to see if I was
following. In short, I followed him and he led me straight to Lipcy. When
I saw Lipcy I wanted to pat the dog or perhaps throw him a piece of bread,
but there was no dog. He vanished before my eyes. I knew then that this was
no dog but a messenger from Heaven.

—Did the Gentile actually hide you?

—I stayed in his hut for many weeks. He cared for me in every possible
way.

The narrator of this incident, Moyshe-Ber, a former shoemaker, unhesitatingly
regards the dog who led him to safety as a messenger from Heaven. Since he also
experiences the kindness of a Gentile who takes grave risks to give asylum to a persecuted Jew, his tale provides a thematically supportive parallel with the story of
Yankev. When he hears Yankev's story, the emissary from Erets Yisroel (Modern
Hebrew: Eretz Yisrael—the Land of Israel) also sees Balaam's role as *hafle vofele,*
"wonder of wonders" (Y 258). If the English-language editors excised the supernatural canine guide as being too blatant a *deus ex machina* device, Bashevis himself may have included him in his original Yiddish text precisely to augment the
theme of communication between animals and humans as part of a beneficent
universe that works in unison to perform the Divine Will.

Vanda's women neighbors call her *a shtume khaye,* "a dumb beast," and much
of the plot of *Der knekht* turns on the subject of dumbness. It is during the period

Leonard Prager

of her enforced and simulated dumbness that Vanda and Yankev communicate most deeply. Communication is something of a mystery, Bashevis seems to be saying. Balaam's ass spoke in human language, having seen an angelic being invisible to Balaam himself.

Heaven Is Also for Animals

Just as Bashevis's use of demons and spirit-figures constitutes a sophisticated psychological notation, so his animal stories and animal scenes may be read as fictionalized pleas for the recognition of higher consciousness in animals, a central notion of modern animal rights movements. The starving cats of Theresa, the widow of the dissolute nobleman Pilitzky, do not eat her corpse after she has starved herself to death—*a tsyekhn az khayes veysn oykh vi optsudanken a voyltuer* (Y 277), "a sign that animals can also show gratitude to those who treat them kindly."

Developments in both medicine and society over the past thirty years have made the subject of animal consciousness a focus of intense controversy, at its extreme fringes shaking the social order. Works gain and lose meanings as time and mores change, and today Bashevis, by virtue of his seemingly eccentric vegetarianism and empathy for animals, has become more contemporary than ever. During the past three decades, the animal rights movement has raised awareness of the moral status of animals. Numerous books and essays in periodicals keep the subject before the reading public. In English alone two journals, *Ethics and Animals* and *Between the Species,* are devoted wholly to issues related to animals. Whereas anthropomorphic discussion of animal behavior was formerly universally scorned as an unscientific projection of human feelings onto brute beasts, today there are scientists who defend such opinions and attribute emotional complexity to many animal species, canines in particular. Jeffrey Masson concludes his recent book *Dogs Never Lie about Love: Reflections on the Emotional World of Dogs* with the credo:

> I am not a religious man, and I pause before using the word soul, but my experiences with the dogs in my life . . . convince me that there is some profound essence, something about being a dog, which corresponds to our notion of an inner soul, the core of our being that makes us most human.[18]

On one level *Der knekht* traces movements of return and retrenchment, yet in its final note it affirms a pattern of extension and inclusion. Yankev as a Jew in his community lives with a tamed and ritualized nature; Yankev as slave herdsman among mountain pagans lives with untamed nature and encounters his libidinal urges without the institutional safeguards against surrendering to them. What is at first alien and savage is somehow brought into a new system of integrated values which harmonizes the seemingly blatant opposition between Jew and Gentile and also between human and animal.

Does a dog have a soul, as Vanda argues? Yankev moves toward acceptance of the notion of a dog enjoying *hashores hanefesh,* "immortality of the soul." This is one aspect of the integration of opposite elements patterned in the novel: the Jewish cemetery goes out to encompass Vanda-Sore; a final vision includes her father as well. And heaven is also for animals.

Notes

1. A typical account of Jewish fear of dogs may be found in Yekheskl Kotik, *Mayne zikhroynes* (Berlin: Klal-Verlag, 1922), pp. 18–20.

2. Yudl Mark, "A zamlung folksfarglaykhn," *Yidishe shprakh* 5:4–6 (1945): 97–139.

3. Psakhye Frimer, "Miluim tsu der zamlung folksfarglaykhn," *Yidishe shprakh* 6:1–2 (1946): 21–29; Mendl Mark, "Dergantsungen tsu der zamlung folksfarglaykhn," *Yidishe shprakh,* 6:3–6 (1946): 133–138.

4. Mendl Mark, "Oftste farglaykh-obyektn," *Yidishe shprakh* 7 (1947): 81. All translations are my own.

5. Ibid.

6. Ibid.

7. Ignats Bernshteyn, *Yidishe shprikhverter un rednsarten* (Warsaw: n.p., 1908); see "hunt," #1 and #45.

8. Yitskhok Bashevis, *Der knekht* (New York: Tsiko, 1967; reprinted Tel Aviv, 1980). All Yiddish quotations in the text of this essay are taken from the Tel Aviv edition and are designated by page numbers after the letter "Y." The published English translation was made from a Yiddish manuscript and appeared five years earlier, in 1962: Isaac Bashevis Singer, *The Slave,* translated by the author and Cecil Hemley (New York: Farrar, Straus, Giroux, 1962). All translations of passages quoted from the novel are mine.

9. See *Der knekht,* p. 20: *er hot keyn mol nisht farzukht keyn fleysh,* "he never ate any meat"; also pp. 60–61, 271. Yankev is disturbed in an almost Jainist manner by the need to kill insects and ends a vegan (p. 287).

10. Simkhe Pyetrushka, *Yidishe folks-entsiklopedye,* 2 vols. (Montreal: Keneder Odler, 1943), vol. 2, p. 842.

Leonard Prager

11. A recent edition of this famous prayer book is *Sidur Korban Minkho* (Jerusalem: n.p., 1971). *Perek shiro* is on pp. 3–8.

12. Ezra Spicehandler, "Hebrew Literature, Modern," in *Encyclopaedia Judaica,* 16 vols. (Jerusalem: Encyclopaedia Judaica, 1971), vol. 8, col. 203.

13. Gershon Shaked, *Shmuel Yosef Agnon: A Revolutionary Traditionalist* (New York: New York University Press, 1989), pp. 146–152.

14. Michael S. Moore, *The Balaam Traditions: Their Character and Development* (Atlanta, Ga.: Scholars Press, 1990), p. 116 (Ph.D. thesis, Drew University, 1988). See also John T. Greene, *Balaam and His Interpreters,* Brown Judaic Studies 244 (Atlanta, Ga.: Scholars Press, 1992), especially pp. xi–xii; Joseph Bar-El, "*Khoyzek* from Zimri and Shelumiel to Balaam and Jesus," in *History of Yiddish Studies* (Winter Studies in Yiddish, vol. 3), ed. Dov-Ber Kerler (Chur: Harwood Academic Press, 1991), pp. 131–140.

15. Greene, *Balaam and His Interpreters,* p. 154.

16. Mordkhe [Mordecai] Kosover writes: *vegn bilomen iz fartseykhnt: bilom iz geven a hunt antkegn im! (zogt men oyf zayer a shlekhtn mentshn); zayn a bilom (a fardorbener),* "It is said of Balaam: 'Balaam was a dog compared to him' (said of a very bad person), and 'to be a Balaam' (i.e., 'corrupted')." Both these expressions are found in Sh. Bastomski, *Baym kval* (Vilna: Naye Yidishe Folks-shule, 1920), p. 27. Yude Elzet [Zlotnik], *Bay undz yidn* (Warsaw: P. Graubard, 1923), pp. 194ff., adds: *biloms moyl hot er (oyf a soyne vos ken sheyn un a sakh reydn),* "He has Balaam's mouth (said of an enemy who talks a lot and well)." See also M. Kosover, "Amolek, mokhe, timkhe = armener" ("Amalek," "mokho," "timkhe" = Armenian), *Yidishe shprakh* 18:1 (April 1957): 6.

17. A. A. Robak in *Filologishe shriftn* 3: 375 (cited in Kosover, "Amolek").

18. Jeffrey Masson, *Dogs Never Lie about Love: Reflections on the Emotional World of Dogs* (New York: Crown Publishers, 1997), p. 191.

Bilom in Bashevis's *Der knekht*

6

Art and Religion in *Der bal-tshuve* (The Penitent)

Alan Astro

Bashevis's novel *Der bal-tshuve,* originally published in *Forverts* in 1973 and translated into English as *The Penitent* ten years later,[1] is cast almost exclusively in the form of a monologue by a Polish Jew named Yoysef Shapiro who has escaped to the Soviet Union during the war and then become a prosperous real-estate developer in New York. Dissatisfied by the spiritual void of American life, disenchanted by the various leftist ideologies espoused by secular Jews, he has decided to return, as it were, to the most Orthodox version of the faith of his forebears.

His monologue follows the form of many of Bashevis's American stories. Shapiro has sought out a famous author—presumably a figure for Bashevis himself—in order to tell him the story of his life. Despite a few adventures—a disappointing marriage, a failed love affair, an encounter with a Hasidic rabbi in lower Manhattan, an attempted tryst with a female passenger on a flight to Israel, a visit to a kibbutz—not much happens, however. Shapiro's monologue consists mainly of a diatribe against modernity in all its forms: novels, theater, and movies; hippies and the sexual revolution; Marxism and liberalism; existentialist philosophy; psychoanalysis; the reading of Scripture divorced from Talmudic commentary; Israeli Hebrew *mit der goyisher sfardisher havore* (Y 153), "in its Sephardic pronunciation with its Gentile flavor" (E 161).

Der bal-tshuve has suffered from weak misreadings from two usually astute critics, Harold Bloom and Ruth Wisse. Bloom writes that Shapiro's voice "is indistinguishable from Singer's own, and there is no way to read this book except as Singer's tirade . . . It is a very unpleasant work, without any redeeming esthetic merit or humane quality."[2] Wisse also equates Shapiro with Bashevis: "despite a technical separation from the author, [Shapiro] clearly speaks with [Bashevis's] full blessing."[3] But since Wisse does not share Bloom's distaste for Orthodoxy, her verdict on the book is less damning. For Wisse, *Der bal-tshuve* is one of Bashevis's later novels, "loose and self-indulgent," in which the "characters reach out for order to the imposed restraints of the anti-modern or pre-modern Jew."[4]

Wisse and Bloom do not get everything wrong about *Der bal-tshuve;* some penetrating comments they make about the novel will be highlighted later. But from greatly different ideological positions, each of them ignores or dismisses the narrative frame within which Shapiro tells his story to a clearly identified authorial persona other than himself. For Wisse and Bloom, Shapiro is simply Bashevis. Yet even in the absence of the kind of narrative structure this novel has been given, one could hardly justify seeing a character — *any* character, whether speaking in the first, second, or third person — as an unmediated mouthpiece for an author.[5] Wisse published her opinion when only the Yiddish original had appeared, but Bloom disregards the following sentence from the epilogue to the English translation, when Bashevis imagines himself being asked whether this novel shows that he has repudiated his own personal doubts about God: "My candid answer is that Joseph Shapiro may have done so, but I haven't" (E 168).

How could Bloom have missed the distance between author and creature, between antagonist and protagonist? It would seem that he did not appreciate the irony implicit in the character's monologue. For Bloom, the unpalatable aspects of Shapiro's diatribes make the novel into "an involuntary satire upon itself . . . Singer seems to be parodying some of Saul Bellow's minor characters . . . in the kind of monologue that in Bellow would be deliberately satirical."[6]

Pace Bloom, there is deliberate irony enough in *Der bal-tshuve,* but it is unstable irony. It is not satirical, corrosive, Voltairian irony. Far more shrewdly than either Bloom or Wisse, Thomas Sutcliffe, a reviewer for the *Times Literary Supplement,* defined Bashevis's stance in this novel:

> Singer has recorded in interviews the fact that he cannot find consolation in the Jewish faith; this novel charts a course which he has decided not to take, and its great achievement is to forgo a false triumph over an alternative refused . . . Singer allows the attractions of faith and its ugliness to exist side by side . . . The success of the book is its own resistance to temptation, the refusal to highlight the bad in Shapiro and play down the good.[7]

Sutcliffe comments on the penitent himself: "His peace of mind at the close of his story is neither mindless nor repellent . . . The decision he makes is to give up the graduated system of choices and values which a secular morality proposes as fundamental."[8] This last observation echoes the epilogue to the novel, where

Art and Religion in *Der bal-tshuve*

Bashevis objects to his character's opting for Orthodoxy: "A total solution would void the greatest gift that God has bestowed upon mankind — free choice" (E 169). No doubt the original Yiddish word in Singer's mind was *bkhire.*

At the end of Bashevis's story "Mayses fun hintern oyvn,"[9] a character asks why God created *di shvartse khevre,* "the company of demons." The answer is that they test humankind. They exist *s'zol zayn bkhire,* "in order that there be free choice" (Y 24/E 75). Likewise, *bkhire* is the theme of a poem Bashevis jotted down on a December 1969 calendar page, which he never intended to publish. Entitled "gadles demoykhin," "The Grandeur of the Mind," the poem begins as follows:

uvokharto bakhayim — bkhire iz gut,
bkhire iz neytik yede minut.
bkhire iz der zin fun lebn —
alts vos got hot undz gegebn:
bkhire in tat, gedank un vort,
bkhire in yeder tsayt un ort.[10]

And thou shalt choose life — choice is good,
Choice is necessary every minute.
Choice is the sense of life
All that God has given us:
Choice in deed, thought, and word,
Choice in every time and place. (my translation)

The Hebrew words *uvokharto bakhayim,* "And thou shalt choose life," are from Deuteronomy 30:19. *Bkhire iz zin in tat, gedank, un vort,* "free choice is sense in deed, thought, and word." Remembering that Bashevis earned some livelihood in Poland translating German novels of the caliber of Thomas Mann's *The Magic Mountain* into Yiddish,[11] we are reminded of the translation scene in Johann Wolfgang von Goethe's *Faust,* where Saint John's *logos* is rendered as *Wort, Sinn, Kraft,* and *Tat,* "word," "sense," "thought," and "deed."[12]

Choice is a central theme in another of Bashevis's novels about a penitent, *Der kuntsn-makher fun lublin* (The Magician of Lublin).[13] Yasha Mazur, its hero, ultimately chooses, like Yoysef Shapiro, to deny himself all choice. Yoysef walls himself in with all the restrictions of Orthodox practice; Yasha does the same and moreover has himself literally immured with brick and mortar. In this regard, it is surely symbolic that *Der bal-tshuve* begins with the encounter between the writer and the penitent at the Western Wall in Jerusalem.

Back in the old existentialist days, one would have said that the choice of both

95

Alan Astro

Yasha and Yoysef not to have to choose is "inauthentic." Was Bashevis the last existentialist writer? Is *bkhire* the *logos* engendering *his* universe? It is hard to imagine Bashevis agreeing, as his creature Yoysef Shapiro summarily dismisses Jean-Paul Sartre as

> *der frantsoyzisher miklompershter filosof, miklompershter shrayber, der shefer fun dem azoy gerufenem ekzistentsyalizm, vos keyner veyst nisht vos er shtelt mit zikh for—azoy fildaytik iz er, azoy umklor, azoy ful mit vidershprukhn.*
> (Y 69)

> the alleged French philosopher, writer, and formulator of existentialism, which no one understands since it is so vague and full of contradictions.
> (E 68)

This diatribe draws our attention precisely because of its weakness, suggesting that Yoysef Shapiro could hardly begin to defend himself against the existentialist's charge of bad faith. Usually Shapiro's ire is more eloquent, if no more judicious. Take, for example, one of Shapiro's many misogynistic moments. Here he is contemplating some women writers, or the wives of writers, in Israel. As the angry eye of Yoysef sees it, even their drinking of lemonade seems to reveal a deep moral flaw:

> *di vayber zeyere—oder efsher zenen dos shrayberins?—murmlen di zelbe kleyne rekhileslekh vos di andere. fun mol tsu mol tuen zey a tsi dem limonad oder dem marantsn-getrank mit zeyere royt-gefarbte lipn. m'darf nisht zayn keyn groyser meyvn tsu zen, az zey hobn di zelbe iluzyes vos di mener, di zelbe umdergreykhbare farvelekhtser, di zelbe khaloymes vegn a glik, vos kon nisht zayn. tsvishn eyn kholem un dem andern leyenen zey an oysgetrakhte mayse vegn a sheynhayt, vos milyonern yogn zikh nokh ir, bavarfn zi mit brilyantn, oder vegn an aktrise, vos krigt tsen toyznt toler a nakht far zingen a lidl in las vegas. fun mol tsu mol khapn zey a blik in a shpigele. derkont men zeyere yorn? iz zey gerotn optsuvishn yedn shpur fun a kneytsh? iz der krem fun helena rubinshteyn virklekh bekoyekh optsushteln dem khurbm vos s'brengt mit zikh di elter?* (Y 97–98)

> Their wives—or were they women writers?—utter the same petty remarks as the others. From time to time they take sips of their lemonade or orange drink with their rouged lips. You don't need any special talent to see that they have the same illusions the men have, the same unattainable urges, the same dreams about a happiness that doesn't exist. Between one dream and the next, they read some ridiculous story about a beauty pursued by millionaires who shower her with diamonds, or about an actress who gets ten thousand dollars a night to sing a little song in Las Vegas. From time to

Art and Religion in *Der bal-tshuve*

time they glance at themselves in mirrors. Is their age showing? Have they managed to erase every trace of wrinkles? Can Helena Rubinstein's cream really halt the destruction [*khurbm*] wrought by time? (E 100, translation modified)

This passage is followed in the text by a blank space, rare in the book. It is though something unspeakable has been said, forcing a silence. Is the depth of these women's narcissism fathomless, as Shapiro seems to believe? Or is the unspeakable really the sheer obscenity of Shapiro's diatribe, the rhetorical excess from which even he must recoil momentarily, as he uses the emotively highly charged term *khurbm* to speak of the ruin of age? After all, the Yiddish term *khurbm,* from the Hebrew *hurban,* is often used to designate three major crises in Jewish history: the destruction of the First and Second Temples in Jerusalem and the Nazi Holocaust. Later on, Shapiro oversteps the bounds of decency even more determinedly, asking the woman with whom he attempted to make a tryst on the plane: *volt ir gekont zayn hitlers gelibte?* (Y 145), "Would you have been able to be Hitler's lover?" (E 152, translation modified). In seeking to show the depravity of his interlocutor, Shapiro simply exposes his own obscenity.

Shapiro places the blame for the Nazis on, among others, *der "groyser shrift-shteler" graf Sad* (Y 107), "that 'great writer' the Marquis de Sade" (E 111), but he himself resembles one of the marquis's torturers, not so much because he takes pleasure in tormenting a potential lover, but because, like Sade's heroes, he drones on in a hermetic discourse, leaving no rhetorical stone unturned in his search for what he has determined to be best for himself. If the Sadean hero's enjoyment resides less in debauchery than in the justifications for it, so Shapiro acknowledges that *aza teyve hot znus—zi farlangt barimeray . . . faktish git farbrekhn veynik hanoe, afile fizishe hanoe. m'muz di hanoe fargresern un gut makhn durkh barimeray* (Y 141), "that's the nature of fornication—it demands boasting . . . Crime actually provides little pleasure, not even physical pleasure. You have to enhance this pleasure through boasting [*barimeray*]" (E 147–148, modified). This moment of insight is also one of blindness: Shapiro does not recognize his own *barimeray* when he repeatedly states, for example, that his sexual excesses make him as evil as a Nazi. The very desire to tell his tale is also a kind of sexual boasting.

Shapiro truly believes he is *der bal-tshuve,* literally not only "the master of repentance," but also "the master of the answer." No one can interrupt him; even the writer to whom he speaks rarely breaks in. The solitary nature of his diatribe is ad-

Alan Astro

dressed in a fairly common moment of lucidity: *kh'hob gevolt zayn aleyn un aleyn makhn—tsum vifltn mol?—dem khezhbm fun mayn lebn* (Y 96), "I wanted to be alone and to take stock, by myself—for the how manyeth time? [*tsum vifltn mol?*] —of my life" (E 98, modified). The published translation proposes a different, but possibly no less ironic, interpretation of *tsum vifltn mol:* "I wanted to be alone and to take stock—for perhaps the first time—of my life." "Take stock" translates into Yiddish as *makhn dem khezhbm,* literally, "take account." *Khezhbm,* "account," one of the most frequently used words in the book,[14] accords well with Shapiro's obsessive-compulsive symptomatology. Bashevis's critique functions not by demonstrating that the penitent's convictions are erroneous, but that his discourse is necessarily exaggerative.

Ruth Wisse notes pertinently that Shapiro's "monologues are sustained by the stunning energy of their antipathy."[15] In this way, they partake of "the spell of Bashevis," to quote the title of Dan Miron's seminal article.[16] Miron writes:

> In spite of its untranslatable, idiomatic juiciness, Bashevis' Yiddish demands of the translator primarily a responsiveness to the feeling of basic narrativity that is actually embodied in the rolling, simple sentences one after the other. The sensitive translator need only revive in his heart the epic, rhythmic sequence of the folk-like tale in his own idiom and he immediately comes upon the recipe that enables a living duplication of the Bashevian narrative charm.[17]

Of course, what is at stake in *Der bal-tshuve* is not the "rhythmic sequence of the folk-like tale," but rather the equally universal tones of the jeremiad, the cadences of "the Moral Majoritarian hovering in each of us, however enlightened we pride ourselves on being," as Bloom felicitously puts it.[18]

Yoysef Shapiro wishes to turn the clock back, not only religiously, but also linguistically. We have already heard him rail at modern Israeli Hebrew and its *goyish* pronunciation. Naturally, speaking English would be *treyf* (ritually unfit), but merely using Yiddish provides no *hekhsher* (rabbinic guarantee of ritual fitness). The first Hasidic rabbi to show Shapiro the way to redemption *hot nisht gekont dem yidish, vos di moderne ortodoksn hobn ibergenumen fun di apikorsim* (Y 58), "didn't know the kind of Yiddish that the modern Orthodoxy had taken over from the unbelievers" (E 56). It is as though Yoysef Shapiro wishes to apply to his life the purely linguistic and esthetic program Bashevis had set out in his 1943 article "Problemen fun der yidisher proze in amerike."[19]

Art and Religion in *Der bal-tshuve*

Arguing against Yiddishist ideologies from that day to ours, Bashevis wrote there that *[di] shprakh heybt on geyn af tsurikvegs, in der tsayt ven dos folk un zayn inteligents geyt foroys* (Y 2), "[the] language is starting to move backward, while the Jewish people and its intelligentsia move forward" (E 5, modified). Yiddish cannot foster a new culture; its purpose, henceforth, is to put us into contact with the old:

> *vi shpanyolish dermont in der shpanisher tkufe—azoy vert yidish alts mer dos loshn, durkh velkhn mir konen zayn gaystik in kontakt mit di letste etlekhe hundert yor fun undzer geshikhte ... der goles—di yidishe kehiles, di kol-layt, di rabonim, shokhtim, nemonim, lomdim; der frumer yidisher kremer un bal-malokhe, di frume yidene, der yeshive-bokher un dos kale-meydl—zaynen un muzn blaybn di tematik ... fun der yidisher literatur.* (Y 10)

> As Ladino recalls the Spanish era, so Yiddish has gradually become the language that links us spiritually with the last several centuries of our history ... The Diaspora—the Jewish communities and their leaders, rabbis, ritual slaughterers, trustees and scholars; the pious shopkeeper and artisan, the fervent housewife, the yeshiva student and the child bride—such are and must remain the subjects ... of Yiddish literature. (E 10, modified)

That does not mean that contemporary life cannot be portrayed: *yidish vet nokh lange yorn dinen vi a mitl tsu farshteyn undzer nekhtn (un teylvayz undzer haynt)* (Y 11), "Yiddish will continue for many more years to serve as a means of understanding our past (and partially our present)" (E 11, modified). Thus those of Bashevis's chief characters like Yoysef Shapiro, living in the present but looking toward the past, fall into the confines of this program. However, *yeder pruv tsu veln traybn undzer loshn foroys iz hofnungsloz* (Y 11), "any attempt to push our language forward is hopeless" (E 11, modified). In other words, Yiddish has a brilliant future behind it.[20]

In *Der bal-tshuve,* Bashevis sets the same limits for *yidishkeyt,* in the sense of Judaism, as he does for the Yiddish language. Yoysef Shapiro says to his author: *ir kont ale khesroynes fun modernem mentsh, nisht mer—ir vilt nisht aroystsien di konsekventsn fun ayer visn. ven ir tut eyn trit vayter, volt ir gevorn a polner yid* (Y 15), "You know all the faults of modern man, but you don't want to draw the conclusions from your knowledge. If you took one step further, you'd become a full-fledged Jew" (E 14, modified). But Bashevis does not follow his creature, because he knows that representing the Jewish past in art is not the same as re-creating it in life.

So how could readers confuse Shapiro with Bashevis? It seems they may have

Alan Astro

swallowed a red herring, though that is probably not the right idiom. Like Bashevis, Shapiro decides to embrace vegetarianism despite the mistrust it calls forth among his fellow worshipers, the *mekhitse* (Y 129), "barrier" (E 134), it places between him and them: *vegetarizm hobn zey batrakht far a shtik veltlekhkayt* (Y 129), "they considered vegetarianism a kind of secularism" (E 134). For example, Sabbath observance obligates enjoyment of meat and fish, if possible. But this matters little to Shapiro: *afile ven s'zol aroyskumen a bas-kol fun himl az hargenen a bashefenish, fargisn zayn blut iz a gute zakh un a mitsve, volt ikh geentfert vi yener tane: eyn mashgikhin bevas kol* (Y 44), "Even if a voice from Heaven decreed the slaughter of animals and the shedding of their blood to be a virtue, I would respond like that Tanna [one of the rabbis whose teachings are included in the Mishnah] who said, 'We don't care about voices from Heaven'" (E 41).

To the very end Shapiro is not sure in his faith; he declares himself *greyt tsu vern a yid afile oyb di toyre iz an oysgetrakhte zakh un keyn got iz kholile nishto* (Y 151), "ready to become a Jew even if the Torah were a figment of the imagination and if there were no God" (E 158, modified); *keyn fulshtendike emune iz efsher in gantsn nisht faran* (Y 154), "Maybe there is no such thing as total faith" (E 161). However, there is one thing about which he has no doubt, as he states, using the Maimonidean formula *beemune shleyme,* "with perfect faith": *ikh gleyb beemune shleyme, az vi lang mentshn veln fargisn dos blut fun gots bashefenishn, vet nisht zayn keyn menukhe af der velt* (Y 44), "I believe with perfect faith that so long as people shed the blood of God's creatures, there will be no peace on earth" (E 41–42, modified).

In a characteristically narcissistic gesture, Bashevis vouchsafes his character one existentially authentic moment: his vegetarianism. Conscience, rather than willfully uncritical obedience, demands this stricture of Shapiro. Unlike Judaism, vegetarianism does not serve him as a foil against modernity, a foil whose limitations are all too apparent to him. He is no dupe of his inauthenticity; he knows his religiosity to be an empty gesture against his *hilflose Zeitgenossenschaft,* his "helpless contemporaneity," to use Robert Musil's expression from *The Man without Qualities.*[21] Shapiro's lucidity extends even to his identity as a *Mann ohne Eigenschaften.* At one point he is *farshtumt—dershtoynt vi dramatish mayn lebn iz gevorn un gepleft fun mayn eygener kharakterlozikayt* (Y 79), "baffled by the dramatic turn of events my life had taken and by my own lack of character" (E 79–80). Shapiro's "lack of character," the absence of profundity which bothered Harold Bloom, is

Art and Religion in *Der bal-tshuve*

actually an element of the allegorical texture of this book, which portrays the competing claims of art and religion on postmodern sensibility.

Shapiro is a disbeliever in Freudian *vilde boykh-svores, narishe pshetlekh* (Y 61), "wild, unfounded theories and far-fetched conclusions" (E 59) and other unfair characterizations of the Jewish mother—he speaks of her as *di emese yidishe mame —nisht yene vos . . . di psikhoanalitiker batrakhtn far der sibe fun ale gaystike krankaytn* (Y 115), "the true Jewish mother—not the one whom . . . psychoanalysts see as the cause of every mental illness" (E 11, modified). Shapiro would, of course, declare his Id and Superego to be something other than psychic agencies: *far aykh efsher iz dos vort yeytser-hore nisht mer vi a simbol. ober far mir zenen der yeytser-hore un der yeytser-tov di same realistishe vezns, di same esents fun der virklekhkayt* (Y 78), "To you, perhaps the expression 'Evil Spirit' has no more than a symbolic meaning, but to me both the Evil Spirit and the Good Spirit are real, the very essence of reality" (E 79). Shapiro's inner psychomachia, his polemics with his good and evil impulses, takes up much of his monologue, providing it with the thinnest possible veil, allowing it to continue by woefully masking its solipsism. In one of these internal dialogues, the *yeytser-hore,* personified both as *der sotn,* "Satan," and *a shretl,* "an imp," points to Shapiro's *hilflose Zeitgenossenschaft:*

> —*kh'hob gezen a sakh azoyne bal-tshuves vi du—hot der sotn getaynet— s'iz bay zey nisht mer vi a kapriz . . .*
> —*oyb kh'kon nisht zayn keyn yid, vel ikh makhn a sof tsu mayn lebn— hob ikh geshrign in mir.*
> —*dos aleyn zenen di verter fun a modernem mentsh—hot a shretl mir arayngeroymt in oyer.* (Y 123)

> "I've seen a lot of such penitents as you," Satan countered. "It's no more than a passing fancy . . ."
> "If I can't be a Jew, I'll put an end to my life!" I shouted within me.
> "These are the words of a modern man," an imp whispered in my ear.
> (E 128)

We have seen Shapiro asking why the writer to whom he tells his tale does not acknowledge his thorough distrust of modernity to become, like him, *a polner yid,* "a full-fledged Jew." We may wonder why, given Shapiro's lucidity—and his vegetarianism—he does not draw the proper conclusions from his doubts and become Bashevis. That, precisely, is Shapiro's problem. He cannot become an artist.

Alan Astro

Of course, he can be forgiven that. We cannot all be artists. But what is worse is that Shapiro refuses to admit the place of art in his own system of values, which is one more example of his inauthenticity. This assertion is based not so much on a reading of Shapiro's numerous diatribes against what he calls *di shmeylike kunst* (y 120) — an expression not rendered in the English version (see e 124), but one might render it as "*shmoly* art," reflecting a possible Yiddishism in English, *holy-shmoly* — as so many examples of neurotic denial, though that cannot be discounted. Likewise, we can imagine that Shapiro is merely feigning indifference toward art when he says: *nokhn davenen hob ikh geton epes vos kon aykh forkumen melodramatish, ober ikh bin nisht keyn literat un mikh art nisht tsi ikh bin dramatish oder melodramatish* (y 56), "After praying, I did something which may appear to you melodramatic, but I'm not a literary man and I don't care whether I am dramatic or melodramatic" (e 53). More pointedly, there is his irrepressible need to tell his story to a *writer* — a writer of whose work he describes himself as *a heyser khosed* (y 9), "a fervent disciple" (e 6) or, more exactly, "an ardent Hasid," before he became a *khosed* of a more literal kind.

Shapiro spins the religious metaphor further: *vu ir zent gekumen in nyu-York darshenen, bin ikh geven tsvishn oylem . . . emes, ir't mikh nisht gekont. kh'hob yedes mol gemuzt zikh far aykh forshteln fun s'nay* (y 9), "Wherever you *sermonized* in New York, I was there in the audience. True, you didn't know me. I had to introduce myself to you each time anew" (e 6; emphasis added in both versions). The artist's failure to recognize the character he has created can be read as symbolizing the character's unawareness of the importance of art in his psyche. Indeed, Shapiro places Madame Bovary, along with Anna Karenina, Raskolnikov, and Taras Bulba, in the category of typical literary characters, all of whom are *rotskhim un noyefim* (y 121), "murderers and adulterers" (e 125, modified). Yet on this score, as elsewhere, he does not hesitate to contradict himself. To illustrate the glory of the endless strictures of Orthodoxy, he asks: *vifl "khumres" nemen af zikh yene, vos zenen arayngeton in literatur . . . ? kh'hob ergets geleyent, az flober hot keyn mol nisht in zelbn kapitl ibergekhazert dos zelbe vort* (y 87–88), "Think of the many restrictions assumed by those who are concerned with literature . . . I read somewhere that Flaubert never repeated a word within the same chapter" (e 88).

Di shmeylike kunst, "*shmoly* art," turns out to be *di heylike kunst,* "holy art," though Shapiro does not say so directly. However, he justifies his choice of faith

Art and Religion in *Der bal-tshuve*

ultimately on esthetic rather than religious grounds, as a matter of taste. He says to the woman whom he has attempted to seduce on the plane:

oyb milyonen daytshn hobn zikh makriv geven far dem gets hitler un nokh azoy fil milyonen rusn un yidn hobn zikh makriv geven far dem gets stalin, bin ikh greyt zikh makriv tsu zayn, oder tsum veynikstn tsu laydn tsulib dem "gets," vos hot gegebn di tsen gebot un di gantse toyre . . . [ikh] vil . . . a gets loyt mayn aynzen un loyt mayn geshmak. (Y 148–149)

If millions of German sacrificed themselves for the idol Hitler, and so many millions of Russians and Jews sacrificed themselves for the idol Stalin, I'm ready to sacrifice myself—or at least to suffer—for the "idol" that gave the Ten Commandments and the whole Torah . . . I want an idol in accordance with my understanding and my taste. (E 156, modified—interestingly, the published English version removes the appeal to taste, rendering instead: "I want an idol that meets my requirements")

Similarly, in the Yiddish original the novel ends with Shapiro's stating that even if the Jewish conception of God should turn out to be false—*az . . . s'vet zayn leys din veleys dayen* (Y 156), "if there is neither Justice nor Judge," another formulation significantly omitted from the English version (see E 163–164)—at least he will have lived *loyt mayn ibertsaygung un loyt mayn geshmak* (Y 156), "according to my conviction and my taste." This last phrase is also omitted from the English version, which ends: "I have accepted the Torah and its commentaries because I am sure that there is no better choice. This faith keeps growing in me all the time" (E 164). The English version ultimately takes a less ironic attitude toward tradition than the Yiddish original; no doubt Bashevis presumed that his Yiddish readership's feelings toward religion were not as reverent as the attitudes nourished by the somewhat puritanical American public.

Shapiro finds his greatest sexual happiness with his new, Orthodox wife. The irony of this is not that the omnipresence of sex in the modern world is castrating, as Shapiro extravagantly suggests:

ven a mantsbil geyt shlofn mit di hayntike nekeyves, geyt er faktish in bet arayn mit ale ire gelibte. deriber zenen faran haynt azoy fil homoseksualistn. der moderner man shloft gaystik mit umtsolike andere mener (Y 154)

When a man sleeps with a modern woman, he actually gets into bed with all her lovers. That's why there are so many homosexuals today, because modern man is sleeping spiritually with countless other men. (E 162)

Alan Astro

Rather, it is that the alluring, chaste Jewish woman literalizes Shapiro's esthetically motivated choice of religiosity.

Shapiro recalls that, before his conversion, he had little truck with those who asked him to support the cause either of religion or of art:

> *di frume hobn farlangt ikh zol shtitsn di toyre, di andere hobn geploydert vegn kultur . . . di yeshives, hob ikh gehaltn, veln oyftsien batlonim, parazitn. nu, un vemen un vos vet oyftsien di kultur? rotskhim un zoynes.* (Y 21)

> The pious Jews demanded that I support the Torah and the secular Jews begged for culture . . . The yeshivas, I felt, would raise daydreamers and parasites. Well, and whom and what would culture raise? Murderers and whores. (E 20–21, modified)

Shapiro comes to suspend his disbelief in Orthodoxy and excuses religious Jews who do not live up to their faith: *s'zenen do shlekhte kharaktern tsvishn zey oykh. dem yeytser-hore hot men nisht derharget* (Y 155), "There are bad people here, too. The Evil Spirit hasn't been liquidated" (E 163). But never will he indulge even the greatest writers: *di azoy gerufene gute shrayber zenen den gut? vos iz dos azoy vikhtik vos elyot oder dzhoys hobn in zinen gehat beys zey hobn gepatshket zeyere puste melitses?* (Y 15), "Are the so-called good writers any good either? What important things did Eliot or Joyce have in mind when they were writing their empty phrases?" (E 14).

This is where Shapiro fails. He proclaims the eternal worth of religion, but dismisses art. He hardly notices that the plane he takes to Israel stops in Rome and Greece. Yet the religious apologist, the *bal-tshuve,* does not have the last word. The ultimate *tshuve,* the final answer, is given by his interlocutor, the writer, who says little throughout and nothing at the end. But as Shakespeare — whose worth even Shapiro grudgingly acknowledges —

> *ikh bin, vi ir veyst shoyn, a knaper onhenger fun modernem mentsh un fun zayn literatur. ober Shekspirs meynung, az di velt iz a teater oder a drama — iz an emes, vos iz farbundn mit dem gloybn in hashgokhe.* (Y 117)

> As you already know, I'm hardly an exponent of modern man and his literature, but Shakespeare's contention that all the world's a stage is a truth that is tied into faith, into the belief in Providence. (E 121)

says in *King Lear,* true love is silent. The apology of art is art itself.

Religious Orthodoxy cannot countenance worldly culture as an end in itself.

Art and Religion in *Der bal-tshuve*

But Bashevis, by portraying both the logic and incoherence of religious discourse, suggests that art can grasp religion more fully than religion can encompass art.

Notes

1. Yitskhok Bashevis, *Der bal-tshuve* (Tel Aviv: Perets Farlag, 1974); Isaac Bashevis Singer, *The Penitent*, no translator listed (New York: Farrar, Straus, Giroux, 1983). All quotations from the novel in Yiddish in the text of this essay refer to the above edition and are designated with page numbers after the letter "Y"; all translations refer to the above-cited English text and are designated by page numbers after the letter "E." For greater precision of meaning, I have occasionally modified the published English translation, as with other source materials cited in both Yiddish and English translation.

2. Harold Bloom, "Isaac Bashevis Singer's Jeremiad," *New York Times Book Review*, September 25, 1983, 3.

3. Ruth R. Wisse, "Singer's Paradoxical Progress," in Grace Farrell (ed.), *Critical Essays on Isaac Bashevis Singer* (New York: G. K. Hall, 1996), p. 112.

4. Ibid.

5. This point is developed by Joseph Sherman, "Author versus Narrator in *The Penitent*: Reconsidering Isaac Bashevis Singer's 'Tirade,'" *Journal of Narrative Technique* 18 (1988): 243–257.

6. Bloom, "Singer's Jeremiad," p. 3.

7. Thomas Sutcliffe, "Making the Leap into Faith," *Times Literary Supplement*, March 23, 1984, 311.

8. Ibid.

9. Yitskhok Bashevis, "Mayses fun hintern oyvn," in *Mayses fun hintern oyvn* (Tel Aviv: Perets Farlag, 1982), pp. 7–25. English translation by the author and Dorothea Straus, "Stories from Behind the Stove," in I. B. Singer, *A Friend of Kafka and Other Stories* (New York: Farrar, Straus, Giroux, 1979), pp. 61–76.

10. "Gadles demoykhin" appears in Jacob Weitzner, "Yitskhok Bashevis Zinger un zayne umbakante poemes," *Yidisher kempfer* 69:2798 (September–October 1998): 11–12.

11. Thomas Mann, *Der tsoyberbarg*, translated by Yitskhok Bashevis, 4 vols. (Vilna: Kletskin, 1930).

12. Johann Wolfgang von Goethe, *Faust*, part 1, vv. 1224–1237 (Munich: Deutscher Taschenbuch, 1983), p. 40.

13. Yitskhok Bashevis, *Der kuntsn-makher fun lublin* (Tel Aviv: ha-Menorah, 1971); English translation by Elaine Gottlieb and Joseph Singer, *The Magician of Lublin* (New York: Noonday Press, 1960).

14. See, for example, *Der bal-tshuve*, pp. 92, 111, 113, 114, 120, 139.

Alan Astro

15. Wisse, "Paradoxical Progress," p. 111.

16. Dan Miron, "Passivity and Narration: The Spell of Isaac Bashevis Singer," translated by Uriel Miron, in Farrell (ed.), *Critical Essays*, pp. 149–61.

17. Ibid., p. 159.

18. Bloom, "Singer's Jeremiad," p. 3.

19. Bashevis, "Problemen fun der yidisher proze in amerike," *Svive* 2 (March–April 1943): 2–13. English translation by Robert H. Wolf, "Problems of Yiddish Prose in America," *Prooftexts* 9 (1989): 5–12.

20. In regard to a Freudian case history, a French psychoanalyst writes: "The Rat Man, like a good neurotic, has his future behind him" (Charles Melman, "On Obsessional Neurosis," in Stuart Schneiderman [ed. and trans.], *Returning to Freud: Clinical Psychoanalysis in the School of Lacan* [New Haven: Yale University Press, 1980], p. 136). Bashevis's Shapiro — with his endless self-reproaches and agonizing choices among options, all of which seem unacceptable — has his place in the pantheon of literary obsessive-compulsives, along with Hamlet and Portnoy.

21. Robert Musil, *Der Mann ohne Eigenschaften,* 2 vols., revised and edited by Adolf Frisé (Reinbek bei Hamburg: Rowohlt, 1981), vol. 1, p. 360; *The Man without Qualities,* 2 vols., translated by Sophie Wilkins and Burton Pike (New York: A. A. Knopf, 1995), vol. 1, p. 391.

Art and Religion in *Der bal-tshuve*

7

"Death Is the Only Messiah"
Three Supernatural Stories by Yitskhok Bashevis

Jan Schwarz

If, to use a simile, one views the growing work as a burning funeral pyre, then the commentator stands before it like a chemist, the critic like an alchemist. Whereas, for the former wood and ash remain the sole objects of his analysis, for the latter only the flame itself preserves an enigma: that of what is alive. Thus, the critic inquires into the truth, whose living flame continues to burn over the heavy logs of what is past and the light ashes of what has been experienced.[1]

Yitskhok Bashevis's first literary portrayal of his psychosexual development as a young Yiddish writer who had just left behind the traditional Hasidic world was his 1928 story "Oyfn oylem-hatoyhu" (In the World of Chaos).[2] In Bashevis's 1981 spiritual autobiography, *Love and Exile: An Autobiographical Trilogy*, he referred to this story as a veiled self-portrait of the writer as a young man:

"In the World of Chaos" might have provided me my first direction as to style and genre. Somehow, I identified with this hero. Just like him, I lived yet was ashamed to live, ashamed to eat and ashamed to go to the outhouse. I longed for sex and I was ashamed of my passions.[3]

Stylistically, this story pointed the way for Bashevis's supernatural storytelling, an art in which he was to excel. Simultaneously, Bashevis transformed his psychological complex of repressed sexuality and shame into what would become his typical alter ego: an isolated individual who, exiled from his community, wanders aimlessly outside the boundaries of normative Jewish society. The significance of "In the World of Chaos" in Bashevis's oeuvre is further substantiated by the fact that he republished this tale in the 1988 issue of *Di goldene keyt*.[4] As far as I know, this is the only story from Bashevis's Polish period (1925–1935) that he later republished in Yiddish after being awarded the Nobel Prize in 1978. Clearly, the story had a crucial importance for the writer in his old age as his first artistic attempt to express his personal dilemma.

"In the World of Chaos" belongs to a series of naturalist stories which Bashevis wrote between 1925 and 1932. Many of his stories from this period highlight the ugliness and depravity of the *shtetl* and its surroundings. "In the World of Chaos," however, expressed a new artistic direction in Bashevis's work, less influenced by Abramovitsh/Mendele's satirical realism than by Y. L. Peretz's symbolist tales. In his 1943 essay "Arum der yidisher literatur in poyln" (Concerning Yiddish Literature in Poland), Bashevis acknowledged Peretz's pivotal influence:

> Two alternatives remained for the Yiddish writer: either he, too, could ridicule the despised and tragic Kabtsansk, to which he was linked by fate; or he could dig into the depths, look backward, seek in poverty [of Jewish life] the great, the profoundly Jewish, the eternal. Peretz had chosen the latter. With talent, one can ridicule only once. On the other hand, the work that Peretz had begun was pathbreaking. It revealed the beginning of the road that Yiddish literature would have to take if it were to exist at all.[5]

Peretz's tales provided an artistic method which would serve as a point of departure for Bashevis's exploration of self, society, and the supernatural. The leading Yiddish writers of the 1920s, in particular Dovid Bergelson, Der Nister, and Israel Joshua Singer, were all, in their own way, protégés of Peretz. They came of age as writers under the auspices of Peretz's humanist ideology and his secular adaptation of traditional Jewish sources. Bergelson's impressionism, Der Nister's symbolism, and I. J. Singer's naturalism suggested divergent artistic and ideological approaches to contemporary Jewish life. However, all three shared a fundamental belief that literature could reflect the social-historical and spiritual conditions of Eastern European Jewry. All of them believed, moreover, in literature's power to inspire the reader to change these conditions. Bashevis, in contrast, returned to a pre-Enlightenment discourse in which literature was used primarily for entertainment and moral edification, for example, as a warning against forcing "the end of days." He refused to employ literature for extraliterary ends such as addressing political, cultural, or religious issues in the rapidly changing environment of Polish Jewry in the 1920s and 1930s.

"Death Is the Only Messiah"

The protagonist of "In the World of Chaos" is Shimen, the son of a rabbi. He is driven by a messianic quest to hasten the coming of the Messiah by destroying "the Evil One." Armed with amulets, ancient Aramaic and Hebrew formulas, and a stubborn, angry will, he is the prototype of the commissar for whom the end always justifies the means. After he has left the *shtetl,* Shimen ignores his parents' exhortation to return home. His parents believe that he has been seduced by Lilith, the mother of the demons, and consider him insane.

At a Leipzig market, Shimen spots a beggar with a deformed face and decides that his search has come to an end. He yells out the Aramaic incantations which are supposed to destroy "the evil forces." The Christian market people misunderstand Shimen's odd behavior, taking it to be a Jew's attempt to steal from a poor beggar, so they beat Shimen severely until he sinks into unconsciousness. Badly bruised, he seeks refuge in a mill, where he encounters a rabbi poring over a holy book. The story ends with the rabbi telling him that *a blinder zet dokh az bist a bar-menen. knepl oyf di kapote, vestu zen az geyst in takhrikhim!*—"even a blind person can see that you are a corpse. Unbutton your coat, and you will see that you are walking about in a shroud."[6]

This plot summary cannot do justice to the elaborate style of the story. Unlike the simple narrative flow of most of Bashevis's short stories, "In the World of Chaos" is narrated in typical naturalist fashion. The author paints a raw, unsentimental picture of the protagonist and his environment by using an abundance of descriptive adjectives in long, winding sentences. In this early short story, Bashevis was still searching for his artistic voice. The story's *muser-haskl* (moral) quoted above is its most interesting feature. It encapsulates Bashevis's unique employment of the image of death, a key concept of his later "philosophy of protest."

In his autobiography *Gloybn un tsveyfl oder di filosofye fun protest* (Faith and Doubt or the Philosophy of Protest), serialized in *Forverts* from 1976 to 1981 and entitled *Love and Exile* in its modified English version, Bashevis elaborated a fantasy about temples where people could study and protest "the various misfortunes God had sent to humans and animals."[7] In this temple, the Book of Job will be used as the new Torah, except for the final segment in which Job's suffering is mitigated through Divine intervention. The protesting prophets of the temple are writers and philosophers such as Otto Weininger, Edgar Allan Poe, and Arthur Schopenhauer, "who rejected life and considered death the only messiah,"[8] a belief that echoes the last words of the English translation of Singer's family saga *Di familye*

Jan Schwarz

mushkat (The Family Moskat, 1950). What keeps Bashevis from committing suicide, the most logical consequence of his "philosophy of protest," is "the idol of literature and the idol of love."[9]

Yet his love life, as Bashevis depicted it in his autobiography, was characterized by promiscuity and lack of true satisfaction. His sexual encounters, all of which took place in secret, occurred in a social vacuum; they were primarily played out as ritual bodily exercises without any deep affection or spiritual meaning. As for his writings, Bashevis considered them a further contribution of falsehoods to "the world of lies/falsehood," the material world or *oylem-hasheker*, far removed from "the world of truth" or *oylem-ho'emes*, the realm of death.

The first artistic expression of Bashevis's "philosophy of protest" in which the image of death plays a crucial role as the ultimate negation of all redemptive, life-affirming impulses had appeared nearly half a century earlier in "In the World of Chaos." In this story Bashevis rejected any allegorized view of death as a reflection of social, political, and existential conditions in the *shtetl*, rejecting in other words the way Peretz had presented death in his 1904 story "Di toyte shtot" (The Dead Town).[10] In that story, Peretz depicted a *shtetl* without legal or socioeconomic foundations. By describing corpses who rise from their graves and take over a *shtetl*, Peretz exposed the *luftmentsh* (the Jewish version of the Russian "superfluous man," who is poor, a dreamer, often a schemer, without a definite occupation—Sholem Alekhem's character Menakhem Mendl is the classic exemplum) mentality of a Jewish society lacking all vision and any ability to transcend its habitual, commonplace way of life. Bashevis, by contrast, focused on the futility of any quest, whether political or religious. His nihilist esthetics viewed social transformation as an impossibility, as a flight from a human condition of chaos that ended only in death.

In *Love and Exile,* Bashevis mentions that he wrote several variations of "In the World of Chaos." One of them is the story "Tsvey meysim geyen tantsn" (Two Corpses Go Dancing),[11] a tale which belongs to a series of demonic monologues under the collective title "The Diary of the Evil Inclination" that were included in his 1943 collection *Der sotn in goray un andere dertseylungen.* Several of the stories in this collection are narrated by the voice of the *yeytser-hore,* the Evil Inclination, who tempts and manipulates the chief characters into performing the most vicious acts.[12]

The *yeytser-hore*'s evocative style is inextricably embedded in a traditional Jew-

"Death Is the Only Messiah"

ish conception of the universe. Many of this conception's specific characteristics have been eliminated from the 1966 English translation. For example, at the beginning of "Tsvey meysim geyen tantsn" the *yeytser-hore* calls out as if he were the *gabbai* (trustee or warden) in a synagogue. But instead of giving the protagonist the honor of being called to the Torah, he exclaims: *yaamud zekl ben flekl, gey tsurik in dayn ru arayn un drey nisht keyn spodek* (Y 289), "Rise, Zekl ben Flekl, return to your resting-place without trying any funny stuff." The English translation renders this irony stodgily as "'Back to your sepulcher, Mr. Corpse,' I order, 'enough of your tricks.'" This is only one of many cases in which the English translation has eliminated *di yidishe tam,* "the Jewish spice" of the *yeytser-hore*'s speech pattern.

Like the eponymous chief character of Peretz's "Bontshe shvayg" (Bontshe the Silent), Bashevis's protagonist in "Tsvey meysim," Itshe-Godl, is a pauper who "lived and died in silence. Like a shadow, he passed through this world." However, unlike the exploited work-horse Bontshe the Silent, Itshe-Godl is depicted as an idle *yeshive bokher* who spends most of his time warming benches in the study house. After his premature death at the age of thirty-six, Itshe-Godl is totally forgotten by both angels and devils instead of being summoned, as Bontshe is, to receive justice in the heavenly court. Only by chance does the *yeytser-hore* learn about "this forsaken cadaver" and decide to have a little fun with it.

The *yeytser-hore* provides Itshe-Godl with a rich man's attire and allows him to visit the marketplace, where he is made to interrogate and subsequently frighten to death his remarried widow. Then the *yeytser-hore* arranges a match between Itshe-Godl and another corpse, that of a wealthy widow. However, in the final morbid scene they are forced to return to their graves before they can consummate their marriage.

In "Bontshe shvayg," Peretz ridiculed Bontshe's passive humility by playing out the traditional theater of reward and punishment in *yene-velt,* the world of the dead. Bashevis, by contrast, parodies any redemptive possibility by replacing the heavenly court filled with angels prosecuting and defending new arrivals devised by Peretz with his own omniscient evil narrator. The *yeytser-hore* derives satisfaction from dragging corpses who exist in a kind of Jewish purgatory through the worst kind of depravity. Bashevis was not interested in psychological realism or historical verisimilitude; instead, he explored the narrative possibilities inherent in his naïve, virtuous characters' potential for Evil.

My final example of Bashevis's use of death imagery in his supernatural stories,

Jan Schwarz

"Di kafeterye" (The Cafeteria, 1968),[13] belongs to his later American stories. In "Di kafeterye," the *yeytser-hore* has been replaced by a semiautobiographical narrator who has lived on the Upper West Side of Manhattan for more than thirty years — that is, for as long as Bashevis himself lived in Poland. This narrator frequents a cafeteria, a hangout for "old bachelors like myself, would-be writers, retired teachers, some with dubious doctorate titles, a rabbi without a congregation, a painter of Jewish themes, a few translators — all immigrants from Poland and Russia" (E 288).

Among these *sheyres hapleytes*, "survivors of the Holocaust," is a young woman named Esther who, along with her father, survived Stalin's labor camps. At their first meeting the sexual attraction between her and the narrator is mutual. However, their relationship remains platonic, based on Esther's admiration of the old writer's literary work and his attraction to the beautiful young woman. A few years later the cafeteria burns down, and when it reopens Esther and the narrator meet again. She tells him that her health is declining and that she might apply for reparation money from the Germans. One night Esther arrives at the narrator's apartment and confides that the night before the cafeteria burned down, she had a vision:

> kh'kum arayn un zey a bild vos kh'l nisht fargesn bizn letstn tog fun mayn lebn, biz der letster minut. ale tishn zenen tsunoyfgerukt un s'zitsn bay zey parshoy-nen ongeton in vayse kitlekh, vi doktoyrim oder sanitarn, ale mit hakn-krayzn oyf di arbeln. oybnon zitst hitler. kh'bet aykh: hert mikh oys. a meshugener hot oykh tayl mol fardint m'zol im hern. (Y 64)

> I went in [the cafeteria] and saw a scene I will not forget to the last day of my life. The tables were shoved together and around them sat men in white robes, like doctors or orderlies, all with swastikas on their sleeves. At the head sat Hitler. I beg you to hear me out — even a deranged person sometimes deserves to be listened to. (E 297)

In the denouement, the narrator sees Esther walking down Broadway arm-in-arm with a man who, he realizes, must be either in his nineties or dead. The story ends on an ironic note of ambiguity: "Yes, corpses do walk on Broadway. But why did Esther choose that particular corpse? She could have got a better bargain even in this world" (E 300).

The cafeteria has replaced Bashevis's father's religious court as the public sphere in which Jews congregate to socialize and unburden themselves about their miserable lives. As a combination of a secular Hasidic *rebbe* (spiritually inspired rabbinic

"Death Is the Only Messiah"

leader) and therapist, the narrator listens to Esther's story with compassion and interest. The image of Hitler reflects the dark side of the survivors' existence in New York. They wander about, lacking any ability to settle down and take control of their destiny. Even Esther, the youngest and most optimistic among them, is caught in a net of Evil, as represented by Hitler. In the story, Esther is transformed from an individual with a personal history into a vague shadow, a figment of the narrator's imagination. Unlike Itshe-Godl, who is eventually honored with a gravestone erected by the community as a means of preventing him from returning to life, both Shimen and Esther exit into oblivion at the end of the story.

Nahman of Bratslav's *Seyfer sipurey mayses* (The Holy Book of Tales, 1815) as well as Hasidic hagiographical material provided models for Bashevis's literary presentation of Shimen's spiritual quest in "In the World of Chaos." In addition, Peretz showed the way in which the traditional *shtetl* could be depicted as a spiritual-religious battleground for characters motivated by modern secular aspirations completely at odds with the traditional environment in which they have been raised.

In "Tsvey meysim geyen tantsn," the supernatural realm is still embedded in a deeply rooted Jewish universe. The story depicts the formulaic Satanic temptation of the righteous man who is at the same time the naïve representative of the folk. Within this narrative structure, it situates the forces of Evil in the inner sanctum of traditional Jewish *shtetl* life. This story effectively turns Peretz's humanist moral universe upside down by presenting instead a moral universe defined by traditionally "good" and "bad" forces. In another story from "The Diary of the Evil Inclination," "Zaydlus der ershter" (Zeidlus the Pope), the epiphany of Zaydlus, the main character, results from his realization that if Satan exists God must also exist. In consequence, he can die peacefully with the assurance that he inhabits a complete moral universe in the terms in which traditional Jewish belief structures it.

Most of the Jewish references and imagery of the first two stories surveyed here are lost in English translation. "Di kafeterye," however, translates without problem into English because of its minimal Jewish style and subject matter. In this story, the supernatural is situated within a realist frame that depicts Holocaust survivors living in New York. The tale's precise historical moment—the immediate aftermath of the Holocaust—and its specific setting, a cafeteria on the Upper West

Jan Schwarz

Side of Manhattan, situate the story in the Gothic, fantastic context of Western literature and place it beyond the pale of the Yiddish supernatural imagination.[14]

In "Di kafeterye" there is no allegorical play on the traditional Jewish categories of "Good" and "Evil." That esthetic and moral construct, it would appear, has lost its meaning after its creators, the Jews of Eastern Europe, have been annihilated in the Holocaust. The only supernatural spark in "Di kafeterye" is kindled by Esther, who stubbornly clings to the Old World values of "true love" and "honesty." Once again, the attraction of Bashevis's narrator to such a "pure" soul triggers his narrative inventiveness.

The narrator proves to be a vampire who sucks dry the life blood of his characters. He turns his encounter with Esther into literary material which, piled up in his apartment in the form of parched manuscripts, he is afraid will ignite. The demonic playfulness of the *yeytser-hore* as he is presented in the earlier stories has been replaced in "Di kafeterye" by a misanthropic Yiddish writer confronted with a rapidly declining readership. His literary production becomes part of the same vicious circle of passivity, forgetfulness, and death that characterizes his Yiddish readers in the cafeteria.

The three stories surveyed here present an extremely bleak view of Jewish life in the twentieth century. For their creator, nothing had changed significantly during the forty years which separated their publication. This static world view, along with Bashevis's refusal to depict himself as influenced by historical, social, or psychological conditions, is perhaps his most distinctively reactionary artistic mark. As Dan Miron has pointed out, Bashevis's depiction of his Jewish characters as passive and victimized is a feature that has made him popular with a non-Jewish readership:

> Bashevis is not just a marvelous story-teller, but, also, some kind of wandering Jew, a modern Ahasuerus whose terrible destiny (the curse of Jesus) drives him on his endless journey and drags him through strange and wild experiences and events—all of them out of the realm of his control.[15]

This stereotypical image of the Wandering Jew exemplified by Shimen in "In the World of Chaos" is, as has been noted by many critics, a characteristic trope of Bashevis's work.

To conclude, it is important to emphasize that the Yiddish original of the two early stories discussed here affords the reader the aesthetic pleasure of partaking in

"Death Is the Only Messiah"

Bashevis's intertextual play with Jewish literary models while, simultaneously, appreciating the narrator's juicy, colloquial Yiddish. What remains in English translation is a set of exotic, fantastic images from a bygone world, minus the richly textured voices of Singer's Yiddish imps, who are so completely at home in the Eastern European Jewish landscape and imagination. Yet it is precisely this folktale style that can be translated so easily into other languages that explains Singer's accessibility to a worldwide audience. As has been demonstrated in the comparison of the three supernatural stories, Singer was able to simplify his narrative style by transforming the naturalism of "In the World of Chaos" into simple folktales modeled on Peretz's neo-Romantic reinvention of the tales of Nahman of Bratslav.

The three stories surveyed here were not scenes from a lost world; they were not like any attempts to resurrect what had been destroyed in historical reality, as were the works of so many other Yiddish writers after the Holocaust. Instead, these stories presented a kaleidoscope of Jewish life, carefully crafted to portray a particularly bleak mythological view of the human condition. As pointed out by many critics, a chaotic, terrifying universe, strangely different from anything else in modern Yiddish literature, can be discerned behind the simple, straightforward narrative flow of Singer's supernatural tales. Singer closed the Yiddish literary canon in late twentieth century America by rejecting humanism and modernism, the two pillars of Yiddish literature which Peretz had created. Instead, Singer offered a nihilist Yiddish scrapbook of supernatural *bobe-mayses* (grandmother's tales) for our postmodern times.

Notes

1. Walter Benjamin, *Selected Writings, Vol. 1, 1913–1926*, edited by Marcus Bullock and Michael W. Jennings (Cambridge, Mass.: Harvard University Press, 1996), p. 298.

2. Yitskhok Bashevis, "Oyfn oylem-hatoyhu," *Di yidishe velt* 1 (Warsaw, April 1928): 53–64.

3. Isaac Bashevis Singer, *Love and Exile: An Autobiographical Trilogy* (Garden City, N.Y.: Doubleday, 1984), p. 151.

4. *Di goldene keyt* 124 (1988): 87–95. I quote from this version.

5. Yitskhok Bashevis, "Arum der yidisher literatur in poyln," *Tsukunft* (August 1943): 471; "Concerning Yiddish Literature in Poland," translated by Robert Wolf, *Prooftexts* 15:2 (May 1995): 119. "Kabtsansk" means "Paupersville" and is the fictional town featured in the work of Mendele Moykher Sforim, the pen-name of Sholem Yankev Abramovitsh.

Jan Schwarz

6. Bashevis, "Oyfn oylem-hatoyhu," p. 95.

7. Singer, *Love and Exile,* p. 350.

8. Ibid.

9. Ibid., p. 169.

10. Y. L. Peretz, "Di toyte shtot," in *Ale verk* (New York: Tsiko, 1947), pp. 75–86.

11. "Tsvey meysim geyen tantsn," in *Der sotn in goray un andere dertseylungen* (New York: Farlag Matones, 1943), pp. 289–305; translated by Joseph Singer and Elizabeth Pollet, "Two Corpses Go Dancing," in *The Séance and Other Stories* (New York: Farrar, Straus, Giroux, 1968), pp. 187–201.

12. Khone Shmeruk discusses "The Diary of the Evil Inclination" in his seminal article "Monologue as Narrative Strategy in the Short Stories of Isaac Bashevis Singer," in David Neal Miller, *Recovering the Canon* (Leiden: E. J. Brill, 1987).

13. Yitskhok Bashevis, "Di kafeterye," published in *Di tsukunft* (March–April 1968) and later included in the collection *Mayses fun hintern oyvn* (Tel Aviv: Farlag Y. L. Perets, 1982), pp. 43–71. English translation by I. B. Singer and Dorothea Straus in *Collected Stories* (New York: Farrar, Straus, Giroux, 1982), pp. 287–300. I have used this English translation.

14. For a compelling analysis of the fantastic as genre and discourse in Western literature, see Tzvetan Todorov, *The Fantastic: A Structural Approach to a Literary Genre* (Ithaca: Cornell University Press, 1975).

15. Dan Miron, "Passivity and Narration: The Spell of Bashevis Singer," *Judaism* 41:1 (Winter 1992): 6–17.

"Death Is the Only Messiah"

III

BASHEVIS'S
INTERFACE
WITH OTHER
TIMES AND
CULTURES

8

Bashevis's Interactions with the *Mayse-bukh* (Book of Tales)

Astrid Starck-Adler

Yiddish is our memory, the bridge between our yesterday and our today.[1]

Obvious in a number of Bashevis's stories featuring demons and ghosts, dybbuks and werewolves, is the writer's extensive deployment of motifs common in traditional Jewish folklore. Moreover, his supernatural narrators repeatedly refer to old Yiddish storybooks and legends—those *mayse-bikhlekh* in *yiddish-taytsh,* bought from itinerant book peddlers or found moldering in old attics—which underprop the tales these supernatural beings relate. This essay seeks to explore some of the similarities and, more significantly, some differences in folk motifs reworked in stories by Bashevis and to suggest reasons for what Bashevis is doing.

The *Mayse-bukh,* from which Bashevis drew his materials for these tales, is the most celebrated of those collections of popular folklore that greatly influenced modern Yiddish fiction dealing with the marvelous, the supernatural, and the forces of the occult.[2] Although Max Grünbaum had published some excerpts from it at the end of the nineteenth century (1882), the *Mayse-bukh* itself was being rediscovered in the 1920s and 1930s. Ludwig Strauss translated some of its tales into German (1934); Bertha Pappenheim and Moses Gaster translated them in their entirety into German (1929) and English (1934), respectively.[3] A variety of incentives evidently impelled Bashevis to draw from the tradition of Jewish narrative born with the *mayse.* Undoubtedly, one reason for his recourse to this material was the possibility it offered him of becoming a kind of demiurge, to create a fictional universe in which the familiar and the strange, the well-known and the bizarre, custom and superstition, terror and desire, could all be yoked together and given material representation as a mirror of both the individual soul and the collective human psyche.

More significantly, however, Bashevis's treatment of old legends and old themes enabled him to treat time as a continuum, as he remarks himself: "In this world of old Jewishness I found a spiritual treasure trove . . . Time seemed to flow backwards . . . I lived Jewish history."[4] His reconstruction of these old stories also becomes a way through which Bashevis can attempt to re-create the culture destroyed by the Shoah, a destruction which, for Bashevis, is embodied in the death of the Yiddish language:

> I like to write ghost stories and nothing fits a ghost better than a dying language. The deader the language the more alive the ghosts. Ghosts love Yiddish, and as far as I know, they all speak it . . . I am sure that millions of Yiddish-speaking ghosts will rise from their graves one day and their first question will be, "Is there any new book in Yiddish to read?"[5]

Integrating his own narratives with traditional folklore, Bashevis sets his tales in a period between the end of the nineteenth and the beginning of the twentieth centuries, for him the most crucially testing time in modern Jewish history. The sources from which Bashevis draws permit him to illuminate the present with the light of the past, among other ways by omitting certain elements from his sources and by accentuating others. Unlike the narrative models on which they are based, Bashevis's reworkings do not feature as their chief characters morally edifying types chosen to present a harmonious view of a justly ordered universe; instead, his characters are strongly individualized so that the tales in which they feature become phenomenological and existentialist explorations of a world of moral uncertainty. Both Bashevis's originality and his message reside in the narrative structure he reconstructs from old models; for him the traditional narrative operates as a function of memory, as a means of questioning the nature of identity, and as a focus of moral perspective.

Although the collection of homiletic tales that makes up the *Mayse-bukh* was compiled by Yakov Pollack, also known as Yakov Buchhändler, the authors of its individual tales are unknown, so that the *Mayse-bukh* as a whole is virtually an anonymous work. Nevertheless, all its stories, printed in one volume for the first time in Basle in 1602, are united by a singularly clear vision. The *Mayse-bukh* does not content itself with merely translating into Yiddish legends — *aggadot* — from the Talmud. Clearly discernible also are specific signifiers that identify the tales as products of the milieu of the Jews during the Middle Ages. Thus the *Mayse-bukh*

Bashevis's Interactions with the *Mayse-bukh*

functions as a "golden chain" linking a partly reactivated antiquity to the emerging modern world, in which the mystical rabbis of the past come alive alongside Hasidei-Ashkenaz like Rabbis Shmuel and Yehudah ha-Hasid as well as non-Jewish characters "converted" to the moral tenets of Judaism. All of them weave their miraculous, magical, or dramatic narratives between the covers of the same book. The *Mayse-bukh* in Yiddish, or, to employ the word by which its language was designated in its own time, in *taytsh,* is the clearest reflection of the world and the moral values of Ashkenazic Jews in Exile, and its compiler presents his collection as a book of ethical edification intended for women, and for men ignorant of Hebrew, to be reserved for reading aloud on the Sabbath as *taytsh-gemore* (commentaries in the Yiddish vernacular for the Jewish masses). In this way, pieces of ethical instruction designed as oral preachments became converted into moral tales for pleasurable reading. The *Mayse-bukh* is a text produced at the point of intersection between the oral and the written traditions of Yiddish literature, between the stable Jewish world view of the Middle Ages and its steady destabilization at the start of the modern period.

The narratives of the *Mayse-bukh,* a work of undisguised moralizing, mix piety and fervor, miracles and magical practices, cosmology and demonology; often its homilies express a wish to hasten the coming of the Messiah and deflect the discriminatory persecutions to which Jews living in Exile were exposed. The *Mayse-bukh* is a work born in Exile and nurtured by Exile, a world where, as in ancient times, no division exists between *oylem-haze,* the world of the here and now, and *oylem-habe,* the World-to-Come—therefore the importance and power of prayer. God is omnipresent (see *Mayse* 50, for example) and will judge all humankind by their acts: nothing Evil remains unpunished—and few are so virtuous that they have nothing with which to reproach themselves—while virtuous lives will be amply rewarded. As in the early Jewish moral tracts of the thirteenth century, later included in *Sefer Hasidim* (Book of the Pious, 1538),[6] the main literary production of the medieval German-Jewish pietists, the presence of Evil is emphasized in the *Mayse-bukh* in such a way as to glorify God and to show His Divine magnificence in vanquishing it. Humankind is shown to move blindly among invisible but innumerable demons, which offer perpetual temptation. In *Berakhot* (tractate of the Talmud) 6a, Aba Benjamin says: "If we could see all the evil spirits standing around us, no man would be able to bear it, for they are massed round us in rows like the vines of a vineyard" (*Mayse* 27). What is required of all humankind is that

121

they should resist all these demons in the way they were resisted by all the saints of blessed memory, whose conduct is offered again and again as moral exempla for us to follow. However, human beings can never attain a state of perfection, because in all instances sanctity is acquired through unceasing struggle and vigilance.

In the cosmogony presented in the *Mayse-bukh,* the virtuous and God-fearing characters are less individuals than types functioning as pillars to support a moral structure built on the opposition between Good and Evil: they also serve to frame the action by introducing historical time and geographical place to lend veracity to what is recounted. Thus tales are often introduced in this way: "Once upon a time Rabbi Samuel the Pious came to Cologne on the Rhine" (*Mayse* 162); "There once lived a man in the Holy Land who was very close to the king. He was rich and pious and knew everything that was going to happen" (*Mayse* 14). We are then made to share all the tribulations, and shown all the merits, of these personages so that their narratives can end on morally upbeat notes like the following: "Therefore, my dear friends, take to heart the moral of this story," or "May God grant us the benefit of their merits."

Bashevis himself employs a reverse strategy. He attempts to recover, behind the writing, the primal voice that recounts the tale, a primal voice that manifests itself, among other forms, in the outcries of a dybbuk in a possessed body forced to respond solely as the dybbuk wishes.[7] The universe Bashevis evokes differs wholly from that presented in the *Mayse-bukh;* his universe does not respond to a system of moral logic that views all events solely in terms of Good or Evil. Instead it is a universe perceived through dual vision and heard in stereophonic sound. To be sure, sometimes a dybbuk present in these stories behaves in a traditional manner by confessing its crimes and enduring punishment in expiation of its sins, as in *Mayse* 152, which is the first story ever told about a dybbuk. In this tale, the dybbuk is a man "about whom the sages say he who is guilty of adultery should have the four kinds of capital punishment inflicted upon him. But [he had] not been punished that way." This is certainly true of the dybbuk that enters into Rechele in *Der sotn in goray;*[8] but then, in a story like "Der toyter klezmer" (The Dead Musician),[9] we are introduced to two dybbuks who were despised while they were living human beings and who, once they are dead, are still scorned. Beyle Tslove is first raped by a supposedly pious prayer-teacher and then consigned to a brothel by a bawd parading as an observant Jewish woman. In Bashevis's folkloric tales, the duplicity of living human beings replaces the *Mayse-bukh*'s abstract dichotomy be-

Bashevis's Interactions with the *Mayse-bukh*

tween Good and Evil. Although individuated by being given personal names, the men or women in Bashevis's tales seem to be not instruments of a Divine justice, but rather pawns in the hands of an unfathomable and silent God or the helpless instruments of a tempting devil.

Taybele, the chief character of "Taybele un hurmiza," [10] is a clear example. When all three of her children have died in infancy and her husband has turned even more morose and silent, this tale's narrator emphasizes, without offering any explanation, that "although punished by the Almighty, [Taybele] still smiled easily . . . it wasn't in her nature to rail at fate or cling to sorrow" (e 10). With little apparent motivation, her husband then suddenly decides to abandon her without giving her a *get* (formal religious divorce), an action that leaves her a powerless *agune* (abandoned wife who cannot remarry):

> God had taken both her children and her husband. She would never be able to marry again; from now on she would have to live alone. All she had left was her house, her store, and her belongings. The townspeople pitied her, for she was a quiet woman, kind-hearted and honest in her business dealings. Everyone asked: how did she deserve such misfortunes? But God's ways are hidden from man. (e 10)

For the most part, in the moral order Bashevis evokes, only Evil exists in the face of a hidden, absent, or mute God, in an absurd world where dereliction is the rule. The moral vacancy is filled by the *yeytser-hore,* the Evil Inclination, which, in a void seemingly cut off from God, finds itself obliged to play the role assigned to it: to be faithful to itself, even if, after the Shoah, the moral parameters of Good and Evil, within which alone its existence has meaning, have long since ceased to exist:

> There are no more Jews, there are no more demons . . . There is no longer an Angel of Good nor an Angel of Evil. No more sins, no more temptations . . . There is no further need for demons. We have also been annihilated. I am the last, a refugee. I can go anywhere I please, but where should a demon like me go? To the murderers? [11]

Human beings seem no longer created in the image of God, but in the image of Satan. This Satanization in literature, the creation of "a Literature of Evil," as Georges Bataille called it, has a double source: it derives in part from a particular kabbalistic vision of the world which stresses the importance of the existence of

Astrid Starck-Adler

Evil and in part from a pessimistic *Weltanschauung* which, since Friedrich Nietzsche, is predicated on the death of God.

In *Der sotn in goray*, Bashevis dramatizes the kind of social order that attends the enactment of the kabbalistic belief that Evil must be pushed to its ultimate limits in order to force the coming of the Messiah. What results is the chaotic universe of the false Messiah, Sabbatai Zevi. This world is the direct antithesis of that postulated by the *Mayse-bukh*, which, situating itself in the historical period between the anti-Jewish persecutions following the Black Plague and the murderous pogroms of Chmielnicki, elects to provide moral uplift, insisting on the unchallengeable existence of the Good both in this world and in the World-to-Come. This Good is promoted by studying the Torah, by observing the Commandments, by performing good deeds. To do good is to overcome Death, the *Mayse-bukh* insists, quoting Scripture: "It is written in the Holy Torah, 'This is thy life and the length of thy days' [Deuteronomy 30:20], that is, the Torah is thy life and prolongs thy days" (*Mayse* 1); "Honor thy father and thy mother, and God will recompense you and lengthen your life" (*Mayse* 127); "Every man should dispense charity, as the verse says, 'Charity saveth from death' [Proverbs 10:2]" (*Mayse* 83). In contrast to shocking ambiguities in the conduct of the universe pointed up by Bashevis, the *Mayse-bukh* insists that by virtuous and pious conduct men and women together hasten the ardently desired coming of the Messiah. At the beginning of the seventeenth century, when belief in the coming of the Messiah was particularly strong, the messianic longings of the *Mayse-bukh* are indubitable, expressed as much in its varied context—"May the Lord . . . send us the Messiah. Amen" (*Mayse* 199)—as in its form: conflating centuries of recorded historical time, the Rabbi Hanina (from the era of the Roman Empire) becomes the principal "hero" of the collection and, acting on behalf of the prophet Elijah, assumes the role of herald to the coming of the Messiah.

In the middle of the twentieth century, Bashevis situates himself directly within this narrative tradition, but with an entirely different purpose. He takes as his mission the need to bear witness to the past and make it live again. Bashevis's work inscribes itself as part of "the catastrophe literature [which] is . . . almost entirely in Yiddish," [12] even that written before the Shoah. Behind all the tales in the *Mayse-bukh* is a total conviction that there exists an interpenetration of the natural and the supernatural worlds, so the dead can reappear on earth, either

Bashevis's Interactions with the *Mayse-bukh*

because they are mysteriously brought back to life — "When the rabbi was dying, he called his children to him and said to them: '. . . I will come back every Friday night to my house and pronounce the *kiddush*' [prayer of sanctification of the Sabbath]" (*Mayse* 125) — or so that they can expiate the sins they committed while they were alive — "Because I took a field away by force from his owner, I have no peace; for I am driven all night long round it" (*Mayse* 253). As messengers from the world beyond, whether welcomed or feared, they bring messages of hope in Divine Providence. While in the work of Bashevis these two worlds are equally imbricated in one another, like the reality of Jewish existence which they reflect and testify to — "The leitmotif of Yiddish was, that if a day passes without a misfortune it is a miracle from heaven"[13] — Bashevis presents the ghosts who play out their various *danses macabres* in his tales as beings displaced even when they existed in this world; they were corpses "even when alive":

Usually, after a man dies the Angel Dumah confronts him, demands his name, and then proceeds to weigh up his good against his evil deeds. But Itche-Godl lay rotting for months without anyone coming to question him, forgotten not only by the angels but by the devils as well. (E 164)[14]

The world of the dead, the existence of which is predicated on a world of the living that has disappeared, is reflected in the narrative structure of Bashevis's stories themselves, in which the end of history is made to coincide with the death of the character around whom the tale is built. This structure defines a double death: the death of narration and the death of the act of writing. Each character in such tales lives only during the time it takes to tell the story that embodies this character, while the story itself is called into existence only as the fiction of a bored demon:

It has always tickled my fancy to amuse myself not only with the living but with the dead as well. That I do not have the power of resurrection is a well-known fact. This is something only the Almighty can accomplish. Nevertheless, I, the Evil One, can for a short time infuse a corpse with the breath of life, with animal spirits as the philosophers choose to call it, and send it to roam among the living. ("Two Corpses," E 163)

In Bashevis's reworkings, the demon is a vitalizing force merely of the second rank, possessing limited powers and capable of breathing life only into mario-

Astrid Starck-Adler

nettes. His existence derives from being a demon-author in search of dead characters. To exist at all, some kind of body is essential. Hence, absence of body obliges
dybbuks to take possession of the living bodies of others in order to make themselves and their demands known. Ghosts, however, ignorant of the fact that they
are dead, do not understand what has happened during the period that has inter-
vened since their decease. They deceive themselves into believing that they have a
semblance of existence, which itself bears all the characteristics of the grotesque.[15]
For example, in "Tsvey meysim geyen tantsn" (Two Corpses Go Dancing) Itche-
Godl marries Finkl, but on their wedding night he finds himself disintegrating in
a tomb because, even though he is unaware of it, the process of decay continues
inexorably.

Drawing on traditional folkloric materials like these, Bashevis reworks them
for his own clearly defined purposes, as in his reconstruction of the story of the
Jewish pope. In the *Mayse-bukh*, Elkhanan, the son of Rabbi Shimen the Great
of Mayence, is abducted as a child by the *shabes-goy*, the Christian servant who
comes to light the fire on Shabbat; he is baptized and, through the great aptitude
for scholarship he has inherited from his father, becomes the pope. Through the
Mayse-bukh's narrator, we know that Elkhanan "remained among the Christians,
as one may well imagine, considering that it went well with him and that he was
held in high esteem" (*Mayse* 188). Nevertheless, as the *Mayse-bukh* presents it, the
Jewish pope Elkhanan never forgets he is a Jew and determines secretly to return
to his people and their ancient community after having written a book "against the
[Christian] faith, locked it in a vault and [given] orders that every candidate for
the papacy should read the book." By way of self-accusation he himself explains
why he does not return to his people sooner: "the good circumstances in which I
was, kept me from returning to my faith." This intensely worldly motive, stressing
the advantages of being a Christian in a Jew-hating world, provides Bashevis with
the perfect starting point for his counterattack on what he sees as a wholly false
lure. Thus he begins his own version of this tale with this offer as the core of the
devil's temptation of Zaydl:

> In ancient times there always lived a few men in every generation whom I,
> the Evil One, could not corrupt in the usual manner. It was impossible to
> tempt them to murder, lechery, robbery. I could not even get them to cease
> studying the Law. In one way only could the inner passions of these righ-
> teous souls be reached: through their vanity. (E 212)[16]

Bashevis's Interactions with the *Mayse-bukh*

In pushing him to convert to Christianity, the devil appeals primarily to Zaydl's vanity and lust for worldly honor. However, caught in the snare of his own erudition, which rapidly degenerates into pedantic casuistry, Benedictus Janovsky, as he is known after his baptism, fails to achieve what in the end is revealed as a delusory objective, and he ends as a blind beggar muttering snatches from the Gemara, the Mishnah, and the Psalms on the steps of the cathedral of Cracow, having lost any sense of reality, of truth. Like the ghosts and dybbuks of those long dead, the living corpse Zaydl has lost both *oylem-haze* (this world) and *oylem-habe* (the next world). On his deathbed, the devil comes to conduct Zaydl to hell, undercutting his newfound faith that if hell exists then God must also exist with the dismissive assertion, "This proves nothing."

Bashevis's folkloric stories form an intertext that continually takes the reader by surprise. If he uses old folklore material to re-create the past, it is a past seen with the unblinkingly realistic eyes of the present, whose vision is finely adapted to the moral emptiness of the contemporary world. In "Der toyter klezmer," Liebe Yentl is possessed on the day of her betrothal by two dybbuks simultaneously, a drunken fiddler and a whore, who end their bouts of abusing each another by contracting a sham marriage for themselves.[17] Stories that center on the plight of a dybbuk, both in the *Mayse-bukh* and in the works of Bashevis, focus on the confession of a sinner. But in Bashevis the persons possessed by these dybbuks are selected in an entirely arbitrary fashion; they simply happen to be living by chance in a convenient earthly vicinity. This very arbitrariness is stressed in the case of Rechele in *Der sotn in goray* by the dybbuk who operates, as always in a world in which Evil predominates, *leys din ve-leys dayen*, "without either Justice or Judge." Rechele's behavior is the expression not of her own but of the dybbuk's sinful life: her legs are permanently parted because it is through "that same place" that the dybbuk entered her. In "Der toyter klezmer," however, according to the boastful insistence of the dybbuk Getsl, he chooses to enter the innocent Liebe Yentl because, as he sneers, "she's a good-looking girl. I hate the ugly ones" (E 37). Where the *Maysebukh* hints at some causal relationship between possession by a dybbuk and the victim's character or morals, there seems often to be none in the reworkings of Bashevis.

As Bashevis presents them, dybbuks are born storytellers who speak openly about what others can or dare not and in whatever brazen manner they choose.[18] In its excess, the dybbuk's confessions in *Der sotn in goray* recall those of the Mar-

127

quis de Sade—but remind us also of the *Mayse-bukh*: "The evil spirit said: 'that youth yonder who is standing among you dressed in white clothes, has committed sodomy, which is as bad as adultery'" (*Mayse* 152)—while Getsl the fiddler is a master of ribald popular storytelling: "The dybbuk knew everyone and had words for each man according to his position and conduct" (E 40). The fact that he is a spirit permits Getsl every extravagance: a protean character, an interpreter of multiple roles (rabbi, cantor, jester), a speaker in multiple voices, playing all the musical instruments to create a whole orchestra by himself, he becomes the Till Eulenspiegel of the *shtetl*, absolutely confident that Evil is more attractive than Good. He blasphemes, sinning in words, telling atrocious stories in an attempt to shatter conventional belief in a just and harmonious world order.[19] In the *shtetl* world Bashevis evokes, Good hardly manifests itself, so that, ironically enough, Getsl enlivens the *shtetl* with his braggadocio: "Winter nights are long, and idlers look for ways to while away the time. Soon after twilight, [all the inhabitants of the *shtetl*] would gather at Zise Feige's house to hear the dybbuk's talk and to marvel at his antics" (E 40). Getsl becomes the inverted voice of moral rebuke for them all, and it is clear from his coarse accusations that all people in the whole world have some hypocrisy for which they can be derided. The bawdy remarks of Beyle Tslove the whore, his companion in possessing the body of Liebe Yentl, provide a counterpoint to Getsl's abuse, pointing to the shared culpability of all who hear them for the degradation of this pair of dybbuks.[20] Helplessly attempting to exorcise these two voices of truth without tongues of their own, Reb Sheftel is powerless, his talismans and amulets derided as superstitious impotence. Like Itche-Godl in "Tsvey meysim geyen tantsn," who is forgotten even by demons, Getsl the fiddler has come back to the "sinful earth" because "there is no place for [him] either in heaven or in hell" (E 175).

Bashevis's stereoscopic vision is perhaps best exemplified in his narrative "Di shvarts-khasene" (The Black Wedding), which relates the marriage of a young woman to a demon.[21] The model for this story is *Mayse* 179: "One day a demon (May God protect us!) in the guise of a handsome young man of royal carriage, bearing beautiful objects of precious stones and pearls, wanted to marry the lord's daughter. He took her home and lived with her until he brought her to the Gate of Hell, where he handed her over to the devils who destroy human beings." We are placed directly at the intersection of the world of Evil and the world of Good. In Bashevis's tale, Hindele, the daughter of the demon-afflicted rabbi of Tzivkev,

Bashevis's Interactions with the *Mayse-bukh*

Reb Arn Naftali, marries Reb Shimen, the rabbi of Yampol, who seeks to unite his Hasidic court with that of her late father. But in the distorted reality perceived by Hindele, an epileptic and neurotic young woman with the dubious gift of double vision, Reb Shimen becomes a demon and her marriage a "black wedding":

> When Reb Shimon lifted the veil from Hindele's face after the wedding, she saw him for the first time. He was a tall man with a broad fur hat, a pitch-black disheveled beard, wild eyes, a broad nose, thick lips, and a long moustache. He gazed at her like an animal. He breathed noisily and smelled of perspiration. Clusters of hair grew out of his nostrils and ears. His hands, too, had a growth of hair as thick as fur. The moment Hindele saw him she knew what she had suspected long before—that her bridegroom was a demon and that the wedding was nothing but black magic, a satanic hoax. (E 38–39)

Hindele dies imagining that in giving birth to her husband's son she is actually bringing forth a demon.

While in "Di shvarts-khasene" the human is Satanized, in "Taybele un hurmiza" the Satanic is humanized instead. The *agune* Taybele has the habit of telling stories she has read in women's storybooks (E 11). Among other similarities between the *Mayse-bukh* and the stories of Bashevis is the special place both accord to women, a place with all its ambiguities and ironies that has not yet been fully explored. In the context of this essay, it is sufficient at this point to note that in "Taybele un hurmiza" Taybele herself plays a number of different roles, as a reader, as a storyteller, and as an actress, and all of them are inverted from the norm. As a reader, she recalls for us the role a woman was required to play from the Middle Ages on, when Old Yiddish literature was produced: on the Sabbath, a woman would read from the *Mayse-bukh* for her ethical instruction and improvement. On this traditional function of women as the main purveyors of stories and the chief agents of storytelling in the *shtetl*, Bashevis himself has commented, "I use the female narrator because among the Yiddish-speaking people the storytellers are either the Hasidim or the old women." [22] Taybele herself lives to be transformed, through an entirely human trick, into a character from one such oft-told tale of supernatural deception, the marriage of a young woman to a demon. Alkhonon, a lowly *belfer* or teacher's assistant in the same *shtetl* who yearns to become a *badkhn* or wedding jester, one day overhears Taybele telling her women friends a tale about a young Jewish woman ravished by a demon who then lives with her as her hus-

Astrid Starck-Adler

band. So he tries his hand at playing the role of that demon himself—a poor devil actually—seducing Taybele and making both her and himself happy in this fictional role-playing relationship that can only take place clandestinely, in the dark, on two nights a week. When Alkhonon falls sick and dies, utterly alone, Taybele is driven by a compulsion she does not understand to follow his pauper's coffin to the grave before resuming her lonely earthly life (E 23). Here Bashevis makes the acting-out of a fiction a means of creating real earthly happiness, however transient, that can never be brought into the clear light of truth.

To trace the varied interactions of Bashevis with the *Mayse-bukh* is not merely to uncover some of his source materials, but also to illuminate the way in which he reconstructs these materials for his own purposes. Bashevis's decision to take the *Mayse-bukh* as a model for some of his stories has a twofold significance: it points to an uneasy oscillation between his wish to restore, even in fiction, the world as it was and his inescapable confrontation with the stark reality of Jewish existence after the Shoah.

In "Mayse tishevits," his last demon is a character through whom Bashevis signifies his mission to bear witness to the murdered speakers of a language of Exile which struggled to find expression during more than six centuries. In the *Mayse-bukh,* the words in which the beneficent dispositions of Divine Providence restore the moral equilibrium of an ordered world are the formulaic responses of the Jewish liturgy which are accepted as unquestionable truth. By wrenching contrast, the last demon in "Mayse tishevits" finds in a ruined attic "a Yiddish storybook, a leftover from the days before the great catastrophe"; the story in the book is even more meaningless and valueless in a post-Shoah world than it was when it was written, being "pablum and duck milk." The demon survives only by sucking on the graph of the tale, the letters of the Hebrew alphabet, a hieroglyph that alone is resistant to the destructive pressures of time and history, for the Hebrew letters in which the Yiddish language is written are all that is left with which to re-create, even in illusion, a destroyed world:

> I found a Yiddish storybook between two broken barrels . . . I suck on the letters and feed myself. I count the words, make rhymes, and tortuously interpret and reinterpret each dot . . . Yes, as long as a single volume remains, I have something to sustain me. As long as the moths have not destroyed the page, there is something to play with. (E 157–158)

Bashevis's Interactions with the *Mayse-bukh*

If any means of Jewish survival—for demons as much as for the Jews they once tempted to sin—can be found in the world that has been destroyed, it will be in the ciphers of this hieroglyph. Consequently Bashevis's position, by the end of his exploration of the *Mayse-bukh* and the sources it provided him, becomes, by the supreme irony of the nature of twentieth-century existence, that of the tormented speaker at the end of Samuel Beckett's *The Unnamable:*

I can't go on, you must go on, I'll go on, you must say words, as long as there are any, until they find me, until they say me . . . [23]

Notes

1. Isaac Bashevis Singer, "We Must Preserve the Heritage of Yiddish," *Yiddish* (I. B. Singer Issue) 6:2–3 (Summer–Fall 1987): 137.

2. The *Mayse-bukh*, an *editio princeps*, was printed in Basle in 1602 by Konrad Waldkirch. It contains 255 stories and legends and was reprinted, with the addition of new stories, nineteen times between the seventeenth and the nineteenth centuries. Modern collections of stories that bear unmistakable signs of its influence are Y. L. Peretz's short stories, H. Leivik's *Golem*, Anski's *Dybbuk*, Der Nister's complex short stories, and the fantastic narratives of Y. Y. Trunk.

3. For translations, see Max Grünbaum, *Jüdischdeutsche Chrestomathie* (Leipzig: F. A. Brockhaus, 1882); Ludwig Strauss, *Geschichtenbuch aus dem jüdisch-deutschen Maassehbuch*, Bücherei des Schocken Verlags, No. 18 (Berlin: Schocken Verlag, 1934), republished in vol. 1 of *Gesammelte Werke* (Göttingen: Wallstein Verlag, 1998); Bertha Pappenheim, *Allerlei Geschichten* (Frankfurt-am-Main: Kauffmann, 1929); Moses Gaster, *Ma'aseh Book,* 2 vols. (Philadelphia: Jewish Publication Society of America, 1934).

4. *In My Father's Court* (New York: Farrar, Straus, Giroux, 1962), p. 290.

5. Quoted in Donald R. Noble, "Isaac Bashevis Singer: Nobel Prize-Winning Novelist," in Grace Farrell (ed.), *Isaac Bashevis Singer: Conversations* (Jackson: University of Mississippi Press, 1992), p. 166.

6. *Sefer Hasidim* (Book of the Pious) was written by Yehudah ha-Hasid (1150–1217), a mystic and leader of the movement of German pietists known as the Hasidei-Ashkenaz. This book, expressing and shaping the popular beliefs, customs, and folklore of German Jewry throughout the Middle Ages, exercised a profound influence on the moral attitudes of Ashkenazic Jewry. See the Hebrew text in *Sefer Hasidim* (Bnei Brak: Hotsa'at Yahadut [reprint: originally published by Josefov, 1870]); English translations can be found in Sholom Alchanan Singer, *Sefer Hasidim* (Northbrook, Ill.: Whitehall Co., 1971), and Yehudah

Astrid Starck-Adler

heChasid, *Sefer Chasidim: The Book of the Pious*, condensed, translated, and annotated by Avraham Yaakov Finkel (Northvale, N.J.: Jason Aronson, 1997).

7. A question that repeatedly demands to be addressed is the meaning of a dybbuk, since it makes innocent people suffer. See J. S. Wolkenfeld, "Isaac Bashevis Singer: The Faith of His Devils and Magicians," in Irving Malin (ed.), *Critical Views of Isaac Bashevis Singer* (New York: New York University Press, 1969), p. 93.

8. See particularly Chapter 13, "Der dybuk fun goray," in *Der sotn in goray* (New York: Farlag Matones, 1943), pp. 174–181.

9. "Der toyter klezmer," in *Mayses fun hintern oyvn* (Tel Aviv: Farlag Y. L. Perets, 1982), pp. 209–251; translated into English as "The Dead Fiddler" by Mirra Ginsburg, in *The Séance and Other Stories* (New York: Farrar, Straus, Giroux, 1968), pp. 31–63.

10. "Taybele un hurmiza," in *Mayses fun hintern oyvn*, pp. 73–88; translated into English as "Taibele and Her Demon" by Mirra Ginsburg, in *Short Friday and Other Stories* (New York: Farrar, Straus, Giroux, 1963), pp. 1–24.

11. "Mayse tishevits," in *Der shpigl un andere dertseylungen* (Jerusalem: Hebrew University, Yidish-opteylung, 1975), pp. 12–22; translated into English as "The Last Demon" by Martha Glicklich and Cecil Hemley, in *Short Friday*, pp. 145–158 (quotation on p. 158).

12. Singer, "We Must Preserve the Heritage of Yiddish," p. 139.

13. Ibid., p. 131.

14. "Tsvey meysim geyen tantsn," in *Der sotn in goray un andere dertseylungen* (New York: Farlag Matones, 1943), pp. 289–305; translated into English as "Two Corpses Go Dancing" by Joseph Singer and Elizabeth Pollet, in *The Séance and Other Stories* (New York: Farrar, Straus, Giroux, 1968), pp. 163–175.

15. See Maximilian E. Novak, "Moral Grotesque and Decorative Grotesque in Bashevis's Fiction," in Marcia Allentuck (ed.), *The Achievement of Isaac Bashevis Singer* (Carbondale: Southern Illinois University Press, 1969), pp. 44–63.

16. "Zaydlus der ershter," in *Der sotn in goray un andere dertseylungen*, pp. 273–286; translated into English as "Zeidlus the Pope" by Joel Blocker and Elizabeth Pollet, in *Short Friday*, pp. 212–226.

17. "That Liebe Yentl has been possessed on the occasion of her betrothal is no coincidence. Like the 'enlightened' young woman of Bashevis's era, Liebe Yentl regards marriage in the world of the *shtetl* as oblivion—a monotonous, claustrophobic existence. When her two demons agree to marry, their wedding songs illustrate Liebe Yentl's ambivalence about marriage. She compares marriage to death and her future husband to a corpse" (Nancy Berkowitz Bate, "Judaism, Genius or Gender: Women in the Fiction of Isaac Bashevis Singer," in Grace Farrell [ed.], *Critical Essays on Isaac Bashevis Singer* [New York: G. K. Hall, 1996], p. 215).

Bashevis's Interactions with the *Mayse-bukh*

18. See David Roskies, "The Demon as Storyteller: Isaac Bashevis Singer," in *A Bridge of Longing: The Lost Art of Yiddish Storytelling* (Cambridge, Mass.: Harvard University Press, 1995), pp. 266–306.

19. For Bashevis, all sexuality that deviates from conventional norms is a manifestation of moral disintegration and the inversion of the natural order of the world. See Joseph Sherman, "Upside-Down in the Daytime: Singer and Male Homosexuality," in Farrell (ed.), *Critical Essays,* pp. 191–208.

20. See Stanley Edgar Hyman's remark that "Singer's demonology becomes a metaphor for repressed sexuality," in his "Isaac Singer's Marvels," in Farrell (ed.), *Critical Essays,* p. 38.

21. "Di shvarts-khasene," in *Gimpl tam un andere dertseylungen* (New York: Tsiko, 1963), pp. 301–309; translated into English as "The Black Wedding" by Martha Glicklich, in *The Spinoza of Market Street and Other Stories* (New York: Farrar, Straus, Cudahy, 1961), pp. 33–45.

22. See Isaac Bashevis Singer and Richard Burgin, *Conversations with Isaac Bashevis Singer* (Garden City, N.Y.: Doubleday, 1985), p. 117.

23. Samuel Beckett, *The Unnamable,* in *Three Novels* (New York: Grove Press, 1968), p. 418.

Astrid Starck-Adler

9

The Role of Polish Language and Literature in Bashevis's Fiction

Monika Adamczyk-Garbowska

When Oyzer-Heszl (Heshl), the protagonist of *Di familye mushkat* (The Family Moskat), first visits Hadassah in her room, he looks at her bookshelf and notices a number of Polish books, among others Adam Mickiewicz's *Pan Tadeusz* and Stanislaw Przybyszewski's *The Outcry,* as well as a thick novel entitled *Pharaoh.*[1] The name of the author of this novel is not mentioned, presumably to indicate that Oyzer-Heszl and perhaps indirectly Bashevis as well are not familiar with this particular work. Oyzer-Heszl declares that he wants to read all these books, and indeed he does read some of them, as we learn later. But we never find out whether he read *Pharaoh* or any other books written by its author, Boleslaw Prus, the best-known positivist Polish writer, famous for his detailed depictions of Warsaw and his creation of compelling characters, including Jews. Does Bashevis purposely distance himself from this writer, whose works come naturally to mind to Polish readers of Bashevis's novels set in nineteenth-century Warsaw, in order to deflect attention from any possible parallels that might exist between them, or perhaps even to conceal some affinities?

When Bashevis received the Nobel Prize in 1978, a number of Polish critics and journalists tried to present him as a Polish writer. This was not the case with Polish critics alone. Even two years later, when Czeslaw Milosz received the Nobel Prize in 1980, the award was characterized in the *London Times* as the fourth Nobel Prize in Literature for Poland, after Henryk Sienkiewicz, Wladyslaw Reymont, and Bashevis.[2] Bashevis himself claimed that if the Poles wanted to consider him a Polish-Jewish writer, he did not mind being so labeled. In a letter to his friend Maria Unger, he wrote:

> In America Poles consider me as one of their writers; that's how I was described in one of the pamphlets published here. I consider myself a Jewish writer writing in Yiddish, an American writer, and also a Polish writer, as

I write almost exclusively about Poland and I know Poland best. It's high time people in Poland learned that they have their writer in America.[3]

This letter, written at a time when Bashevis was completely unknown in Poland, shows that he cared about his popularity there. When Bashevis's works finally appeared in the country of his birth, there were speculations in Poland about how well he knew the Polish language and how well read he was in Polish literature. There are various opinions, ranging from those who express admiration for Bashevis's excellent command of Polish to those who claim that he did not know it at all.[4] Bashevis himself was inconsistent in his own estimation of his knowledge of Polish. It is not necessary to speculate on this matter. Depending on the criteria adopted, Bashevis's knowledge of Polish could be considered either very good, taking into account the fact that he wrote exclusively in Yiddish and that he left Poland as a young man, or very poor, taking into account the fact that he spent as many as thirty-one years of his life in Poland. Bashevis mentioned on various occasions that he learned Polish quite late, when he was already an adult, and that he read some secular literature in Polish, including not only original works written in Polish but also translations into Polish from other languages. What is certain is that Polish was necessary for Bashevis in his daily existence while he lived in Poland and served him as a helpful tool in rendering the speech of Poles and assimilated Jews in his own later fiction.

A number of critics have noticed a striking resemblance between *Der hoyf* (The Manor and The Estate) and works by Polish positivist writers, especially Boleslaw Prus. A superficial acquaintance with Bashevis's work, coupled with ignorance of Yiddish literature and support from Bashevis's rhetorical statements, has led commentators to far-fetched conclusions. Some critics and readers in Poland believe that Bashevis knew Polish literature very well and patterned his works on it. Most of these assertions, however, no matter how flattering they may be for Polish literature, are not well founded. Despite seeming similarities, Bashevis's Polish characters are created from a completely different perspective, usually a critical one, which contrasts strongly with the patriotically heroic point of view characteristic of many Polish authors. Moreover, this perspective not only is determined by the fact that Bashevis writes about Poles from the point of view of an "outsider" but also is shaped by Bashevis's imagination and literary technique, his tendency toward hyperbole and caricature.

135

Monika Adamczyk-Garbowska

Bashevis himself admitted to reading a number of Polish writers, but there is no doubt that he never faced the dilemma confronted by a number of Jewish writers living in Poland, the need to make a choice between writing in Yiddish, in Hebrew, or in Polish. Unlike Y. L. Peretz or Sholem Asch, Bashevis never attempted to write in Polish. Indeed, Bashevis's personal attitude toward Jews who did write in Polish was highly negative. Incredibly, he claims that he came across Bruno Schulz's name only while reviewing Schulz's work in English translation during the 1960s, and he goes on to observe that only after reading Schulz in Polish could he see the power of his prose. In its own way this assertion testifies to Bashevis's continued, even if sporadic, interest in Polish literature and his ability to evaluate texts written in the Polish language. Bashevis claims nevertheless that if Schulz had written in Yiddish he would have been a better writer.[5] He expresses similar opinions of assimilated Polish-Jewish authors like Julian Tuwim, Marian Hemar, and Jozef Wittlin, whom he described as "good enough but nothing special." Only later in America did he admit that perhaps he had judged them too harshly since that was exactly what Jewish writers did in America: they "assimilated to" the English language. Bashevis added, however, that in his view it was a pity that such talented authors did not know Yiddish, because they might have enriched that language and, what is more, it would have been easier for them to have a readership in America since, by comparison with Polish, Yiddish was a living tongue in the United States — unquestionably a grossly inaccurate assertion.[6] His critical stance aside, there is no doubt that Bashevis was to some extent influenced by Polish literature and that he used Polish in multiple ways for his own artistic purposes.

Reading Yiddish literature in tandem with Polish literature is often helpful and illuminating. To give a few examples, in Y. L. Peretz's plays there are echoes of Stanislaw Wyspianski's poetics, and each stanza of Avrom Sutzkever's poem "Tsu poyln" ends with a quotation from Juliusz Slowacki's famous poem "Smutno mi Boze" (I'm Sad, God). Yankev Glatshteyn uses a quotation from one of Maria Konopnicka's poems as the motto to his book *Ven yash is geforn* (When Yash Set Forth), and it is highly probable that the name Yash itself is a reference to Konopnicka's poetic story for children *O Janku Wedrowniczku* (On Yash the Wanderer), in which the protagonist, a young boy from a village, travels far and wide in his imagination, including a voyage to America, and then returns to his mother and his native village. Some critics have noticed parallels between Wladyslaw Reymont's *Ziemia obiecana* (The Promised Land) and I. J. Singer's *Di brider ashkenazi* (The

Brothers Ashkenazi) and have suggested that the latter can be regarded as a literary polemic against the former.[7]

In the case of Bashevis, the most striking example in his work — a situation parallel to that of I. J. Singer in relation to Reymont — is his novel *Der kenig fun di felder* (The King of the Fields), which bears a clear resemblance to Jozef Ignacy Kraszewski's *Stara basn* (The Old Fairy Tale). When Jerzy Kosinski published *The Painted Bird*, one of the many accusations raised against him was that of plagiarism — he was accused of having lifted long excerpts from Henryk Biegeleisen's ethnographic study published in Poland before World War II. A similar accusation was raised some years later when Kosinski published *Being There*, a novel that most Polish critics immediately recognized as a version of *Kariera Nikodema Dyzmy* (Nikodem Dyzma's Career) by Tadeusz Dolega-Mostowicz, a very popular novel from the interwar period, and Kosinski was again accused of plagiarism.[8] No accusations of this kind have ever been leveled against the Singer brothers, since apart from any similarities that might exist their respective novels are very different in tone and treatment of their Polish subject matter and can rather be regarded as literary polemics, often quite ironic, against their Polish predecessors.

For many years, contacts between Polish and Yiddish literature and their respective authors were one-sided. To a lesser or greater extent Yiddish writers in Poland knew Polish literature, while very few Polish writers were familiar with Yiddish literature. This alienation is perhaps best encapsulated in Arn Tsaytlin's mystery play *Esterke*, in which the shades of Mickiewicz and Peretz appear: Peretz says to Mickiewicz, *ver du bist — dos veys ikh, nor ver ikh bin — dos veystu nisht,* "I know who you are, but who I am — you do not know."[9] Even if Polish writers expressed some interest in Yiddish works at the end of the nineteenth century, or during the period between the wars, they would not really have drawn inspiration from them. Paradoxically, the situation has been to some extent reversed in recent years as a result of translations of Bashevis's works into Polish. And ironically enough, just as the first translations from Yiddish into Polish were done via Russian, so Bashevis's translations reach the Polish reader predominantly via the English language. The interest in them, however, is enormous by comparison with that shown in the works of Mendele Moykher Sforim, which were translated into Polish by Klemens Junosza-Szaniawski in the late nineteenth century. In contemporary Polish literature from the 1980s and 1990s, for instance, we encounter some references to Bashevis: in Jaroslaw Marek Rymkiewicz's *Umschlagplatz* (Depor-

Monika Adamczyk-Garbowska

tation Place [in Warsaw, to Treblinka extermination camp]) there is a character clearly based on Bashevis; allusions to both Bashevis and his brother I. J. Singer also appear in Hanna Krall's stories.

Bashevis's use of the Polish language and its literature has received little critical attention outside Poland. One of the earliest American critics to mention the subject was Irving Buchen, who compares *The Family Moskat* to *Pan Tadeusz,* the epic poem by Adam Mickiewicz.[10] According to Buchen, both Bashevis and Mickiewicz have similar aims—to preserve a picture of a vanishing community. One might also add that both Bashevis and Mickiewicz wrote their works in exile, Mickiewicz in Paris after the failure of the November Uprising of 1830, and Bashevis in New York soon after World War II ended. Undoubtedly, however, the import of *The Family Moskat* is far more tragic, since the Jewish population of Poland was destroyed in an exceptionally brutal way. Nevertheless, in both works we have detailed descriptions of holidays and local customs as well as a multitude of distinct and vivid characters. Buchen also notices that Oyzer-Heszl's philosophical ideas are influenced both by Stefan Zeromski's *Syzyfowe prace* (The Labors of Sisyphus) and by Przybyszewski's *Homo Sapiens,* with its Nietzschean protagonist Eryk Falk.

The examples cited above, as well as a number of others, deserve more than a passing digression. Therefore, this discussion will deal briefly with a variety of ways in which Bashevis uses Polish language and literature in his work by dividing these usages into separate categories. The first three refer to literary aspects of Bashevis's oeuvre, while the remaining five belong more properly to the sphere of linguistics.

Direct Reference to or Literary Polemic against Polish Works

The King of the Fields is the most striking example of this type. Kraszewski's novel *Stara basn,* published for the first time in 1876, was part of an entire historical cycle written during the period of the repeated partition of Poland. In the whole of Kraszewski's voluminous output, this novel is the one most respected and has become a classic, while his other novels have largely been forgotten. *Stara basn,* written in an archaized Polish, depicts the origin of the Polish state and is based on both legendary and historical sources. By contrast, Bashevis's novel is written in modern language—he does not use the stylization he earlier employed in *Der sotn in goray* (Satan in Goray), although he does make use of some archaic words— and is based almost exclusively on Yiddish legends according to which Abraham,

Polish Language and Literature in Bashevis's Fiction

a Jewish trader, almost became the king of Poland. While Kraszewski has some-times been condemned by Polish critics for his depiction of the early Slavic tribes as cruel, his descriptions are mild compared with those of Bashevis.

The functions and contexts of these two novels are obviously very different. Kraszewski's novel was written when Poland as an independent state did not exist, and it constitutes part of a long historical cycle depicting different periods of Polish history. Bashevis's *The King of the Fields* also constitutes part of a cycle devoted to tracing Jewish presence in Polish lands throughout the centuries, but it is only ostensibly a historical novel. Its thematic thrust can be interpreted in a post-Holocaust context as the absence of Jews in Poland, since the novel's sole Jewish character, Ben Dosa, is compelled to leave the country in order to prevent un-rest, and his memory is only later recalled with nostalgia by some of the native inhabitants he has left behind. Bashevis borrows some names and episodes from Kraszewski, but gives them different functions. There are parallels in the usage of names: for instance, the tribe of Leszeks in Kraszewski and Leshniks (in Polish, Lesniks) in Bashevis, as well as the characters Znosek/Nosek and Jaga/Jagoda, re-spectively. In Kraszewski's novel, Znosek, although very clever, is a negative char-acter, while in Bashevis Nosek is one of few positive characters. They are, however, alike in physical appearance. In Kraszewski, Znosek is a small fellow with cropped hair and catlike eyes, wearing a tight garment.[11] In Bashevis, Nosek is "slightly built, with neither hair nor beard, and a pale face."[12] There is a striking parallel between the titles of the two novels—Kraszewski's *The King of the Peasants* and Bashevis's *Der kenig fun di felder*. This is not the first example of a Yiddish writer being inspired by Kraszewski—Arn Tsaytlin creates the characters in his mystery play *Esterke* after the figures presented in Kraszewski's *Krol Chlopow* (King of the Peasants), which deals with the legend of King Casimir and Esterke. Considering the close relationship that existed between Bashevis and Tsaytlin, there can be little doubt that they discussed Kraszewski's novels.

Jewish Characters' Readings in Polish Literature

Bashevis, among other Polish-Yiddish writers, often presents Polish literature as a step toward assimilation, since it is a central production of the Enlightenment and secularization. Reading secular (Polish) literature often leads indirectly to a Jew-ish individual's religious and ideological crisis and increases that person's sense of being lost, set adrift from all known moorings. Reading widely in secular Polish

Monika Adamczyk-Garbowska

literature may lead characters to a state of intellectual, emotional, and spiritual suspense between traditional Jewish and Polish Catholic culture. Jewish women from wealthy Orthodox homes are shown to be especially vulnerable to this indirectly destructive influence. This is most visible in the tormented vicissitudes of Miriam Lieba, one of the chief characters in *Der hoyf.* Her extensive reading in Polish Romantic fiction, creating impossible idealizations in her fantasy, leads her to marriage with the depraved Polish aristocrat Lucjan Jampolski, conversion to Christianity, isolation from her family and friends, and, eventually, death in poverty. Less drastic in its consequences, but similar in its influence, secular Polish literature also leaves its mark on the life of Hadassah in *Di familye mushkat.* Such young women as these are characterized almost stereotypically by their physical appearance, which is made to resemble that of Polish young ladies from noble families — they are blonde, blue-eyed, and fragile, doomed to lives of unhappiness and desolation as they abandon their cultural and spiritual tradition. In Bashevis's creation of female characters of this type, one senses echoes of Peretz's ironic comment about Jewish women enchanted by Polish culture:

> *khsidishe tekhter lozt gemakh! kemen zikh azoy fayn! di faynste parfumes, un blase azoyne — un ale lezn przhybyshevskin un zeromskin, un ale zenen farlibt in osterwa — un oygn hobn zey vi di gazeln, un azoyne bremen, lange, un azoyne shotns unter di oygn . . .*[13]

> Let us not disturb our Hasidic daughters! They dress their hair so elegantly! The finest perfumes, and they are so pallid — And they all read Przybyszewski and Zeromski and all are in love with Osterwa [Juliusz Osterwa was a famous Polish actor and stage director] — And they have eyes like gazelles and such long eyebrows and shadows under their eyes . . .

The name of Przybyszewski, often recalled by Bashevis in his fiction, is especially meaningful and performs a subtly ominous function in a number of cases, because this author of decadent prose led his wife Dagny, a Norwegian and hence a foreigner in Poland, to her own destruction.

"Fictional" Translation

Der man fun khaloymes (The Man of Dreams), published in installments in *Forverts* in 1970, is presented as a book that was originally written in Polish and then translated into Yiddish. The narrator, Adam Stanislaw Kordecki, is a man of various identities: now a repenting Jew, but earlier a convert to Protestantism and

Catholicism. He explains that he does not want to recall the profane vicissitudes of his stormy and sinful life in Hebrew, the holy tongue, and that his Yiddish is no longer good enough for him to use it in writing, so he chooses to write in a profane language with which he is familiar, and that language is obviously Polish. According to its putative author, the manuscript is supposed to remain in a safe for a hundred years before it can be revealed to the outside world. This literary device chosen by Bashevis was so successful that it has even led to misunderstanding by some critics who claim that the novel was indeed actually written in Polish.

Symbolic Function of the Polish Language

Bashevis often uses Polish to create distance between characters or between characters and their social environment, and this usage is often accompanied by estrangement. For example, in *Di familye mushkat,* when Hadassah starts speaking Polish, her tone changes:

> *vi nor zi iz ariber oyf poylish, hot zikh geendert der ton. frier iz ir shtim geven kindish, di zatsn zaynen aroys say tsetsoygene, say opgerisene. itst zaynen ir di poylishe verter mit di ale veykhe un halb-veykhe konsonantn aroysgenumen fun moyl daytlekh un sharf.* (Y 59)

The moment she switched over to Polish, her tone changed. Earlier her voice had a childish quality; her sentences were either drawn out or cut off. Now the Polish words with all their soft and half-soft consonants fell from her lips precisely and clearly.

On the other hand, on Oyzer-Heszl's lips Polish becomes more *heymlekh:*

> *er hot geredt gramatikalish. er hot nisht farbitn, vi der foter irer, dem dritn fal oyf dem fertn. nor der zatz-boy is geven an oysterlisher. dos goyishe loshn hot bakumen in zayne lipn a nogndike heymishkeyt, vi poylish volt durkh epes a nes gevorn yidish.* (Y 59–60)

He spoke grammatically. Unlike her father, he did not confuse the third case with the fourth. Only his syntax was strange. In his mouth the Gentile language took on a hauntingly intimate tone, as though, by some sort of miracle, Polish had suddenly become Yiddish.

Later, however, the daughter of Oyzer-Heszl and Hadassah can speak only Polish and cannot communicate with her Yiddish-speaking grandmother. By contrast, in stories from *Mayn tatns bezdn-shtub* (In My Father's Court) when the young narrator goes to out into *yene gasn,* "those streets," meaning the Christian dis-

Monika Adamczyk-Garbowska

tricts of Warsaw, he hears in the Polish language a foreign tongue that he does not understand, and this increases his sense of being lost.

Linguistic Usages to Differentiate the Speech of Various Characters in a Multilingual Society

Bashevis often uses Polish, especially in dialogue, to mark the speech of Polish or polonized Jewish characters, as in this dialogue between the mother of Klonia, Hadassah's Gentile friend, and Oyzer-Heszl:

> *di panna hadasa, khotsh fun altn zakon, iz bay mir vi an eygn kind . . . panna hadasa iz nit far a kapotshazh, a khosed. zi kon baym gloybn zikh haltn, nor ir kharakter iz an adeldiker. der khlopak fun der gnoyne gas, mit di lange peyes, iz nisht keyn man far ir.* (Y 173–174)

> Miss Hadassah, although a member of the old order, is like my own child to me . . . Miss Hadassah isn't for one of those fellows who wears a long gaberdine, one of those Hasids. She can cling to her own faith, but she's refined by nature. That boy with the long sidelocks from Gnojna Street is not a suitable man for her.

Here Polish expressions like *stary zakon,* literally "the old order," a euphemistic phrase to describe Jews, *kapotshazh* (in Polish, *kapociarz*), a contemptuous word for traditionally clad Jews, and *khlopak fun der gnoyne gas* (in Polish, *chlopak z Gnojnej,* and in Polish *gnojna* means "dung") all evoke a range of characteristically Polish connotations and consequently define the character much better than if only Yiddish words and expressions had been used.

Folk and Fairytale Elements

Bashevis uses Polish words in folkloristic or fairytale contexts to add variety and exoticism — characters like Topiel or Baba Jaga, for example. In his folk stories and fairy tales, he often makes nouns function as proper names: for instance, he calls a cat Kot, a hog Wieprz, a city Miasto. Sometimes his usage of Polish is particularly strange — a pagan princess is named Koza, meaning "goat" in Polish; the word is also used to describe a lively young girl.

Polish First and Family Names

The linguist Maria Karpluk has noticed that Bashevis makes a clear class distinction in his use of Polish names.[14] For example, peasants bear names like Antoni,

Antosia, or Jadwiga, while their family names are often not mentioned—and if they are, they are usually signifiers that refer to objects or living creatures; in turn, representatives of the gentry are often called Felicja, Zbigniew, or Zdzisław and bear family names ending in *-ski* and *-cki,* which is consonant with the class realities of Polish society. Sometimes a name is a kind of nobilization or demotion: a likeable shoemaker bears the name of Zawadzki and a vicious priest is called Dziobak, a name that can only carry a connotation for a reader familiar with Polish, however; literally it means "platypus," but it can also suggest "prodding" or "stabbing." On the whole, compared with the variety of Yiddish names he can call upon, Bashevis is quite limited in his choice of Polish onomastics. He often uses similar names to depict similar types, and this seems to coincide with his use of types and stereotypes, since on the whole his Polish characters are more stereotypical than his Jewish ones. Some of the Polish names he uses were earlier used by I. J. Singer or other Yiddish writers. This may testify to his limited contact with Polish-speaking circles or his lack of interest in more thorough research. His favorite names are Wilk, Piorun, Zbigniew, and Tekla. The first two are used in reference to both animals and people.

Proverbs and Sayings

These give additional flavor and sometimes serve to express ideas that, according to the narrator and characters, are difficult to render in Yiddish. Such elements are usually introduced with some additional information to underline their foreign origin: "As the Poles say . . ." or "As the *goyim* say . . ." Usually Bashevis has good intuition and uses Polish expressions in the right context. The most problematic of these usages, however, is his deployment of Polish in *Der kenig fun der felder,* where he is inconsistent and uses expressions that sound bizarre in their contexts even if we do not treat the novel as historical. Apart from archaic words that are often derived from Kraszewski, Bashevis uses words and expressions from other historical periods. For instance, he uses the form *Pan Cybula,* an unknown form in the period he is trying to portray, or *Niech zyje Polska,* "Long live Poland," absurd because Poland as an independent state did not exist at that time. His use of the word *kulak* is theoretically correct because in Old Polish the word means "fist." However, as this term was used pejoratively in the Stalin era to refer to allegedly rich peasants, it now has a strange resonance for contemporary readers. Because we know that Bashevis had some contact with Polish-speaking people in America,

Monika Adamczyk-Garbowska

this inaccurate usage might have been caused by his lack of contact with the Polish language used in Poland after the war.

Polish Place Names

These are very important in Bashevis's works, as they are deployed to convey numerous connotations. A good example can be found in *Di familye mushkat* in the following fragment from Hadassah's diary, where she expresses her love for Warsaw:

> *varshe, shtot mayne, vi tustu mir bang! ikh benk shoyn foroys nokh dayn marshalkovske un nayer velt, nokh dayn alt-shtot un povishle. ikh vel afile benken nokh dem gzhybov un di andere yidishe geslekh . . . es is gevis gut tsu lebn in oysland nor oyb mir iz bashert tsu shtarbn, vil ikh lign oyf der genshe gas, nebn meyn bobeshi.* (Y 194–195)

> Warsaw, dear city of mine, how sad I am! Even before leaving you I long for Marszalkowska and Nowy Swiat [New World Boulevard], for the Old Town and Powisle. I will even long for Grzybow and other Jewish streets. It is assuredly good to live overseas, but when my time comes to die I want to lie in the Gesia Street [cemetery], near my dear granny.

This enumeration of various streets in Warsaw and the distinction it draws between the elegant and predominantly Christian parts—Marszalkowska and Nowy Swiat—as opposed to Grzybow and other Jewish streets inform the reader about Hadassah's position in the fictional world of which she is a part,[15] a position that lies uneasily on the border between worldliness and traditional Jewishness.

It is necessary to emphasize that most of these literary allusions and elements of the Polish language employed by Bashevis in various contexts for multiple purposes can be fully appreciated mainly in their Yiddish originals, which were written for readers with a rudimentary knowledge of Polish. Usually Bashevis places Polish words in his Yiddish texts without providing explanations, as he evidently assumes that they will be understood by his readers; only rarely does one encounter explanations offered in parentheses. Reading Bashevis in the original, one knows immediately in what language—Polish or Yiddish—the characters speak. Most often the use of Polish is marked by the use of polite form *pan, pani,* or *panna* (Mr., Mrs., or Miss). In most English translations additional explanations are necessary,

Polish Language and Literature in Bashevis's Fiction

but usually the language the characters actually speak is not mentioned; readers can only guess. This distinction also disappears, of course, in Polish translation.

Finally, reading Bashevis in the original Yiddish permits a fuller sense of the world he is creating, in which different cultures and languages existed together and were mutually used. Apart from Polish, we also encounter in his work elements of Russian, Ukrainian, and, naturally, in his later works set in America or involving American characters, English.

Bashevis is celebrated as an excellent stylist who explores different literary conventions; his Yiddish idiom is rich, and it is enriched even more by his use of Polish, including Polish proverbs, songs, and even curses that express the various emotional states of his characters. It could be said that *how* he writes is more interesting than *what* he writes, especially in his novels. This is certainly true about his 1957 novel recently and posthumously published in English as *Shadows on the Hudson* (1998). His characters like to talk, and the variety of their idiom is more fascinating than the content of their often repetitive and pseudo-philosophical discussions. Aunt Yentl and Gimpl the Fool, Bashevis's paradigmatic *shtetl* figures, are not the only monologists to appear in his oeuvre; a number of them also live on Manhattan's Upper West Side after World War II. Unfortunately, this rich variety can be fully appreciated mainly by the kind of reader that is becoming more and more rare. But as Joseph Sherman recently proved by his excellent rendering of *Shadows on the Hudson,* one can translate Bashevis into fluent English and still preserve much of his linguistic variety.

In sum, Polish language and literature can add exoticism and color, can signify progress but at the same time danger, can sound familiar but also foreign and hostile, can unite two communities and divide them. Wanda in *The Slave* and Jadwiga in *Enemies: A Love Story,* Polish partners of the Jewish chief characters, express their love for them in their native tongue. This problem over the use of language leads Wanda, after she has married Yankev, to pretend to be mute while she lives in the Yiddish-speaking community, for otherwise her broken language and accent would betray her. At the same time, characters in other novels who are trying to pass as Polish-speaking are met with hostile looks accompanying the contemptuous and offensive pejorative *zydy,* "kikes," heard often from anonymous lips in streets or on trains.

The function of the Polish language and its literature in Bashevis's work is as

Monika Adamczyk-Garbowska

ambivalent as that of Poland itself, a country in which the Yiddish-speaking Jewish community felt both at home and alien, but at the same time it also testifies to the centuries-long intertwining of the two languages and cultures — Polish and Yiddish — and their mutual absorption.

Notes

1. Yitskhok Bashevis, *Di familye mushkat,* 2 vols. (New York: M. Sh. Shklarski, 1950), vol. 1, p. 58; published in English as *The Family Moskat,* translated by A. H. Gross (New York: Knopf, 1950). All translations from Yiddish in this essay, however, are my own.

2. In a polemical essay, Ryszard Wasita argues that it is the language that determines a writer's affiliation, and not the country the writer comes from. See R. Wasita, "Decyduje jesek" (Language Is the Decisive Factor), *Polska* 2 (1981): 1.

3. Quoted by Elzbieta Wolicka, "Wsrod swoich obcy: Problem stosunkow zydowsko-polskitch w utworach Izaaka Bashevisa Singera" (Stranger among Neighbors: The Problem of Jewish-Polish Relations in Isaac Bashevis Singer's Works), *Krytyka* 40 (1993): 214.

4. According to the Polish-American critic Jerzy R. Kryzanowski, Bashevis spoke eagerly and fluently in Polish, quoting Adam Mickiewicz's opening verses to *Pan Tadeusz* as well as folksongs, visibly enjoying speaking in Polish, as if enchanted with the sound of the language. See J. R. Kryzanowski, "Spotkanie z Singerem" (An Encounter with Singer), *Archipelag* 12 (1985): 120. This assertion is supported in an article by Marian Turski, a Polish journalist who reports that while speaking Polish Bashevis would sometimes stop and hesitate, searching for the right word, but on the whole he spoke without errors, with proper intonation, in the Polish "preserved" as it had been in the first half of the twentieth century, without inelegant colloquial expressions and other "novelties." See M. Turski, "Wieczor z Singerem" (An Evening with Singer), *Polityka* 27 (1984): 11.

5. Yitskhok Varshavsky [Bashevis], "A bukh fun poylish-yidishn shrayber in english," *Forverts,* December 1, 1963. See also Philip Roth, "Roth and Singer on Bruno Schulz," *New York Times Book Review,* February 13, 1977, p. 50.

6. I. B. Singer, "Kilka godzin z Polakami" (A Few Hours with Poles), in *Felietony, eseje, wywiady* (Feuilletons, Essays, Interviews), translated from the Yiddish by Tomasz Kuberczyk (Warsaw: Sagittarius, 1993), pp. 95–96, 98–99.

7. See Monika Adamczyk-Garbowska, "Between Art and Stereotype: I. J. Singer's *Brothers Ashkenazi* and W. S. Reymont's *The Promised Land,*" in *Proceedings of the Twelfth Congress of Jewish Studies,* forthcoming.

8. On Kosinski's reception by Polish critics, see Monika Adamczyk-Garbowska, "The Return of the Troublesome Bird: Jerzy Kosinski and Polish-Jewish Relations," *Polin: Studies in Polish Jewry* 12 (1999): 284–294.

Polish Language and Literature in Bashevis's Fiction

9. Used as the epigraph to Ch. Shmeruk's study, *The Esterke Story in Yiddish and Polish Literature: A Case Study in the Mutual Relations of Two Cultural Traditions* (Jerusalem: Zalman Shazar Center for the Study of Jewish History, 1985), p. 72. The study itself contains much valuable information on contacts between Yiddish and Polish literature and points to areas that require further research.

10. Irving Buchen, *Isaac Bashevis Singer and the Eternal Past* (New York: New York University Press, 1968), p. 48, n. 2.

11. Jozef Ignacy Kraszewski, *Stara basn* (The Old Fairy Tale) (Warsaw: Ludowa Spoldzielnia Wydawnicza, 1972), p. 98.

12. Isaac Bashevis Singer, *The King of the Fields* (New York: Farrar, Straus, Giroux, 1988), p. 46.

13. Y. L. Peretz, "Nokh a greserer blof," *Haynt* (Warsaw), 240 (November 1, 1912); *Ale verk* 9 (New York, 1947–1948): 295–296; also quoted in Shmeruk, *The Esterke Story*, p. 72.

14. Maria Karpluk, "Imiona i nazwiska Zydow polskich przykladem jezykowej interferencji" (First Names and Family Names of Polish Jews as Examples of Linguistic Interference), *Onomastica* 29 (1984): 207–208.

15. In the English translation, *The Family Moskat*, all these names except Genshe (in Polish, Gesia) were omitted.

Monika Adamczyk-Garbowska

IV

INTERPRETATIONS
OF BASHEVIS'S
AUTOBIOGRAPHICAL
WRITINGS

10

Revealing Bashevis's Earliest Autobiographical Novel, *Varshe 1914-1918* (Warsaw 1914-1918)

Nathan Cohen

By the time Bashevis had been thrust into the forefront of world literature by winning the Nobel Prize in 1978, his works had been translated into a great many languages. The translations were so widespread, and enjoyed such extensive popularity, that at times readers may actually have forgotten the language in which the original work was written. Hence it is particularly necessary to emphasize that Bashevis's chosen literary language was Yiddish, chiefly because error-ridden translations have led to awkward textual corruptions that detract from the quality of the writing and the integrity of the author.

Despite the profusion of works by Bashevis published in translation, many others still remain hidden in the yellowing pages of *Forverts* and other Yiddish newspapers and periodicals—enough to provide years of work for translators, publishers, and researchers alike.

Bashevis's prolific literary output during his years in New York, specifically those books translated under his supervision and hence regarded as his major achievements, became the focus of research. As a result, his earlier works, written in Poland over a period of eleven years and most important to an understanding of his later work, have been relegated to the fringes of analysis and have drawn the attention of very few serious studies.[1] Apart from his superb narrative skill, clarity of style, wealth of expression, and lifelike presentation of character, abilities already apparent even then, it is also possible to identify in these early stories recurring motifs that became the hallmark of his unique style in his later work. These motifs include the moral decline of individuals and their society, the erosion of religious faith, the disintegration of family and community structures, the directionless and generally fruitless search for meaning and happiness in life, and, of course, elements of eroticism.

This essay will focus on one forgotten work from Bashevis's early period, a work missing not only from current bibliographies of his work and thus from subsequent research papers,[2] but also from his own rich memory, as is clear from its omission from any of Bashevis's own published interviews and memoirs. This work is a novel entitled *Varshe 1914–1918,* which appeared serially but irregularly in twenty-one issues of the Zionist daily *Dos naye vort* (The New Word) between September 17, 1935, and January 31, 1936. Apparently the section of this novel which appeared in print was all that Bashevis left behind in the offices of *Dos naye vort* before he left Poland, and it covered only the first year of World War I (1914–1915). Perhaps the upheaval in Bashevis's life and the new commitments he took on, such as writing regularly for *Forverts,* kept him from completing the novel. This may also be the reason for his neglecting even to mention it in later years.

Despite the short time that elapsed between the publication of this unknown novel and the appearance of his first book, *Der sotn in goray* (1935),[3] *Varshe 1914–1918* is a fundamentally different work. While *Der sotn in goray* is, in theme and treatment, largely a natural extension of Bashevis's earlier writings, *Varshe 1914–1918* differs from all of these in genre as well as in theme. It casts new light on the shaping of Bashevis's artistic profile and unique style and greatly assists in revealing the sources of his later works.

At the outset of this novel, the chief character of which is a twelve-year-old boy, it is evident that the reader is confronting a literary work firmly rooted in autobiography. Prior to the appearance of this novel, all of Bashevis's chief characters were men and women of various ages, but certainly never children. Children began appearing again as prominent characters only in Bashevis's works written in the 1960s and after.[4] In many of his stories for children the chief character or the first-person narrator is obviously the author himself.[5] In his fictional works — novels such as *Shosha,* for example — that have explicit autobiographical motifs as well as in memoirs of his childhood, Bashevis appears as one who even in his earliest years absorbed the stories he heard in his immediate environment. His mother, grandmother, and aunts recounted many folktales, fables, and legends drawn from *mayse-bikhelekh,* traditional Yiddish morality books written for women, and anecdotes drawn from their personal memories. His sister Hindele spoke of sensational novels that appeared serially in the Yiddish daily newspapers. His brother Israel Joshua spoke in what was regarded in their father's rabbinical home as the voice of heresy by discussing maskilic and European literature, while from his father himself, Rabbi Pinkhes Menakhem, young Itshele heard Hasidic tales and an abun-

Bashevis's Earliest Autobiographical Novel

dance of stories whose mystical themes were remote from the understanding of a child. When young Bashevis was able to read on his own, he read, as he himself testified, anything and everything, much of which he did not understand: his parents' religious texts, *belles-lettres,* philosophical works brought home by his brother, traditional tales, Sherlock Holmes mysteries, and serial novels. After his sister's marriage and his brother's departure, when whole newspapers no longer appeared in his home, Bashevis had only single sheets used as wrapping paper to read.[6] This literary baggage nourished his fertile imagination, and by an early age he displayed proficiency as a spellbinding storyteller and had an audience of followers of his own age and even older.[7]

In *Varshe 1914–1918,* the chief character, Menashe, often fantasizes and indulges in daydreams, yet he lacks all talent as a storyteller. By contrast, another boy of his own age named Khanine "toter" (the Tartar) holds his friend spellbound with complex and fanciful tales, with his knowledge of geography, natural sciences, and esoteric sexuality, and with his boasts of possessing enough kabbalistic learning to work miracles and even to destroy the world with a single utterance. This sort of bragging is highly characteristic of Bashevis, the child-narrator of his later works.[8] A character like Khanine — dark-haired with dark eyes, disheveled in appearance, and showing off his erudition and mysterious origins — can be found in Bashevis's detailed autobiography, *Fun der alter un nayer heym,*[9] in the short story "The Mysteries of the Cabala," where he is named Moyshe, and in the memoir *In My Father's Court,*[10] where he is called Borekh-Dovid.

One episode which appears in *Varshe 1914–1918* and recurs with modifications at least twice in works Bashevis published years later enables us to follow the gradual development of the boy — identified with Itshele Singer — from passive listener to active storyteller, as his peer loses his narrative ability in an odd process of reversal. This episode is a trip to the countryside initiated by Khanine in the wake of wonderful tales he has told Menashe about exotic fruit trees and wild cows grazing in the wide expanse. Although the boys find neither the trees nor the grazing cattle, the visions revealed to Menashe through the fantasies related by Khanine lead him to live in a dream world of imagination. Khanine obviously takes advantage of Menashe's innocence to make fun of him.[11] Almost identical episodes appear in both *In My Father's Court* and *Fun der alter un nayer heym.* In the former, Bashevis emerges as a disciplined though not entirely passive listener,[12] while in the latter he is transformed into a narrator in his own right who engages in a tale-fabrication contest with his friend.[13] In later writings the boy identified with Bashevis himself appears as the sole narrator. This is the case in *Shosha* and in the short stories "A Hanukkah Eve in Warsaw," "Naftali the Storyteller and His Horse, Sus," "Menashe and Rachel," and "Growing Up."[14] In the last-named story a boy appears with the nickname "Black Fayvl," who is clearly identified with the characters of Khanine "toter," Moyshe, and Borekh-Dovid; although he is presented as lacking any talent for storytelling himself, he is portrayed as a great admirer of Itshele Singer, the teller of wondrous tales.

Menashe is the son of a *dayen* (rabbinic judge) who lives in house number 12 on a narrow and busy street in the center of Warsaw's Jewish quarter. Although this street remains unnamed in the narrative, both description and context make it clear that the street in question is Krochmalna Street. This becomes noteworthy when it is recalled that the Singer family moved from number 10 to number 12 on Krochmalna Street shortly before the outbreak of war.[15] Khanine "toter," who never mentions either his parents or his home, allegedly lives in number 16—the same address that Bashevis notes as the home of Moyshe, his childhood friend who is the prototype of Khanine.[16] Menashe does not attend *kheyder* regularly, but studies a little with his father and less by himself, spending most of his time playing in the street with his friends.[17]

The business of the rabbinical court was conducted in the home of the *dayen,* and one session, described in detail, begins with the words, "The door opened and in walked . . ."[18]—a hallmark opening phrase in many of Bashevis's later memoirs built round the activities of his father's court. In addition, the single event described here appears again with minor changes in later works—once in the Yiddish text of *Mayn tatns bezdn-shtub* (pp. 52–56) and again under the title "The Betrayer of Israel" in *The Collected Stories of I. B. Singer.*[19] The *dayen* himself is depicted as a *khosed* (a follower devoted to his spiritual guide, the *rebbe*) who spends months of the year wandering about in search of a *rebbe* to follow. He allows nothing to stand in the way of this quest, not even the outbreak of war. Even during the time he spends at home, he deals primarily with matters of the spirit and is not particularly concerned with his family's grave economic plight, which actually reaches starvation point shortly after the outbreak of war. Apart from the extent of this rabbi's absences from home, there are other points of similarity between this *dayen* and Rabbi Pinkhes Menakhem Singer as he is described *in propria persona* years later

Bashevis's Earliest Autobiographical Novel

by his son.[20] Menashe's mother is easily identified with Basheve Singer (the source of Isaac's chosen name Bashevis): her physical features, her sharp facial lines, her unstable health and depressive tendencies, and her neglect of household chores in favor of reading her books while continually bemoaning her fate all correspond with Bashevis's mother's sense of grievance at the consequences of her unhappy marriage to a *batlen* (impractical, idle person).[21] Menashe's mother is made to differ from Basheve Singer only in that her father is presented as a wealthy publisher and not as the rabbi of Bilgoray.

Menashe is given a sister, Dinele, a young girl with laughing eyes who loves to dress elegantly, to read novels serialized in the Yiddish newspapers, to hobnob with her friends in the Saski Park and attract the attention of young men. It is rumored that she even goes to the theater. She has been engaged to marry a young man from a good home; but as a result of her family's loss of fortune during the early stages of the war this engagement is broken off. In these difficult days, when her father is so often absent from home and her mother is barely able to function, Dinele runs the family home with great devotion, although she fails to control the mischievous Menashe. This contrasts with the actual events of Bashevis's own life: by the time he wrote this story his own older sister, Hinde-Esther, had married in 1914 and was living in Antwerp; her relationship with her mother was strained and intensely complicated. Despite these discrepancies, one can find many similarities between the real Hinde-Esther and the fictional Dinele.[22]

Menashe's brother Oyzer becomes what his father regards as an *apikoyres,* one who no longer believes in the tenets of Orthodox Judaism, and in consequence is expelled from his father's rabbinical home. During Khalemoyed Sukes (the intermediate days between the first two days of Sukkot and the last two days) in 1914 Oyzer suddenly reappears to announce that he is about to be drafted. All attempts by his mother to convince him to inflict some sort of self-mutilation in order to gain exemption from military service are to no avail, as is her physical attempt to block his departure from the house. After an extended period of no communication with his family, Oyzer reappears in the middle of the night and to his family's horror recounts his incarceration with criminals and his escape from prison.[23] As a deserter he has adopted a false identity and has moved in with his girlfriend without marrying her. Menashe is shown often to frequent his brother's new home; his brother first introduces Menashe to a modern library, where he begins reading voraciously.[24] All these details conform with the biography of Israel Joshua Singer as his younger brother recounted it years later. The closeness of the two brothers in this early novel is an accurate reflection of their actual relationship. For the sake of historical accuracy it should be noted that at the time this novel takes place the real I. J. Singer himself lived in the home of the sculptor Avrom Ostziga, which was a meeting place for Jewish bohemia in Warsaw.[25]

As the title of this novel suggests, Bashevis devotes much effort to describing the atmosphere of Jewish Warsaw during the early days of World War I. As one who spends much time on the streets, Menashe absorbs rumors of the impending war and is a witness to the run on the shops, the hoarding of food supplies—although not of course in his own poverty-stricken home—the soaring prices, and the generally uneasy atmosphere resulting from the widespread military draft. Within a short time the expulsion of Jews from peripheral towns begins, and thousands of Jews are depicted reaching Warsaw destitute and helpless. In parallel historical terms, it was at this time that the Jewish population of Warsaw as a whole began suffering from starvation and disease and died in large numbers. Toward the summer of 1915, with the advance of the German forces, Russian soldiers stood on the streets of Warsaw selling a variety of goods that included items easily identified as garments and household effects looted from Jewish homes in the peripheral towns.[26]

Menashe and Khanine spend entire days wandering the streets, and in an attempt to keep warm they enter various prayer-houses, where they overhear adult discussions and strategic analyses. On one occasion a clandestine *maskil*, Reb Zaynvl, introduces himself to them, invites them home, and feeds them well. He makes them privy to his secret plan to escape from his overbearing wife and his stepdaughters and to make his way on foot to Erets Yisroel. Khanine is enthusiastic and suggests that both he and Menashe join Reb Zaynvl. In order to survive the long journey, they plan to pass Reb Zaynvl off as a *rebbe* and themselves off as two boys acting as the *rebbe*'s attendants or *meshamshim*. One day Reb Zaynvl's wife discovers this odd group rehearsing the proper behavior required at a *rebbe*'s *tish* and puts a swift end to her husband's meetings with the boys. The novel ends abruptly with a description of the Germans occupying Warsaw, the concomitant exhilaration of the local Jewish population, and their keen anticipation of considerable improvement in their condition.

Bashevis's Earliest Autobiographical Novel

That the autobiographical corpus is a major component of Bashevis's works is well known. It includes at least fourteen extensive works comprising memoirs — chronological or random[27] — direct autobiographies,[28] novels in which it is easy to identify the chief character with the author,[29] as well as various combinations of these genres.[30] In addition to all these, one can identify numerous short stories and pieces of reportage in which the autobiographical element is obvious from the outset, while in others it is only hinted at.

Bashevis himself attached great significance to his autobiographical writing, going so far as to declare that "all of my writing is actually memoirs . . . I see no basic distinction between novels and memoirs."[31] In his introduction to the series *Mayn tatns bezdn-shtub* and *Der shrayber-klub* (The Writers' Club), Bashevis openly declares that his objective is a literary experiment to synthesize memoirs and *belles-lettres*.[32] Despite this, very little research has centered on this rich literary corpus, which still awaits a thorough and exhaustive examination.[33]

Although here and there one may encounter insignificant biographical hints in his earlier stories, *Mayn tatns bezdn-shtub* (New York, 1956), translated into English as *In My Father's Court* (New York, 1966), is generally thought of as Bashevis's first autobiographical composition. Janet Hadda has suggested that Bashevis's earlier work *Di familye mushkat* is the beginning of his autobiographical writing.[34] According to Hadda, the impetus for Bashevis to combine autobiographical elements with his fictional works derives from his subconscious difficulty in dealing directly with "too painful reality" — the unexpected death of his beloved brother and the loss of the natural environment of his youth to which he was intimately bound.[35] In his introduction to the interesting reportage series *Mentshn oyf mayn veg* (People along My Path), Bashevis observed:

> Unfortunately, a human being doesn't possess the ability to revive the dead. But I wanted at least to bring to life in literature those who had been annihilated, to provide the Yiddish reader with images of individual men and women, with all the features and peculiarities that are characteristic of an individual. This is, in fact, the purpose of everything that I write.[36]

While there is certainly no reason to doubt either the sincerity of the author's claim or Hadda's logical assumption, both are inadequate to explain why Bashevis wrote an autobiographical novel as early as 1935, at the age of thirty-one, a decade,

Nathan Cohen

if not two, prior to what has been thought of as the beginning of his autobiographical writing. This question is all the more puzzling because in this early novel we are taken into a period during which the Jews of Poland still lived and functioned in relative tranquillity, and all members of the Singer family, except for the father, were still alive. Since we are unable to pose the question to the author himself, we may attempt to suggest an answer by elaborating on what has been stated thus far: Bashevis's autobiographical writing derives from an inner subconscious need which arose from familial and national catastrophes.

Between the Chmielnicki pogroms and the Holocaust—a period of three hundred years—World War I is considered the most traumatic period in the collective memory of Polish Jewry. Many literary works, particularly by younger writers and poets in independent Poland, focus on these fearful years.[37] Yitskhok Bashevis, while still only a child, experienced these events with great force and no doubt felt the need, years later, to give written expression to the trauma he had undergone. Moreover, the immediate Singer family confronted two devastating bereavements during the first half of the 1930s. The first was the death of Bashevis's father, even though it is not entirely clear to what extent it affected the writer, and the second was the wholly unanticipated death of Bashevis's young nephew Yasha, a death which moved him deeply.[38] With the destruction of Polish Jewry, the author's inner urge to commemorate their memory, as well as the memory of his brother, undoubtedly grew.

The abundant monuments in print that Bashevis has left us still await their deserved study, which will undoubtedly add to our appreciation of his work and give us a deeper acquaintance with the world to which he felt such close kinship throughout his life.

Notes

1. The best works dealing with this subject are Moshe Yungman, "The Poland Period in I. Bashevis-Singer's Literary Career (1924–1935)," *Ha-sifrut* 27 (1978): 118–133 (in Hebrew); Eliyahu Shulman, "Di ershte tsen yor fun yitskhok bashevis-zingers shafung," *Di tsukunft* 89 (1983): 96–100, 152–155, 185–188; 90 (1984): 28–30; and David N. Miller, *Fear of Fiction: Narrative Strategies in the Works of Isaac Bashevis Singer* (Albany: State University of New York Press, 1985), pp. 1–27.

2. It is not mentioned either in David N. Miller, *Bibliography of Isaac Bashevis Singer: 1924–1949* (New York: P. Lang, 1983), or in Yungman, "The Poland Period," pp. 126–127.

Bashevis's Earliest Autobiographical Novel

3. *Der sotn in goray* was first published serially in the literary journal *Globus* (Warsaw) two years earlier.

4. Khone Shmeruk, "Isaac Bashevis Singer as Children's Storyteller," *Chulyot* 3 (1996): 163–196 (in Hebrew); Janet Hadda, *Isaac Bashevis Singer: A Life* (New York: Oxford University Press, 1997), pp. 154–158.

5. See a list of examples in Shmeruk, "Children's Storyteller."

6. *Fun der alter un nayer heym, Forverts,* October 25, 1963, November 1 and 15, 1963. Hereafter cited as *Heym.*

7. For example, Reb Avrom-Shmuel, his *melamed* (teacher); *Heym,* October 26, 1963.

8. See, for instance, Isaac Bashevis Singer, *Shosha* (New York: Farrar, Straus, Giroux, 1978), pp. 13–15; *Mentshn oyf mayn veg, Forverts,* May 25, 1958, March 7, 1959; *Heym,* October 25, 1963, November 8, 1963; "The Mysteries of the Cabala," in Isaac Bashevis Singer, *A Day of Pleasure* (New York: Farrar, Straus, Giroux, 1969), pp. 125–136.

9. *Heym,* November 2, 1963.

10. Isaac Bashevis Singer, *In My Father's Court* (Philadelphia: Jewish Publication Society of America, 1966), pp. 175–182 (hereafter cited as *Court*), and in a story that appears in Yiddish only in *Mayn tatns bezdn-shtub* (Tel Aviv: Farlag Y. L. Perets, 1979), pp. 219–224.

11. *Dos naye vort,* October 10, 1935.

12. *Court,* pp. 175–182.

13. *Heym,* November 2 and 8, 1963.

14. Isaac Bashevis Singer, *Stories for Children* (New York: Farrar, Straus, Giroux, 1984), pp. 53–70, 122–129, 167–183, 217–230, respectively. In the original these stories were printed in *Forverts* as "An erev khanike in varshe," December 13, 1975, January 7–9, 1976; "Naftole der mayse-dertseyler un zayn ferd sus," December 4, 5, and 11, 1975; and "Vuks," February 13, 19, and 20, 1976. "Menashe un rokhele" was published in *Bay zikh* 19 (1981): 24–29.

15. *Heym,* November 8, 1963.

16. Khanine's mother, it is rumored, sells household utensils; similarly, Moyshe's mother earns her living by selling pots and pans. See *Heym,* November 2, 1963.

17. Ibid., November 1 and 2, 1963.

18. *Dos naye vort,* September 21, 1935.

19. *The Collected Stories of I. B. Singer* (New York: Farrar, Straus, Giroux, 1970), pp. 505–511.

20. *Heym,* November 1, 1963; and especially *Court,* pp. 51–57, 156.

21. *Heym,* November 23, 1963; *Court,* p. 50; Hadda, *Singer,* pp. 27–30, 33–34.

22. See *Court,* pp. 151–155; and especially Hadda, *Singer,* pp. 31–41.

23. *Heym,* November 15, 1963; *Court,* pp. 281–282. In both sources the father is also recorded as being present at all these events. Both sources record the efforts made by the

Nathan Cohen

grandfather, the rabbi of Bilgoray, to free Israel Joshua from prison and from being drafted into the army. In *Varshe 1914–1918*, it is an uncle who is mentioned as the person who tries to help Oyzer. For fuller details about the relationship between Israel Joshua and his parents, see Hadda, *Singer,* pp. 31–38.

24. According to Bashevis's own testimony, he first went to a lending library on his own initiative. See Isaac Bashevis Singer, *Love and Exile* (New York: Penguin, 1986), pp. 32–35. This library was probably Bresler's Library in Warsaw, which is mentioned in the serial *Mentshn oyf mayn veg, Forverts,* October 30, 1959.

25. *Heym,* November 15, 1963.

26. *Dos naye vort,* January 13, 1936.

27. The serial *Figurn un epizodn fun literatn farayn* (Figures and Episodes from the Writers' Union), *Forverts,* June 28, 1979, to January 10, 1980, is an example of random memoirs, while *Heym* is a serial of chronological memoirs.

28. For example, *Di mishpokhe* (The Family), *Forverts,* February 2, 1982, to February 4, 1983.

29. Two examples of such novels are *Shosha,* originally serialized in Yiddish under the title *Neshome ekspeditsyes* (Soul Expeditions), *Forverts,* April 26, 1974, to November 14, 1974, and *The Certificate* (New York: Farrar, Straus, Giroux, 1992), originally serialized in Yiddish under the title *Der sertifikati, Forverts,* January 13, 1967, to May 27, 1967.

30. Such as *Court,* according to the author's own words (see below), and *Mentshn oyf mayn veg, Forverts,* January 24, 1958, to October 8, 1960.

31. Richard Burgin, *Conversations with Isaac Bashevis Singer* (Garden City, N.Y.: Doubleday, 1985), pp. 78–79.

32. The introduction to *Mayn tatns bezdn-shtub* appears only in Yiddish in *Forverts,* February 19, 1955, and in the English translation. For the introduction to *Der shrayber-klub,* see *Forverts,* January 13, 1956.

33. The most exhaustive studies of this subject to date are Anita Norich, "The Family Singer and the Autobiographical Imagination," *Prooftexts* 10 (1990): 91–107; Khone Shmeruk, "Bashevis-Singer — In Search of his Autobiography," *Jewish Quarterly* 19:4/108 (1982): 28–36; and Khone Shmeruk, "Between Autobiography and Fiction," the introduction to Yitskhok Bashevis Singer, *Mayn tatns bezdn-shtub: hemshekhim-zamlung* (Jerusalem: Magnes Press of Hebrew University, 1996), pp. v–xvii (in Yiddish); Miller, *Bibliography,* pp. 79–82, also deals with the subject, as does Hadda, *Singer,* pp. 111–121.

34. *Forverts,* November 17, 1945, to May 1, 1948; in English, *The Family Moskat* (New York: Knopf, 1950).

35. Hadda, *Singer,* pp. 110–119.

36. *Forverts,* January 23, 1958.

37. For a partial list of books dealing with this period published in independent Poland, see Wolf Gliksman, "Cultural and Social Trends of the Jews in Poland as Reflected in Yiddish Literature 1914–1918," *Gal-Ed* 2 (1975): 373–379 (in Hebrew). See also David G. Roskies, *Against the Apocalypse: Responses to Catastrophe in Modern Jewish Culture* (Cambridge, Mass.: Harvard University Press, 1984), Chaps. 4 and 5.

38. See Hadda, *Singer,* pp. 78–79.

Nathan Cohen

11

Folk and Folklore in the Work of Bashevis

Itzik Gottesman

Recent Yiddish literary criticism has focused on the issue of how modern Yiddish literature has incorporated Jewish folklore, sometimes romanticizing it, at other times parodying it, and at still other times using it with a modernist sensibility.[1] It seems that as consensus for a canon of Yiddish fiction emerges, many of the established works' entry into literary immortality is owing in large measure to their connection with Jewish life through folkloric material. Yitskhok Bashevis, considered one of the great fiction writers in Yiddish, has certainly exemplified the Yiddish author who successfully wrote "folklorically," going beyond the genres of folklore to create something fresh and modern. The fact that Bashevis is often called a "storyteller" rather than a "writer" in the mass media attests to the folk image that has attached to him internationally as a consequence of his style and portraiture.

Yet the history of folklore has demonstrated that underlying the collection, the printing, and the use of folklore there is often an ambivalence toward the subject of study. In other words, the folklore of the nation is praised and greatly valued, but the "folk" itself is often denigrated and held in low esteem. It becomes evident that while the collectors greatly admire the "folk treasure" or "folk creation," their feelings for the "folk" are less than positive. This has been true at least as far back as the Grimm brothers in Germany at the beginning of the nineteenth century, who sought out and recorded folktales and legends from the peasants and working class to manifest the greatness of the German folk. At the same time, however, they often edited the texts they collected, essentially silencing the voice of the folk, so that the Grimms' vision of the tales and the nation would predominate.[2]

No one can accuse Bashevis of silencing the voice of the folk. First, he is a master of the Yiddish language and revels in recording the rich spoken Yiddish of the poorer Jews of Poland. Second, he is a fiction writer and not a folklorist and is consequently under no obligation to transcribe folk texts. What could be claimed, however, is that Bashevis manifests an ambivalence in his attitude toward the folk and its folklore. This argument finds firmer ground in his various memoirs, where, it can be argued, the writer often celebrates the Jewishness of his youth while simultaneously underlining the weaknesses of the Jews. This essay explores the Jewishness/Jew dichotomy running through much of Bashevis's work, fiction and nonfiction alike.

Bashevis's use of Jewish folklore has become one of the identifying features of his fiction. Demons and devils are integral components of Bashevis's novels and short stories, and in his own words, "[using them] helps me to express myself" because they represent "the ways of the world."[3] They are symbolic, bearing a considerable interpretative burden, and cannot be dismissed as simply a gratuitous display of Jewish superstition or belief, whether the interpretation of the work in which they appear leans toward parable, politics, psychology, or anything else.

The difference between this deployment of folklore in Bashevis's fiction and its deployment in his memoirs is striking. This analysis particularly relies on a recently published Yiddish collection entitled *Mayn tatns bezdn-shtub [hemshekhim-zamlung]* (My Father's Court [Sequel-Collection]),[4] containing items selected from various autobiographical series that Bashevis published in the Yiddish newspaper *Forverts*. They include some episodes not published in the original Yiddish *Mayn tatns bezdn-shtub* (1956),[5] some episodes from a series entitled *Der shrayber-klub* (The Writers' Club) published in *Forverts* in 1956, and several episodes from the series *Mentshn oyf mayn veg* (People along My Way), published in the same newspaper from January 1958 to October 1960. Khone Shmeruk, the editor of this new collection published five years after Bashevis's death, assembled the pieces chronologically according to the known facts of Bashevis's biography. The young Bashevis lived in Warsaw until World War I and then moved with his mother and brother to his maternal grandfather's small town of Bilgoray for a few years before returning to Warsaw. Hence this collection is divided into three parts, respectively entitled "Warsaw," "Bilgoray," and "Back to Warsaw."

In terms of Bashevis's interest in folklore, the first two parts are of most interest. "Warsaw" describes his father's *bezdn,* the rabbinical court which operated from the Singers' apartment and where Bashevis's father, the rabbi, interacted for the most part with the indigent of Warsaw. Bashevis's English readers first became acquainted with his father's rabbinical court in the memoir *In My Father's Court,*[6]

Itzik Gottesman

which was an edited and slightly abridged version of the original Yiddish. One of the clearest examples in English of the folk/folklore dichotomy in Bashevis's memoirs can be found in the introduction to the first publication of the Yiddish text of *Mayn tatns bezdn-shtub*. In essence the memoir, set in the period before World War I, centers on the Jews of Krochmalna Street, one of the poorest Jewish streets in Warsaw. Here, incongruously thrust together, the gangsters of the Jewish underworld, traditional Hasidic Jews, laborers, and rabbis of all kinds lived, worked, and rubbed shoulders. Although Bashevis's episodes describe the way these Jews interacted with his parents and sometimes with Yitskhok himself, no reference to his parents or to any of these distressed Jews can be found in the book's introduction. Instead, almost the entire introduction deals with the institution of the *bezdn*:[7]

> *di bezdn-shtub farshvindt itst bay yidn, ober ikh bin zikher az zi vet vider zikh banayen un vet vern an algemeyn-mentshlekhe institutsye. di ideye fun der bezdn-shtub iz, az s'kon nisht zayn gerekhtikeyt on getlekhkeyt un az der bester mishpet iz yener, vos di baley-dinim nemen oyf zikh mitn gutn viln un mit a gloybn in di hekhere koykhes. der heypekh fun der bezdn-shtub iz di inkvizitsye, un ale yene gerikhtn vos banutsn zikh mit koyekh un gvald-tat, alts eyns tsi zey zenen rekht oder link.*
>
> *di bezdn-shtub iz meglekh geven bay a folk fun tifn gloybn un greser hakhnoe. zi hot dergreykht ir hekhste madreyge in der tsayt ven yidn hobn nisht gehat keyn shum makht, keyn shum takifes. dos vafn fun dem dayen iz geven di keshene-fatsheyle vos mit ir hobn di baley-din mekabl kinyen geven.*
>
> *in mayn tatns bezdn-shtub iz a matseyve oyf a mes, vos vet oyfshteyn tkhies hameysim. di bezdn-shtub bay undz yidn iz efsher an umendlekh kleyner un tunkeler muster fun dem bezdn-shel mayle, gots mishpet vos iz, vi mir yidn gloybn, durkhoys khesed.* (Y-BDS)[8]

The Bet-din is disappearing now among Jews, but I am certain it will once again be renewed and will become a general human institution. The motivating principle of the Bet-din is that there can be no justice without morality and that the best judicial sentence is the one that the litigants accept with goodwill and with a belief in the higher powers. The antithesis of the Bet-din is the Inquisition and all those courts that use power and force, no matter whether of the left or right.

The Bet-din was possible among a people of deep faith and great humility. It reached its highest level at the time when Jews were totally helpless, with no political power. The emblem of the judge's authority was the pocket handkerchief, by touching which the litigants confirmed their agreement.

In My Father's Court is a gravestone for a corpse that will be resurrected.

Among us Jews the Bet-din is perhaps an infinitely small and dark example of the heavenly court which is on high, God's judgment which is, as we Jews believe, full of mercy.

Bashevis foregrounds his memoir's Jewishness, but not its Jews. Here he idealizes the Jewish religion, but the Jews themselves, the folk, fade into the background. Jews were no better and no worse than other peoples, but Judaism, particularly the kind of religion as practiced by the oppressed and politically helpless Jews of Eastern Europe, should—as Bashevis views it—serve as a model for the rest of the world. Bashevis was quite aware of a Yiddish literary tradition that had two sites of emphasis, the community and the individual character. He was also aware that he was not part of the tradition that emphasized the community. He had been criticized in the Yiddish world for this very reason—for placing character above the community.[9] Bashevis's portrayal of Jews in anything but a nostalgic manner is one of his work's most distinguishing markers, and one for which he was often castigated in the Yiddish press. In the episode "In a klem" (In a Quandary), the author writes:

ikh muz do zogn, az ven es kumt tsu kharakter-eygnshaftn, helft nisht tsi men iz a khosed, a misnaged, an oyfgeklerter, a yid, a krist, a toter. shlekhter mentshn zenen shlekht, alts eyns in vos far a levush zey zoln zikh nisht onton. gotloze mentshn blaybn gotloz, afile ven zey davenen zeks mol a tog. ikh hob ge-zen khsidim opton miese un beyzvilike zakhn, punkt vi ikh hob gezen khsidim zikh firn zeyer laytish un groys. es iz emes, az religye derheybt dem mentsh. ober ez zenen faran azoyne mentshn, vos zenen mamesh fun der natur tayv-lonish. zey banutsn zikh mit religye bloyz far zeyere tsvekn, oft miese tsvekn. mir veysn az frume kristn hobn ayngeordnt an inkvizitsye. Es zenen geven— un ez zenen filaykh nokh do— "frume" yidn azoyne vos zenen feyik af etlekhe umverdikeytn. ober dos iz nisht di shuld fun religye. es iz di shuld fun a min mentsh vos iz feyik tsu bahaltn rishes hinter di same hekhste ideyaln. (Y-HZ 153)

I must state here that when it comes to individual character, it doesn't help if one is a Hasid, a *misnaged*, a secularist, a Jew, a Christian, a Tartar. Evil people are evil, no matter what external guise they don. Godless people remain godless even when they pray six times a day. I have seen Hasidim pull off ugly and cruel things, just as I have seen Hasidim behave very decorously and with nobility. It is true that religion exalts an individual. But there are individuals who are literally devilish by nature. They use religion solely for their own purposes, often ugly purposes. We know that religious Christians instituted an Inquisition. There were—and perhaps there still are—"obser-

Itzik Gottesman

vant" Jews who are capable of various outrages. But this is not the fault of religion. It is the fault of the kind of person who is capable of hiding wickedness behind the highest ideals.

In Bashevis's view, the ideals of Judaism are worthy and pure; it is only individual people who ruin and denigrate them. The passage just quoted makes the writer's plea not to throw the baby out with the bath water or, as the Yiddish proverb puts it more aptly, *az men iz in kaas afn baltfile, shpringt men nisht kedushe?* "If one is angry with the prayer-leader, does one then not bow at the appropriate moment during the recitation of the Eighteen Benedictions when God's Name is sanctified?" Simply because some Jews are bad, one should not abandon the ethical and moral supremacy of Eastern European Judaism. Writing for a post-Holocaust Yiddish readership, many of whom no longer practiced the observances of Orthodox Jewish law, Bashevis's view was conservative indeed.

In this memoir, the distinction that Bashevis draws between *reb yisroel* and *klal yisroel,* between the individual Jew and the Jewish people, is embedded in the opening paragraphs of his chapters. As Shmeruk points out in his introduction to the new volume, the scenes that take place in the *bezdn* often begin with the door of the apartment opening and descriptions of the Warsaw Jews who enter. One is immediately thrust into the middle of a social interaction, with the child Yitskhok observing and sometimes participating. The author describes a specific, unique scene and type. In his chapters on Bilgoray, however, Bashevis tends to open with generalizations about human relations and character, avoiding, for the moment, the immediacy of his *bezdn* incidents.

The episode "A tumtum vos hot khasene gehat un der rebe get zikh un hot khasene" (A Hermaphrodite Who Married and the Rebbe Who Divorces and Marries) begins, *yeder shtot hot ire tsadikim, ire reshoim, ire moyre-shkhoyrenikes, un ire leytsim* (Y-HZ 139), "Every city has its saints, its wicked, its melancholiacs, and its clowns." Similarly, in the episode "Mendl turbiner der takif" (Mendl Turbiner the Big-Shot), the narrator begins:

fun vanen nemen zikh takifim? vi azoy bashlist epes a mentsh bay zikh, az er iz a shtarker un az der darf umetum hobn a deye? es iz a retenish vi ale retenishn. (Y-HZ 165)

Where do influential people spring from? How does a person decide that he is powerful and that he needs to have a say in everything? It is a riddle like all riddles.

Folk and Folklore in the Work of Bashevis

"He Achieved His Goal" opens with the statement, *faran mentshn azoyne, vos zeyer goyrl iz a gants lebn tsu zayn umgliklekh farlibt* (Y-HZ 172), "There exist the kind of people whose fate is to be unhappily in love their entire life." And finally the chapter "Di bord" (The Beard) begins, *faran mentshn vos kenen zayn gliklekh bloyz demolt ven zey hobn a sakh fraynd un ven zey krign fun der svive di fardinte onerkenung* (Y-HZ 187), "There are people who can only be happy when they have many friends and when they receive an earned recognition from their circle." Ironically, here in Bilgoray, in the *shtetl* which Bashevis viewed as more quintessentially Jewish than Warsaw, the author opens his stories with universalizing statements. Though the Jews of Bilgoray are Jewish to the bone, nevertheless they are universalized in their similarity to both Jews and non-Jews all over the world.

In Bilgoray Bashevis found his Jewish town of yore, a town that amply provided him with folkloric material for both his fiction and his nonfiction. But his uses of folklore in these two genres should be differentiated. The function of folklore in *Der sotn in goray* has been interpreted, among other ways, as parable and as political allegory. In all of these readings, the folklore has been perceived not simply as a display of Jewish belief or custom, as if to say, "This is what Jews believed in: isn't it interesting?" This type of presentation of folklore is highly evident in S. Anski's popular play of the 1920s, *The Dybbuk,* which contains a parade of old beliefs and lifestyles that has no central bearing on the course of the play. Anski's *The Dybbuk* was so popular and so influential that any subsequent Yiddish fiction dealing with a dybbuk must be read intertextually with it. In this regard Bashevis's dybbuk, the possessing spirit in *Der sotn in goray,* is a manifest reaction against Anski's Romantic use of the dybbuk. Whereas Anski removed almost all the Evil from the dybbuk in his drama, Bashevis filled his own with ferocious cruelty and made him Satan, Evil Incarnate. As a reaction against Anski's use and incorporation of dybbuk folklore—a reflection of nineteenth-century Romanticism—Bashevis responds with a powerful anti-Romantic interwar reaction. Traditional dybbuk tales lay somewhere in between their presentation by these two writers: customarily there is some pity shown for the dybbuk, but the chief focus in dybbuk folktales is essentially on the exorcism and the power of the *rebbe.* These folktales were hagiographical and were more concerned with the exorcist than with either the victim or the possessing dybbuk. In Bashevis's deployment of this folk material, the dybbuk comes closest to the sensational Hollywood film *The Exorcist,* which draws on the Roman Catholic tradition and is hence further removed from the Jewish

Itzik Gottesman

tradition. In general terms, Bashevis is intent on using folklore for its power to depict the moral universe, while Anski's moral focus is on a tale that is ultimately a love story. While both Bashevis and Anski are careful to be faithful to the traditional belief and rite of exorcism, in *Der sotn in goray* Bashevis goes beyond the folk tradition to turn the dybbuk into a metonym for wickedness and his novel into a parable of Evil.

In his memoirs, however, Bashevis takes a very different attitude toward folklore. Dvorah Telushkin, in her reminiscences of her years as Bashevis's secretary, quotes Bashevis as responding to an interviewer's question, "In your folklore, are you trying to pass down traditions?" with the remark, "Folklore is tradition. Nothing is old-fashioned and vee [*sic*] should never look down on tradition."[10] In the same interview, Telushkin also quotes Bashevis as saying, "One should never lose his roots," so that he sets up an equation in which a good Jew needs folklore to stay Jewish. These statements, however, apply only to his nonfiction. In his fiction, folklore is much more than tradition. Bashevis certainly understood the usual definition of folklore and, under his other pseudonyms, wrote numerous articles on the subject in *Forverts* under such titles as "Old Wives' Tales in Jewish Life of Long Ago," "The Significance of the Customs Related to Holidays," "Jews of Long Ago Were Not the Only Ones Who Believed in Transmigration or a Dybbuk," and "Interesting Customs and Songs about Purim." In his memoirs, these folkloristic beliefs and customs, together with their spirits and demons, are made an integral part of the Judaism he idealizes, and in this respect he follows his father's ways.

In Warsaw Bashevis did not find the characters and inhabitants he came across in the *shtetl* of Bilgoray. When similar characters do enter his father's *bezdn* in Warsaw, Bashevis immediately labels them *fartsaytike* (Jews of yore), "old-fashioned." Though Bashevis immensely enjoyed meeting those Jews dressed and behaving as *fartsaytike*, he nevertheless occasionally describes them with irony. In the story "A zokn fun hundert yor" (An Ancient Man Aged One Hundred), Bashevis describes one such "old-fashioned" character, Reb Moyshe Berishes, who remembers when the town of Bilgoray was nothing but empty fields:

> *nokh mer vi di vilde khayes hobn geloyert arum bilgoray un in shtot gufe*
> *—sheydim, leytsim, lapitutn, volkalakn, un alerley andere nisht-gute. hinter*
> *yedn piekelek iz gezesn a lantukh, a hoyz-shedl, un opgeton alerley shtiklekh,*
> *oder a mol geton a toyve der baleboste. nokh yeder mageyfe, hot men getrofn*

Folk and Folklore in the Work of Bashevis

arumgeyn in di nekht geshtorbene vos hobn nisht gehat keyn menukhe in key-ver. (Y-HZ 134)

Outnumbering the wild animals, all around Bilgoray and in the town itself lurked all manner of demons, spirits, elves, werewolves, and various other evil spirits. Behind every oven skulked a *lantukh,* a house spirit that performed various mischievous acts or sometimes a good deed for the woman of the house. After every plague, one came across the dead who could find no rest in their graves and would wander about at nights.

Here Bashevis displays evident ambivalence toward the *fartsaytike* character. When someone comments to Reb Moyshe, "Cold, isn't it Reb Moyshe?" he replies:

dos rufstu kalt? a mol iz geven kalt. feygl zenen gefaln fun di dekher. der bronfn iz gefroryn gevorn in fesl. velf hobn gehoylt in di velder. zey zenen gekumen in shtot arayn un oyfgegesn a ferd . . . (Y-HZ 137)

You call this cold? Once upon a time it was really cold. Birds fell from the roofs. Whiskey froze in the barrel. Wolves starved in the woods. They entered the town and devoured a horse.

Bashevis enjoys the folkloric wonders of *fartsaytns,* of long ago, yet he smirks at the unreality and fantasy of that world. Folklore, *fartsaytns,* the Jewish religion, and the whole concept of what is broadly called *yidishkeyt,* Jewishness, all are parts of the same piece. This episode concludes:

di nakht iz tsugefaln un yidn zenen gekumen davenen minkhe vi mit a hundert yor tsurik, vi far toyznt yor tsurik.
—moyshe, zog "karbones"! . . . (Y-HZ 138)

The night had come and Jews came to pray at the afternoon and evening service as they had come a hundred years ago, a thousand years ago.
—Moyshe, lead us in the prayers relating to the sacrifices in the Temple of Old!

This last sentence is filled with nostalgia for times and customs far in the past and a belief that the old people who lived then were more Jewish than they are now. At the same time, however, through exaggeration in his account, Bashevis ironically highlights the humorous possibilities of that past and the manner of its recounting.

The same ironical attitude toward folklore is found in the episode entitled "The Beard," in which a Jew leaves Bilgoray for America; the further he travels from his hometown, the further from Judaism the world becomes. Almost immediately after he has left Bilgoray, people on the train seem alien and foreign to him: *vos*

Itzik Gottesman

vayter fun shtot, alts fremder, umgelumpeter, beyzer hobn oysgekukt di pasazhirn (Y-HZ 188), "The farther from town, the stranger and more brutal the passengers appeared." On the ship the situation worsens, but only in America itself is the truth revealed—that Jews, as it seems to the immigrant, have all but converted to Christianity. So the disillusioned traveler returns to his *shtetl* world of Bilgoray. In this contrast between the folkloric old-fashioned town and the new apostate city of New York where a man's beard, the authentic signifier of his Judaism, is cut off, one finds great sympathy for the old ways, yet also a gentle humor, poking fun at the inability of those old ways to survive in the modern world. Bashevis articulates a world view that simultaneously expresses regret for the passing of such old-fashioned people and their lifestyle yet offers a narrator who is clearly aware of the inherent absurdity of these anachronisms.

Whether Bashevis himself in fact believed in spirits and demons as he claimed is less important than his conviction that those Jews like his father, who did believe in the truth of such folklore, were good Jews of the highest moral and religious integrity. Their belief in folklore did not render them "superstitious"; rather it expressed their faith in God's wonders and miracles. And when cynical or rationalistic Jews reveal these demons to be an illusion, as Bashevis's mother did in the classic episode "Farvos di gendz hobn geshrign" (Y-BDS 15–19), "Why the Geese Shrieked" (E 11–16), their literal-mindedness does not diminish the admiration the narrator feels for those who by contrast had complete faith in miracles and the mysteries of Divine power.

In a similar episode in the new collection, an old Hasidic *rebbe* marries a young bride who falls pregnant. All the *rebbe*'s Hasidim consider this a great miracle, but the young Yitskhok's mother, always the cold, skeptical *misnaged* (religious rationalist and opponent of mystical Hasidism), is convinced that the world is being deceived. His mother is proved right; it is soon revealed that the bride has placed a pillow under her clothes, and "the miracle was no longer." His believing father, unable to tolerate his wife's rationalism, accuses her: "Because of you, the children have been ruined," establishing a causal relationship between not believing in miracles and apostasy. Bashevis, commenting on why this deception practiced on a supposedly all-knowing *rebbe* did not destroy his following, offers this reflection:

ven a mentsh investirt lange yorn gloybn in emetsn oder in a zakh, kon er nisht mit a mol zogn, az er hot zikh ale yorn opgenart. eyntslene konen dos efsher yo, ober di mase vi a gantse hot nisht dem dozikn koyekh (Y-HZ 144)

Folk and Folklore in the Work of Bashevis

When a person invests many years of faith in someone or something, he cannot suddenly say that he has deceived himself all these years. Perhaps individuals can do this, but the masses as a whole do not have such strength.

Bashevis's acute observation is a basic truism in the anthropology of religion. When something goes wrong and calls into question one's religious faith, the answer cannot be found by discarding the whole religious system, but should rather be sought elsewhere. Indeed this kind of thinking has sustained the Jewish people over thousands of years in their belief that the Messiah will ultimately come. Traditional Jewish Orthodoxy teaches that the fault for the delay in the Messiah's arrival is to be sought in the sins of each particular generation of Jews, not in the Messiah himself. Bashevis does not conclude with this observation; instead he goes further by justifying Hasidic faith on "scientific" grounds, namely the view that anything is possible:

> es iz oykh a fakt, az kastrirter mener hobn gelebt mit froyen. mit a tsayt tsurik iz a yapanisher mansbil gevorn "shvanger" un m'hot aroysgenumen fun zayn boykh a halb-antviklt kind. faln vu mener hobn gehat milkh in di bristn zenen fartshteykhnt gevorn a sakh. der fakt vos der radzyminer rebe hot gehat iluzyes un vos di frishe radzyminer rebetsin hot gevolt m'zol ir opshraybn a hoyz — dos vayzt nisht az s'zenen nishto keyn hekhere koykhes.
>
> di mentshlekhe iluzyes, di mentshlekhe ligns, un di mentshlekhe shvakhkeytn bavayzn az der mentsh iz kleyn. ober zey nemen gornisht tsu fun der getlekher groyskeyt. (Y-HZ 144)

It is a fact that castrated men have lived with women. A little while ago, a Japanese man fell pregnant and a half-developed child was removed from his belly. Many times there have been records of cases when men had milk in their breasts. The fact that the Radzyminer *rebbe* had illusions and that his brand-new *rebbetzin* [wife of a rabbi] wanted to have a house made over in her name does not prove that there are no higher powers.

Human illusions, human lies, and human weakness show that man is small. But they take nothing away from Divine greatness.

Bashevis is fond of the term "higher powers," an expression which I believe he translates directly from the English into the Yiddish because it seems to carry a "scientific" connotation.

This concluding quotation sums up a number of the ideas expressed in this essay about Bashevis's relationship with folk and folklore, particularly as he reveals it in his memoirs. He does not appear to hold the folk in very high esteem; however, their simple faith in the heavens and their old-time religion that embraces

171

Itzik Gottesman

and includes folklore, spirits, customs, tenets, and miracles kept the folk together and humble and could serve as a model for humanity.

Notes

1. See David G. Roskies, *A Bridge of Longing: The Lost Art of Yiddish Storytelling* (Cambridge, Mass.: Harvard University Press, 1995); Seth L. Wolitz, "Between Folk and Freedom: The Failure of the Yiddish Modernist Movement in Poland," *Yiddish* 8:1 (1991): 26–39; Dan Miron, "Folk and Anti-Folklore in the Yiddish Fiction of the Haskala," in Frank Talmadge (ed.), *Studies in Jewish Folklore: Proceedings of a Regional Conference of the Association for Jewish Studies*, Spertus College of Judaica, Chicago, May 1–3, 1977 (Cambridge, Mass.: Harvard University Press, 1980); Ken Frieden, *Classic Yiddish Fiction: Abramovitsh, Sholem Aleichem, and Peretz* (Albany: SUNY Press, 1995); Ruth R. Wisse, *I. L. Peretz and the Making of Modern Jewish Culture* (Seattle: University of Washington Press, 1991).

2. See Jack David Zipes, *The Brothers Grimm: From Enchanted Forests to the Modern World* (New York: Routledge, 1988); Ruth B. Bottigheimer, *Grimms' Bad Girls and Bold Boys* (New Haven: Yale University Press, 1987).

3. Joel Blocker and Richard Elman, "An Interview with Isaac Bashevis Singer," reprinted in Irving Malin (ed.), *Critical Views of Isaac Bashevis Singer* (New York: New York University Press, 1969), p. 23.

4. Yitskhok Bashevis-Zinger, *Mayn tatns bezdn-shtub: [hemshekhim-zamlung]* (Jerusalem: Magnes Press of Hebrew University, 1996). Hereinafter cited as Y-HZ. All translations are my own.

5. Yitskhok Bashevis, *Mayn tatns bezdn-shtub* (New York: Der Kral, 1956). Hereinafter cited as Y-BDS. All translations are my own.

6. Isaac Bashevis Singer, *In My Father's Court* (New York: Farrar, Straus, Giroux, 1966). Hereinafter cited as E.

7. See Roskies, *A Bridge,* p. 272.

8. Introduction to the original Yiddish text, Yitskhok Bashevis, *Mayn tatns bezdn-shtub,* no pagination. This introduction differs slightly from the introduction to the English translation.

9. See Marshall Breger and Bob Barnhart, "A Conversation with Isaac Bashevis Singer," in Malin (ed.), *Critical Views,* p. 39.

10. Dvorah Telushkin, *Master of Dreams: A Memoir of Isaac Bashevis Singer* (New York: William Morrow, 1997), p. 62.

Folk and Folklore in the Work of Bashevis

12

Bashevis at *Forverts*

Janet Hadda

It was a mismatch made in heaven — Bashevis Singer and Abe Cahan. The many years Isaac Bashevis Singer spent in Cahan's kingdom at *Forverts* were central to his professional development as a novelist and to his private experience as an immigrant. Had it not been for the twists of family history that brought Bashevis to *Forverts,* he would have missed both his greatest opportunity and his deepest humiliation. What was it in Bashevis's upbringing and sensibility that brought him into such an unhappy relationship with the formidable Abraham Cahan?

American Yiddish culture as it looks today would not exist without Bashevis and Cahan. In his own way, each revolutionized the perception of Eastern European Jewish life on American soil. The two shared important individual traits. Each had a grandfather who was an influential rabbi. Each made the move from birth in the Old Country to permanent residence in New York. Each possessed intellectual brilliance and intuitive foresight; each was passionate about literature and ruthless in its pursuit. And each contributed long years of service to *Forverts.*

Yet the two could hardly have been more different, and their conflicts were profound and painful. Cahan was the ultimate mediator, viewing diversity as vital challenge. Bashevis was the frightened adversary, viewing opposition as deadly betrayal. Cahan was a modernist, looking forward to the developments of history with energy and determination. Bashevis was a conservative, looking backward to validate his criticism of the present. Cahan was an optimist who always landed on his feet. Bashevis was a pessimist who perennially fought, and sometimes succumbed to, paralytic depression. Cahan embraced building. Bashevis skirted nihilism.

The man who brought these two unlikely collaborators together was Bashevis's older brother, Israel Joshua. I. J. was a man after Cahan's own heart: politically progressive, socially enlightened, personally dependable, artistically straightforward.

Early on, Cahan had taken a central role in promoting I. J.'s career. In 1923 *Forverts* had published I. J.'s short story "Perl" (Pearl) and had put the young writer on the Yiddish literary map. The story had originally been published in the Soviet Union but had provided scant recognition for I. J. Cahan took pride in having discovered a rising talent. He also invited I. J. to join the staff of *Forverts* as a correspondent, a position the Warsaw-based writer accepted. But in a well-known incident, when the publications *Bikher-velt* (Book-World) in Warsaw and *Frayheyt* (Freedom) in New York both denounced him for stooping to write journalism for *Forverts,* I. J. vowed that he would never create fiction again.

Cahan was dismayed. As he later recalled:

> *ikh hob zikh mit zingern etlekhe mol gezen in eyrope un yedes mol hob ikh im*
> *gepruvt bavayzn, az zayn tsurikhaltn zikh fun der literatur iber yene geshikhte*
> *iz naiv. es hot alts nit gevirkt. er hot geshribn glentsende korespondentsn, ober*
> *tsu literatur hot er zikh alts nit genumen.*[1]

I saw Singer several times in Europe, and every time I tried to prove to him that his withdrawal from literature over this incident was naïve. Nothing worked. He wrote brilliant pieces of journalism, but he still refused to return to literature.

As we know, I. J.'s resolve eventually crumbled. In the spring of 1932 he presented Cahan with the manuscript of *Yoshe Kalb,* which the editor hailed in *Forverts* as "thrilling."[2]

But I. J. was not only a talented writer. He was also a good older brother who took care of his delicate and complicated sibling, Yitskhok, with all the devotion of a father. Yitskhok arrived in the United States on May 1, 1935, following I. J., who had moved to New York the previous year. I. J.'s situation enabled him to help his brother — by then the promising young novelist who called himself Bashevis. Both through I. J.'s influence and because of Bashevis's own success with *Der sotn in goray,* Cahan invited the 31-year-old author to publish a novel in installments. Moreover, Cahan granted Bashevis an extraordinary privilege: he did not require him to complete his novel before the serialization commenced. This allowance was a major concession, and it was certainly a gift. But whereas I. J. had once kept silent because of a petulant vow, Bashevis was silent for other reasons. Afflicted by a monumental writer's block, depressed and inhibited, he simply could not produce.

Bashevis's novel *Der zindiker meshiekh* was eventually completed after a fashion, but thereafter Cahan relegated him to the task of writing nonfiction. Bashevis later recalled his reaction to the fiasco:

> I avoided showing my face to the *Forward* [*Forverts*] writers and I always dropped off my copy late in the evenings when all the staff members were gone . . . The night elevator man at the *Forward* already knew me. He always made the same joke — that I dropped off my column like an unmarried mother disposed of a bastard.[3]

Although Cahan continued to carry him, Bashevis hardly felt supported. Cahan had not written a single word of welcome for him in the pages of *Forverts;* the sole reference to his arrival was a haunting photo of the brothers in the rotogravure section. In a 1936 letter to Meylekh Ravitch, Bashevis tried to affect an upbeat tone, but his sense of failure jumped from between the lines:

> Here in New York, I am just barely all right. I have finished the novel in *Forverts.* Now I am writing articles about literature. That represents great trust on the part of Cahan, but it doesn't constitute a living. At *Forverts,* they have mastered the craft of paying badly.[4]

And lest he forget that even this small favor was due to I. J., Bashevis was not even allowed to feel like a full-fledged contributor to the paper. As he put it: "There was a box for received mail . . . with separate compartments for the various staff members. My brother had his own box where letters to me were deposited as well."[5]

What was it about the chemistry between Cahan and I. J. on the one hand, and between Cahan and Bashevis on the other, that rendered the relationships so utterly different? The temptation is to view the chasm as literary: I. J. was a realist, a social critic, whereas Bashevis was a dreamer, a creator of tales. I. J.'s message was often political. Bashevis's moral, where it existed, was generally personal rather than collective. He was more likely to rail against hypocrisy than against poverty, against spiritual starvation than against physical hunger. His characters were more often psychologically depressed than politically oppressed.

But this division is not the essence. Closer scrutiny proves that Cahan was as interested in the mysterious qualities of *Yoshe Kalb* as he was in its realism; moreover, he and Bashevis came closest to blows over one of Bashevis's most realistic works, *Di familye mushkat.*

It is arguable, rather, that Cahan and Bashevis wound up on a collision course with one another because of upbringing and consequent self-image. I. J., although

Janet Hadda

he was Bashevis's brother, resembled his boss much more closely than he resembled his younger sibling. While constitutional and genetic factors always play a significant role in development, psychological influences count enormously as well. Family systems theorists make the point that everyone in a family assumes, or is assigned, a particular position. From this perspective, no two children experience exactly the same environment. In the Singer household, I. J. was both the eldest son and, according to available accounts, his mother's favorite. Logical and skeptical like his mother Basheve, I. J. disdained the softness, flights of spirituality, and inefficiency of his father, Pinkhes Menakhem. He sparred with his father, who eventually threw his rebellious son out of the house because of his secular and artistic activities.

By the time Yitskhok came along, Basheve Singer had borne four children. Two little girls had died. The family was set in its ways, the fights were ritualized, and neither mother nor father had time to invest in the young boy's development. The only one who could be relied upon to get things done was I. J., who understood how the child was being raised and could see possibilities for him that Basheve and Pinkhes Menakhem could not. He was both the role model and the forceful guide in some of Bashevis's most important life decisions.

Bashevis grew up longing for attention and warmth, unable to trust that the people he needed would be there when he was afraid, lonely, or sad. He was no one's favorite; no one, with the exception of his strange and dramatic sister, fussed over him. And even his sister's ministrations were geared to providing affection and consolation for herself, rather than encouragement and inspiration for him.

The brothers grew into very different men. I. J. was widely respected. He took stances — of which the vow to leave *belles-lettres* was one of the more eccentric. He could be relied upon to deliver. Yitskhok Bashevis, on the other hand, found himself sexually attractive to women, but not much admired by men or women until later in life — and then from a distance rather than close up. He eschewed commitments, personal or political, and he was notoriously unreliable. The stories of his marital and literary infidelities — affairs, broken contracts, betrayals — are legion. By contrast, I. J. was exemplary in integrity and conduct.

Cahan was just the sort of man whom I. J. could idealize. Thirty-four years I. J.'s senior, Cahan was Olympian, indefatigable, compelling, apparently able to pursue his vision without fear that his actions would lead to personal consequences. Unlike Pinkhes Menakhem, who cringed before authority and who needed others to take care of him, Cahan was the authority and the caretaker. Even in his dotage, when he was ensconced at the Algonquin Hotel, he managed to put an over-whelmed and diffident young graduate student named Moses Rischin at ease.[6] Where Pinkhes Menakhem was unable to accept his son's secular bent and artistic aspirations, Cahan encouraged and endorsed them. Simply put, for I. J., Cahan was a father figure who, in turn, admired him.

Unlike the Singer boys, Cahan had grown up in a home where he was doted on and treated as special and significant. An only child, he thrived on attention from both parents, Shakhne and Sheyne-Sore, and from an extended family. One of Cahan's first recalled experiences shows how early on he was taught to think highly of himself. His paternal grandfather, a respected rabbi and *magid* (Jew-ish preacher), had come to visit. He was ushered into his son's home by admiring townspeople, and the three-year-old Avrom understood his own father's impor-tance as the great man's son. Then:

der zeyde hot mir genumen tsu zikh afn shoys un mir gegebn a "tsener"—a groyse, kuperne finf-kopikene matbeye. imitser fun di ongevezende hot tsu im gezogt: "er iz dos gor nit vert!" un er hot af dem geentfert: "oyb er iz nokh nit vert, vel er vert zayn!"[7]

My grandfather sat me on his lap and gave me a *tsener*—a big, copper, five-kopeck coin. One of the people present said to him: "He isn't worthy of that!" And my grandfather replied: "If he's not worthy yet, he *will* be!"

Cahan's father was a *melamed,* and when Avrom was very small he would sit on his father's lap while Shakhne tutored his pupils. In later years, Cahan recalled that, although he was still too young to study, he had managed to repeat some of the words with their translations, to his father's pride and delight.

The family was not without hardship. When Avrom was not yet six, Sheyne-Sore's family, who were Vilna Jews, brought the Cahan family from the nearby town of Podbreze to the city. They set the parents up as innkeepers, an occupation to which Shakhne was ill-suited. There were tensions within the extended family, and income was meager. Nonetheless, the boy was nourished on his father's dreams for him:

. . . az got vet mir helfn, vel ikh dir dingen lerer af rusish, af daytsh, af frant-soyz, af fidl-shpiln. du muzt ober zayn a frumer yid, alter! hunderter mol hob ikh dize troymen fun im gehert.[8]

177

Janet Hadda

. . . with the help of God, I will hire teachers for you in Russian, German, French, violin. But you must remain a pious Jew, little one! Hundreds of times I heard these dreams from him.

Cahan grew into a self-sufficient, hard-working man — an impressive writer and charismatic public speaker. He assumed leadership roles easily. As editor of *Forverts,* he helped shape an entire immigrant generation. Although Cahan later described having to coax I. J. back to writing fiction,[9] he never lost faith in the young writer. He appreciated I. J.'s responsible nature, which never faltered, despite his emotional scars and apparent melancholy.

But Cahan had no patience with Bashevis's combination of arrogance and failure to deliver. Even when Bashevis burst through his writer's block and began to pour forth his famous fiction, the two clashed; and when Bashevis emerged from his years of creative slumber, he published elsewhere than in *Forverts.* Consider his great 1945 stories "Der kurtser fraytik" (Short Friday) and "Di kleyne shusterlekh" (The Little Shoemakers), both published in *Di tsukunft* (The Future: a leading Yiddish political/cultural monthly published in New York for over 100 years), and "Gimpl tam" (Gimpel the Fool), published in *Yidisher kemfer* (an important Yiddish journal of political and cultural opinion published in New York), or his masterly 1943 essays "Problemen fun der yidisher proze in amerike" (Problems of Yiddish Prose in America), published in *Svive* (a fine Yiddish library journal published in New York by the Yiddish poet Kadie Molodovsky), and "Arum der yidisher proze in poyln" (Concerning Yiddish Prose in Poland), published in *Di tsukunft.*

How, then, did Bashevis manage to hold his own with an editor who clearly did not esteem him? And why did he stay at *Forverts?* Two answers are possible: first, once Bashevis began to write again, his generative powers were immense, and his audience appreciated him. Second, by the mid-1940s, Cahan was well into his eighties, perhaps too old to engage any longer in his notorious micromanagement.

Still, according to Bashevis's account, the lion of *Forverts* did not succumb easily. As Bashevis tells the story, he and Cahan came to intellectual loggerheads over *Di familye mushkat.* Cahan had a well-known habit of intrusive editing, delivering lectures about how a writer should proceed. His attitude toward Bashevis was no exception, but in the matter of this novel, the young author rebelled. This was his elegy to Warsaw, to Eastern European Jewry, and to his brother, who had died the previous year. Among other things, Cahan had objected to Bashevis's extensive and serious attention to the world of Hasidism, viewing the lack of critical distance as a flaw. One day Cahan came to deliver his sharp suggestions, and Bashevis found himself replying: *s'tut mir layd, Mr. Kahan, ober der gantser plan fun roman is shoyn fartik,* "I'm sorry, Mr. Cahan, but the whole novel is planned out."[10]

Cahan blanched, looked at Bashevis with a mixture of shock and contempt, and walked away. The battle lines were drawn: Bashevis would not accept Cahan's judgment, and Cahan could not retreat from his position. Moreover, Cahan was known as a fighter who would not quit; his victories were the stuff of legend far beyond the confines of East Broadway. Bashevis contemplated his future as a ruined writer. Some days later, Cahan called Bashevis to his office and told him that the novel was not doing well — which was a lie — and that he would have to wrap it up. As a gesture of supposed magnanimity, he offered Bashevis four weeks to get the job done. But Bashevis had planned a novel that would take two years to unfold, and he had reached an apotheosis: he would not write another word. Furthermore, as he told members of the staff who tried unsuccessfully to mediate between the two men, he would not write another word until he had a contract guaranteeing that he could keep publishing the work until he decided it was complete. This was defiance of immense proportions, because *Forverts* did not issue contracts. Even his allies thought Bashevis was ungrateful.

In the end, Bashevis prevailed and got his contract. Moreover, Cahan fell ill and was never the same again. He threatened a complete exposé of *Di familye mush-kat*'s flaws but never wrote it. With one stroke, Bashevis had vanquished multiple demons, at least externally: he had stood up to Cahan, the tyrant. He had shown that his will had to be respected. He had taken a stand, as his brother had done so many years earlier, and he had been even more successful than his brother in proving the strength of his resolve. He had received concrete proof of his value as a writer. He was now, theoretically, a man who could hold his own among his fathers. And, on the surface, that was the case. Cahan withered and died, I. J.'s reputation faded, and Bashevis became the darling — albeit a controversial one — of *Forverts.*

Janet Hadda

But the inner truth was different. As Bashevis put it twenty years later, when he was a decade away from the Nobel Prize, the effect of the struggle left lasting torment. Racing to get copy to the typesetters after the debacle, Bashevis threw himself into his writing:

ikh hob geshribn mit nervezitet. di zatsn zenen aroysgekumen opgehakt un men hot mamesh gefilt in zey dem shraybers tseyakhmert gemit.[11]

I wrote nervously. The resulting sentences were choppy and one could literally feel the writer's agitated spirit.

Even years later, when he had the opportunity to rewrite that particular section for the publication, in book form, of *Di familye mushkat* both in Yiddish and in English, he was not able to clean it up completely: . . . *nokh afile itst kon ikh aroysleyenen fun di kurtse zatsn di opgehakte bilder fun mayne demolsdike gefiln,* ". . . even now I can still read the short sentences and discern the choppy images of my feelings at the time."[12] As he could not eradicate it from his memory or from his work, his victory at *Forverts* had been Pyrrhic. He had failed to win Cahan's regard, and he would never, ever, supersede his brother I. J. — neither in the great editor's eyes nor in his own vanquished heart.

Notes

1. *Forverts,* May 21, 1932, p. 8. My translation.

2. Ibid.

3. Isaac Bashevis Singer, *Love and Exile* (New York: Penguin, 1986), pp. 286, 287. This volume consists of three earlier published volumes: *A Little Boy in Search of God, A Young Man in Search of Love,* and *Lost in America.* These were originally serialized in *Forverts* as *Gloybn un tsveyfl* (Faith and Doubt) between November 14, 1974, and January 3, 1975; between April 29 and August 12, 1976; and between February 3 and December 7, 1978. Hereafter cited as *Love and Exile.*

4. Letter to Ravitch, April 1936. Letters to Ravitch are in the Ravitch Archives, Jewish National and University Library, Hebrew University, Jerusalem. I thank the Bergner family for granting me permission to read the correspondence. The translation is my own.

5. *Love and Exile,* p. 287.

6. I thank Ms. Vera Hannenberg for providing me with this vignette.

7. Abraham Cahan, *Bleter fun mayn lebn,* 5 vols. (New York: Forverts, 1926–1931), vol. 1, p. 15; my translation.

8. Ibid., vol. 1, p. 95.

9. *Forverts,* February 20, 1944, pp. 2, 5.

10. Isaac Bashevis Singer (as Y. Varshavsky), *Fun der alter un nayer heym* (From the Old and the New Home), *Forverts,* published September 21, 1963, to September 11, 1965. This extract is from *Forverts,* March 27, 1965, p. 2.

11. *Forverts,* March 27, 1965, p. 2.

12. Ibid.

Janet Hadda

V

BASHEVIS'S
UNTRANSLATED
"GANGSTER"
NOVEL:
YARME UN KEYLE

13

A Background Note on the Translation of *Yarme un keyle*

Joseph Sherman

Introduction

Among the many valuable papers housed in the Singer Yiddish archive in the Harry Ransom Humanities Research Center at the University of Texas in Austin is a large section in holograph, and the first five chapters in print as they appeared in *Forverts,* of a novel by Bashevis, remarkable in being entirely different in genre from any of the fiction that made him so celebrated in his lifetime.

This novel, entitled *Yarme un keyle* (Yarme and Keyle), serialized in *Forverts* between January 1956 and January 1957, is set in the Jewish underworld of Warsaw in the years before World War I. Its chief characters are Yarme, a thief and pimp, and Keyle, his lover, who is a prostitute. The novel is peopled with Jewish criminals of varying illegal accomplishments—forgers, blackmailers, gangsters, seducers, white slavers, even murderers. The world Bashevis evokes in this novel is radically different from the worlds by which he is best known—either one of piety and Orthodox Jewish observance or one intruded upon by demons, dybbuks, and evil spirits.

Yet this novel is intimately part of a well-established genre: the "gangster" novel has a long history in modern Yiddish literature. Although to the Western reading public perhaps the best-known depiction of Jewish gangsters is that found in Isaac Babel's Odessa stories, written in Russian and published in various Russian newspapers and magazines between 1921 and 1924, the criminal underworld made its appearance in Yiddish fiction much earlier than Babel's tales, which were, in their turn, influenced by Semyon Yushkevich, an early twentieth century Russian-Jewish writer.

As early as 1865, in his second major novel *Der vintshfingerl* (The Magic Ring), Mendele Moykher Sforim (S. Y. Abramovitsh) depicted the entire Jewish underworld of Glupsk (Foolstown)—a thinly disguised portrait of Berdichev, the town in which Abramovitsh had settled at that time—putting on display a highly organized gang of thieves and white slavers. In his third major work, *Fishke der krumer* (Fishke the Lame, 1869), Mendele again portrayed a Jewish vagabond, named *der royter ganef* (the red thief), who belongs to a roving gang of beggars who now and then visit Glupsk. These Jewish underworld motifs were strengthened in the expanded, later editions of both these novels (1888). A similar presentation of a Jewish underworld can be found in Mordkhe Spektor's *Aniim ve'evyonim, oder gliklekhe un umgliklekhe* (The Poor and the Miserable, or the Happy and the Unhappy, 1885).

Although writing in a lighter vein, Sholem Aleykhem (S. Y. Rabinovitsh) did not hesitate to depict the seamy side of *shtetl* life. In *Stempenyu* (1888), one of his earliest novels, he presents a lively picture of *klezmorim,* traveling musicians who perform at weddings and other Jewish celebrations, as part of an underworld, since they use their own slang and follow a bohemian, dissolute way of life. In another interesting example, this time deploying a version of the Robin Hood motif in a Jewish setting in his short story "Moshke-ganef" (Moshke the Thief, 1903), Sholem Aleykhem transforms the local *shtetl* thief into a heroic figure when he kidnaps a young Jewish girl from a convent where she is about to undergo a forced conversion to Christianity. In his volume of train tales, *Ayznban-geshikhtes* (1909), in the monologue entitled "A mentsh fun buenos-ayres" (A Man from Buenos Aires), Sholem Aleykhem offers a satiric picture of a wealthy white slaver who obliquely discloses his occupation and immorality in boastful conversation during a train journey.

As a reaction to the neo-Romanticism of Y. L. Peretz and Sholem Asch, both of whom presented highly idealized portraits of *shtetl* life, writers in the years immediately following the failed "first" Russian revolution of 1905 uncompromisingly sought to depict the *shtetl* in all its squalor, poverty, backwardness, and decay. I. M. Weissenberg's *A shtetl* (1909)—deliberately so called to undercut Asch's 1904 novel of the same title—delineated the life of Jewish workers with ruthless intensity, sparing no details of the revolutionary violence to which Jews fully abandoned themselves; Weissenberg portrayed the *shtetl* Bundists as nothing more than thugs. After World War I, Weissenberg's admirer and protégé Oyzer Varshavski published his novel *Shmuglyars* (Smugglers, 1920), ruthlessly exposing the moral degradation of the *shtetl* in Poland during the German occupation, when smugglers, thieves, prostitutes, and illicit liquor-peddlers came into their own, in this

A Note on the Translation of *Yarme un keyle*

way pointing to the irretrievable decay of the traditional Jewish world. Every sign of goodness and virtue is eradicated from Varshavski's *shtetl,* and only the inner worthlessness of the chief characters is apparent.[1]

Joseph Opatoshu took a gentler, more romantic approach to the Jewish underworld. In 1912, five years after Opatoshu had emigrated to New York, he published *A roman fun a ferd-ganef* (Romance of a Horse Thief), which eschews the violence of Weissenberg in favor of a nostalgic affection for Jews who, although earning their living by theft and lawbreaking, nevertheless seek at the same time to live observant, God-fearing lives. Their turning to crime is presented as part of a socio-economic and political dispensation that leaves Jews helpless victims of an unjust society and so obliged to fend for themselves in the best way they can.[2] A few years later, Opatoshu wrote a series of stories about Jewish criminals in New York entitled *Fun nyu-yorker geto* (From the New York Ghetto), which were later collected and published in one volume under the title *Untervelt* (Underworld).

The first major work Sholem Asch wrote after he settled permanently in the United States in 1914 was his own response to this aggressively realistic trend in portraying Jewish criminals. In 1916 he published his novel *Motke ganef* (Motke the Thief), in which he contrasted the simple, static life of the Jewish poor in a Polish *shtetl* with the sordid squalor of Jews living in Warsaw's slums. Asch's Motke is unburdened by moral scruples and suffers no pangs of conscience, living like a stray dog, only with more cunning and determination to survive. The world Motke inhabits is populated by vagrant circus performers, debauchees, and whores, and the story climaxes with his murder of the pimp of the young prostitute with whom he has fallen in love. Even the mystical symbolist Soviet Yiddish writer Der Nister, in his masterpiece *Di mishpokhe mashber* (The Family Mashber, 1939, 1948), vividly depicts the Jewish underworld in his birthplace, Berdichev, ironically pointing out its close links with a number of Hasidim.

In the first instance, those writers who introduced Jewish crime into Yiddish fiction rejected sentimentality in earlier presentations of the *shtetl.* They reacted against what they regarded as falsification by their more "respectable" counterparts, whom they believed guilty of hypocrisy. Those who wrote gangster novels in Yiddish set out to indict through their fiction what they despised as bourgeois gentility. By contrast, they were determined to present the Jewish world of Eastern Europe as "normal," displaying *shtetl* Jews in the grip of the same proclivity for criminality, erotic sexuality, and violence as their non-Jewish compatriots.

187

Joseph Sherman

In the wake of the Holocaust, however, Yiddish critics, horrified by the complete destruction of Eastern European Jewry, came to be ashamed of these motifs in Yiddish literature. The eminent poet and critic Yankev Glatshteyn, for example, attacked even Mendele's *Fishke der krumer* as an inappropriate representation of Eastern European Jews:

> fishke der krumer *is nit keyn shilderung fun yidisher dershlogener oremkeyt
> . . . [es] iz a mayse fun a shnorerisher untervelt, fun profesionele betlers, vos
> lebn a farbrekher-lebn, fun vagabondn, parazitn un ummentshn.*[3]
>
> *Fishke the Lame* is not a portrait of depressed Jewish poverty . . . [it] is a
> tale about an ignominious underworld of professional beggars who live a
> criminal life, of vagabonds, parasites, and nonhumans.

Glatshteyn's intemperate language typifies the post-Holocaust burden of guilt borne by American Yiddish writers, clearly articulating their despairing attempt to evoke a nostalgic, elegiac vision of Eastern Europe as a land of holiness, totally sanitized of any dirt, squalor, or human depravity. Indeed, the determination of those Yiddish writers still left alive after the Holocaust was now to memorialize the vanished world of the *shtetl*, to foreground beauties, pieties, and traditions now effaced from existence.[4] The attempt to "normalize" Jewish life in Eastern Europe through Yiddish fiction was wiped away by the ultimate illustration that Jewish life in Eastern Europe had always been "abnormal." Its ultimate "abnormality" was, appallingly, the Nazi genocide; after it, there would no longer be any Jewish life in Eastern Europe to "normalize" any longer.

Given the period during which Bashevis published this novel in *Forverts*—the mid-1950s—and with a clear picture, as we now have, of Bashevis's skill at repeatedly reconstructing established forms of Yiddish fiction to polemicize with the world view or literary tradition they promoted, there can be little doubt that he turned to the gangster genre for the same purpose. While he was clearly determined not to follow those Yiddish writers who demanded a sentimentalization of Eastern European Jewish life, he was equally determined to memorialize that destroyed world in his own distinctive way.

Equally interesting is the fact that there were definite plans to publish this novel in English shortly after Bashevis received the Nobel Prize for Literature in 1978. In the first biography written about him, *The Magician of West 86th Street* (New York, 1979), the author, Paul Kresh, states quite specifically that at the time his

A Note on the Translation of *Yarme un keyle*

own book went to press, plans were already well advanced for *Yarme un keyle* to appear in English translation. Kresh's assertion is supported by the existence in the Singer archive of a typescript, in English, of the first five chapters of this novel, translated by Bashevis's nephew, Joseph Singer. Unusually for material in the archive, the English typescript is accompanied by a file of carefully clipped-out and numbered episodes of the novel's serialized Yiddish text. The typescript is clearly a rough draft — blank spaces are left for the later insertion of many words and phrases, mostly those in Hebrew, evidently awaiting consultation with the author. On the other hand, the typescript, which exists in both original and carbon copy, is wholly unmarked, and the typewritten pages show no signs of having been well handled. So the mystery arises — what prevented the translation of this novel from being completed and published in English? Did the publishers reject it? Or did Bashevis himself decide to withhold it from publication?

Although it is impossible to know for certain from the papers in the archive what the real reason was, it is feasible to speculate a little. If the decision was that of the publishers, one might have expected to find some notes on the existing typescript or some correspondence relating to it from the publishers' readers. No such evidence exists in the archive. It is possible that Bashevis, having made his literary and philosophical point to his Yiddish readers through his *Forverts* serialization, decided that the polemic he had engaged in would be lost on his English readership, for whom he had spent years creating the particular persona of I. B. Singer, the wise and lost representative of a annihilated world. For most of his readers in English, Singer's presentation of that world was a tribute to its piety and sanctity. It was a world in which the forces of Evil, represented wittily in an endless parade of Satan's emissaries, are ultimately — for his English readers at least — vanquished by the superior strength of goodness, piety, and fear of God. Perhaps Bashevis felt that his carefully crafted public image would suffer if he permitted this novel to appear in English; perhaps he felt that the project of his whole writing career — to memorialize the dead world of Polish Jewry — would be compromised, at least for those who read his work only in English, with no knowledge of the Yiddish tradition on which he drew so abundantly and of which, for all his many disclaimers, he was inextricably a part.

The answers to these questions are not available at present. What is available however, is this extraordinarily mixed novel, which deepens our awareness of the range of Bashevis's creativity, his singular capacity for manipulating established

Joseph Sherman

Yiddish fictional genres and subverting them for his own sharp-minded purposes. So it seems especially appropriate in a volume like this, which points to the disparity between the Yiddish writer Bashevis and the English author Isaac Bashevis Singer, to offer the reader the opportunity to glimpse an unusual side of his multifaceted experiments. Published here is the novel's entire second chapter, in a new translation.

Setting the Scene

The novel is set in the period between the failed "first" Russian revolution of 1905 and the outbreak of World War I in 1914. The action opens in 1912 in Warsaw, still inside the tsarist empire. The Jewish world, in ferment, quivers with conflicting political and national ideologies, with intense struggles about the ideological and political future of the Jewish people. Zionism, Bundism, and revolutionary Marxism are all contending for possession of what has come to be called "the Jewish national soul." All this contention over the future of the Jewish people is, however, a matter of indifference to the novel's main characters, all of whom are enclosed in the hermetically sealed world of Warsaw's criminal underworld.

The opening chapter introduces the reader to Yarme, nicknamed "Yarme Burr" from the name given in Warsaw to the prickles that boys throw into the beards of the pious on Tishebov (the traditional day of mourning for the destruction of Jerusalem), because he likes to needle his comrades and the women with whom he is involved. At thirty-two, Yarme, an expert lock-picker, has already served four prison sentences for theft and is an experienced smuggler and pimp. He is married to Keyle, nicknamed "Red Keyle" because of her fiery red hair, who at twenty-nine has gone through service in three brothels and is an eagerly sought prostitute. Although Yarme and Keyle love each other, they have an "open" marriage which leaves each of them free to have sexual relationships with others on the sole condition that they keep no secrets from each other.

The violence and immorality of the world they inhabit is dramatically illustrated in the opening moments of the novel: Keyle, paying a sick-bed visit to a fellow criminal, Blind Itche, who is recovering in the hospital from a stab wound from a competitor, is dragged into his bed and raped by Blind Itche, who years before had been the first to take her virginity. This incident does not disrupt the relationship between Yarme and Keyle, nor their friendship with Blind Itche, whom they visit again in the hospital, where virtually the whole of Warsaw's Jewish crimi-

A Note on the Translation of *Yarme un keyle*

nal underworld has gathered at his bedside. There various robbery plans to make vast amounts of money quickly are discussed.

Important for the novel's later development of Singer's theme is the emphasis placed at a very early stage on the fact that all these thieves and whores come from pious Jewish homes; some of the men have even studied in *yeshives*. The shadow of their religious upbringing hangs over most of them, especially Yarme and Keyle, on whom "the Sabbath always cast a gloom." Yarme himself "even remembered the first page of the middle section of the Gemara by heart," while Keyle never neglects to light memorial candles for her deceased relatives.

The night after visiting Blind Itche, Yarme and Keyle go to the Yiddish theater, where Yarme encounters Stumping Max, a forger and thief who has served time in prison with Yarme years before and who, ostensibly a very rich man, has now returned to Warsaw from extensive traveling abroad. Stumping Max, so-named because he has a permanent limp, is now chiefly engaged in the white slave trade. Years before, he enjoyed a sexual relationship with Keyle, who detests and distrusts him. Yet after the theater they all go drinking in a tavern where Keyle, who is dependent on liquor, gets drunk and behaves loudly and coarsely with Max and others. Yarme, enraged by her conduct, punches her in the face, swearing to have nothing further to do with her as Keyle, in her drunkenness, begs to be taken away to brothels in South America.

Notes

1. For more specific details, see, for instance, Charles Madison, *Yiddish Literature: Its Scope and Major Writers* (New York: F. Unger, 1971); Sol Liptzin, *The Maturing of Yiddish Literature* (New York: Jonathan David, 1970).

2. Both Weissenberg's *A shtetl* and Opatoshu's *Romance of a Horse Thief* have been published in English translation. For these texts, and valuable introductory material on these novels and the underworld genre in general, see Ruth R. Wisse (ed.), *A Shtetl and Other Yiddish Novellas* (Detroit: Wayne State University Press, 1986).

3. Yankev Glatshteyn, "Fishke der krumer," in *In tokh genumen: esayen 1945–1947* (New York: Matones, 1947), pp. 453–469.

4. I am deeply indebted to Dr. Mikhail Krutikov for his generosity in sharing with me his knowledge and overview of the underworld genre in Yiddish literature, to which the foregoing summary owes much.

Joseph Sherman

Yarme and Keyle
Chapter 2

Isaac Bashevis Singer

Translated from the Yiddish by Joseph Sherman

1

Yarme had broken his vow. After Keyle had sobered up, she'd wept bitterly, kissed his feet, and sworn by her dead mother's memory that if he didn't forgive her, she'd go straight to the Kalisz railroad line and throw herself down on the tracks. She tore her hair, beating her head against the wall with a face bathed in tears the size of lima beans. When Yarme finally took her back to bed, she proved to him that he wasn't yet familiar with all the cunning tricks she knew for arousing and satisfying a man. Yarme demanded to know who had taught her all these skills, and among the names of pimps and thieves Keyle mentioned a clairvoyant who owned a black mirror that paraded images of lost husbands and former lovers as well as of the dead who yearned to couple with those who lusted for them. She spoke so wildly and told such fearful stories that shudders kept thrilling up and down Yarme's spine. How could he possibly cast aside someone like this? He determined to go to the rabbi and have himself absolved of his vow.

Yarme had encountered Stumping Max several times, and even though Max at first claimed that he'd simply slipped into Poland on a whim, to look around the old towns and renew acquaintance with old cronies, it gradually emerged that he had plans to recoup all his expenses and perhaps make a substantial pile at the same time. In Buenos Aires, in Rio de Janeiro, in all of South America, there was a shortage of available females, and they had to be imported from Europe. The newspapers luridly described the way white slavers cruised about in carriages, abducted girls, raped them, and then shipped them off in shackles to faraway places.

But these, Max maintained, were all the fantasies of sensationalists. How could grown women be abducted? How could they be transported across borders and put aboard ships against their wills? Nonsense! Trash! These trulls obviously went of their own free will. A street-wise frigger could seduce as many girls as he wanted. Other girls were simply longing to claim they'd been seduced. These were new times. Women had the same appetites as men. They didn't want to marry plodding nonentities, fall pregnant, bear brats, and waste their best years on swaddling clothes and diapers, wet-nurses and pacifiers. All one needed was to know how to sweet-talk them.

To Yarme, Max outlined a scheme he wanted Red Keyle to be part of. She had a fiery mouth and knew how to shoot it off. In America she'd be able to make a fortune.

Yarme tried to say that he wanted Keyle for himself, but Max countered, "Honestly, Yarmele, you talk like a ninny. You can't keep anybody for yourself. Even a *rebbetzin* remarries as soon as her old man kicks the bucket. You've got as much chance of keeping Red Keyle at home managing the housekeeping and darning her husband's socks as you have of harnessing the wind in the field."

Slowly Max outlined his plan. He'd read in an American newspaper about an alluring woman who'd made a career of marrying rich men and, after the wedding, either wheedling or cheating them out of their fortunes and leaving them high and dry. This cunning piece had drawn dozens of such dupes into her net and had grown hugely wealthy. What could be done in America could be done here in Poland as well, Max argued. Many of the Jews here had amassed fortunes. A woman of Keyle's sex appeal and glib tongue could turn the heads of saints and sages. While Max and Yarme were seducing a clutch of girls and getting them ready for the voyage to South America, Keyle could easily snare a few hundred thousand rubles for a start. With money like that, the three of them could set up the grandest bordellos in Argentina, Brazil, Bolivia, and Uruguay and live like kings. Yarme and Max might even marry a couple of rich widows each, before they took their floozy freight abroad.

"Yarmele, gold lies about in the streets over there," said Max. "All you have to know is how to scoop it up. I'm as rich as Croesus. If I wanted to, I could buy a palace and live like a prince. But that's only good for old washouts, not for someone my age. I can't rest. I've got ants in my pants. If I don't keep on the go, I get weak at the knees and start hallucinating. You're made of the same stuff, Yarmele.

193

Yarme and Keyle: *Chapter 2*

The moment I saw you at the theater the other night, I knew we'd have to become partners. Your Keyle's a treasure, and no mistake!"

"What do you want? — for us to become a threesome?"

"Not necessarily. I'm not starving, God forbid. I traveled first class on the ship from Rio to London and if I told you what I did during those weeks at sea, you'd call me fat lip. Brother, you don't have to dance around skirts with any kind of come-on any longer. I get straight down to business: 'One way and another, you appeal to me. I've got my own cabin. As soon as I saw you, you aroused me.' How's it written in *Ethics of the Fathers?* 'Don't waste time blabbing with women.' Yes is yes and no is no. I don't know about others, but with me it's always 'yes.' I don't have to tell you that I'm no beauty: I'm short, bald, and crippled. Can you understand it?"

"Yes, I can," replied Yarme.

"What do you think it is? Do they pity me?"

"It's everything together."

"What kind of everything?"

"Your mouth. You could charm a stone."

"Yes, yes, it's a kind of — what's it called? — animal magnetism. If a magnet can attract a pin, why can't a man attract a fancy miss? You've only got to sell the right kind of line. The three of us could take on the world."

Max chatted on with Yarme over coffee and cheesecake at the thieves' den at Mila number 6, later at Lurs's café [kawiarnia "lourse"], and later still at Samodeni's on Theater Place. That night, in bed, Yarme reported everything to Red Keyle.

At first Keyle protested, "No, no, a hundred times no!"

Keyle no longer wanted others. She wanted only one God and one Yarme. But Yarme argued, "How long can we rot here at number 8 Krochmalna worrying ourselves sick over every groschen we spend? Even dumplings get polished off, and too much pear compote can become tasteless. Warsaw's a backwater. You're either walking from Krochmalna Street to Smocza or from Stawka to Niska and back again. It makes me sick in the guts. America's a new world. Ignoramuses left Poland and became millionaires in America. All we need is to scrape together the first few thousand. After that, everything runs on greased wheels."

"What's he want us to do?" asked Keyle.

Isaac Bashevis Singer

"To team up. He'll put up the money for the business. He wants to deck you out like a princess. He wants us to move into a hotel."

"Yarmele, he'll want something else too. He ate me up with his eyes."

"Partners are partners."

"Oh, Yarmele, I'm afraid."

"If you're afraid, say your prayers."

"Hold me tight! With both your mitts! Like this!"

Keyle clung so tightly to Yarme that he was afraid she'd break his ribs. She seemed to be trying to tear her way into his guts with her pointed knees. Her mouth bit into his and she seemed to have stopped breathing. For a long while they both lay still, passion exhausted.

Then Keyle said, "Yarmele, perhaps dying would be better?"

"How could it?"

"I've always wanted to die for someone."

"There's always time for that. The Angel of Death never runs away."

"I want to die young, not old."

"Your kind stays young."

"I want you to murder me so I can kiss your hands till my breath stops."

"Before dying, we ought to grab a bit of living."

For as long as they could, they restrained their desire for one another.

They fell asleep at daybreak, and at nine Yarme started out of a dream. For a second it all came back to him, but a moment later he'd forgotten it. Nothing was left but a memory of bloodied faces, wild yelling, disemboweled guts, cascades of blood. Was this a pogrom, an attack by murderers, a demon dance? Perhaps all of them at the same time.

"Why's a dream so quickly forgotten?" Yarme wondered.

He'd slept only a few hours, but he woke completely rested. He glanced at Keyle. She lay half uncovered with bared breasts and red nipples, laughing in her sleep. One of her eyes was open a slit.

"My God! She's lain with thousands of men, yet she's remained as fresh as a rose. How's this possible?" Yarme mused in amazement.

Naked, Yarme went over to the window. A strip of early morning sky glowed blue over the courtyard. The sun gleamed crookedly across the wall. Windows opened. Early as it was, young women were already airing bedding. One vendor was hawking fresh bagels, a second was peddling herring. Soon there'd be a swarm of acrobats, beggars, and people who belted out ditties about the sinking of the *Titanic,* together with the blind and crippled victims of the Russo-Japanese War. At one end of the courtyard lived a ritual slaughterer, not one who slaughtered strictly according to Jewish law and was registered by the Jewish community council, but an unlicensed slaughterer who operated in a cellar at far less charge and had to bribe the police so they wouldn't lock him up. There was also a Hasidic study house here where morning prayers were already in progress. Yarme heard the blowing of the *shofar* [ram's horn blown on high holidays to bring the sinner back to repentance]. Was it already the month of Elul? he wondered. The summer had zipped past like a rat down a drain.

Yarme heard the prescribed notes of the *shofar:* a blast, a trill, a quaver. He recalled what was said about blowing the *shofar* in the *shtetl* where he'd grown up: that it was meant to frighten Satan into thinking that the Messiah had come so he wouldn't accuse Jews of sinning. The *shofar* also called on Jews to repent.

"Maybe I ought to repent as well?" Yarme murmured absently. Perhaps one's whole life would speed away as quickly as the summer had?

In reality he was only toying with the notion, though. He wasn't yet ready to grow a beard and earlocks, to marry some housewife in a ritual wig and pack a house with brats as observant Jews did. In any case, since God didn't exist, who gave a damn about repentance?

Keyle opened one eye.

"What's the time, Yarme?"

"Go back to sleep, it's early."

"Right."

And she immediately fell asleep again.

2

Events moved swiftly. Stumping Max had renewed his old acquaintance with Bertha Stein, or Misbegotten Bertha, as she was commonly known. Bertha had been raised in Krochmalna Street, but she'd moved to Ptasia Street. Once she'd run a brothel for well-heeled clients on Wronia Street, but she'd long since given this up and opened a set of furnished rooms instead. Bertha was everything at the same time — the landlady of a rooming-house, an employment agent who supplied maids to wealthy homes, and a procuress of women for rich and discreet clients

Isaac Bashevis Singer

who had wives and families and were therefore obliged to keep their sins out of the public eye.

By her first husband, Bertha had two daughters whom she'd sent to boarding-school so they'd know nothing about their mother's affairs. Her first husband had died and her second had divorced her. For a long time she'd kept a lover, Khat-skele the Coachman, but she'd thrown him over and replaced him with a swindler, so Khatskele had stabbed her. For his crime, Khatskele had spent three years in the Mokotow Prison, after which he'd gone off somewhere, abandoning a wife and five children to God's mercy. Bertha's current lover, Hertz Kalashnik, was the care-taker of the house where Bertha rented an entire floor for her furnished rooms. Hertz Kalashnik supplied false passports for those who needed them, forged birth certificates, and counterfeited other official documents.

Like Shmuel the Skimmer, he bribed the police all the way up to the deputy chief, and helped out all those willing to pay his price. Kalashnik had a wife, one son studying to be a doctor, and an older son who'd supported the revolution-aries in 1905 and caught a bullet in his belly during a demonstration in front of the town hall. After serving two years in the Pawiak Prison, he'd become a penitent, one of the "dead Hasidim" as they called those who visited the grave of Nahman of Bratslav, a rabbi who'd died almost a century before. They traveled to the rabbi's grave in the cemetery of Uman [in the Ukraine], where a prayer-house had been erected.

Yarme Burr, Red Keyle, Stumping Max, and Misbegotten Bertha met for lunch at the restaurant at number 2 Krochmalna. This restaurant was famous not only on Krochmalna but also in the neighboring streets. Its food was kosher, and its regu-lar patrons consisted mainly of thieves, forgers, and pimps, as well as wholesale fruit dealers from Mirowska Street and street vendors in Yanash's Court [Dwor Janasza] and Goscinny Dwor. At night, music was played in the big dining room. The restaurant was renowned for its traditional appetizers of tripe, calf's foot jelly, and lungs-and-liver. All bets laid in Krochmalna Street on how much an individual could eat or how many mugs of beer he could down were settled in this eating-house. Here Moyshe Gorbelly had wolfed down half a goose with twenty bread rolls, washing down the lot with fifteen mugs of beer. Here a certain Lame Ley-bele, in trying to emulate Moyshe Gorbelly, had suffered a stroke in the middle of his blow-out.

Here there was also a separate gaming room, where people played blackjack, euchre, dominoes, and solo. Here a certain Khayim Bigtalk gambled away his wife at twenty-one, and when the winner came around to their house to claim his prize, he found that both husband and wife had gassed themselves.

Bertha was already past fifty, perhaps in her sixties, but she looked no older than forty. She had a full head of black hair — either natural or dyed — a beak-like nose, and the round black eyes of an owl. She always wore black dresses with long sleeves and high collars because Khatskele's attack had scarred her throat. Bertha liked to prattle and wouldn't be interrupted. In the restaurant Max had hired a private room that, quite apart from food and drink, cost him fifteen rubles; its walls were covered with wine-colored wallpaper, and a carpet was spread over its stone floor.

At first Bertha talked in generalities. Times were changing. Today wasn't yesterday. Not only enlightened people, but even Jews who regularly attended synagogue, even wealthy Hasidim, were no longer as fanatical as they had been in the old days. The younger generation, in particular, wanted education. The father still visited the *rebbe*'s court, but he sent his daughters to a *gymnasium* [the German term for the model for the "middle school" and "lycée," adopted in Russia]. The son split hairs in the study house and swayed over the Gemara, but when the mother took the waters during the summer, she threw off her ritual wig, put on a fancy hat, spoke Polish or German, and strolled along the promenade. The daughters of Hasidic families fell in love with students, traveling salesmen, and — would that such things didn't happen — even with officers.

Bertha boasted that if she were to tell all the secrets she knew, any number of families might break up. But she'd never reveal other people's secrets; as the saying went, she'd carry everything to the grave with her.

The situation here in Poland was such, Bertha observed, that as inflation soared the poor grew poorer while the rich grew richer. Alongside their wealth, people's appetites swelled. What was a man to do if his wife had been ill for years and wouldn't let him near her? Some wives grew so bloated it was disgusting to look at them. They lived not for their husbands but for their sons, their daughters, their grandchildren.

There were also rich widows in Warsaw who didn't want to marry again because they were ugly and old, and they knew that the men who courted them lusted only for their money, not for their bodies. When a woman took a man into her house, he became the boss and could squander everything. But if a woman like

198

Isaac Bashevis Singer

this could find a decent lover to travel abroad with every year, to a place where no one knew them, she'd gladly do it. Quite possibly later on genuine love might spring up between a couple like this. All those who wanted to knew quite well that she, Bertha, could supply everything from a furnished room for a night to a furnished apartment for months or years; from a permanent nurse for a helpless invalid to an abortionist for a girl in trouble; from a mistress for life to a woman who could not only cook but could also keep her employer company at the theater or the opera on the quiet while his wife prowled after a match for her daughter in Karlsbad or Franzenbad. For the most part one could get everything for money, but one had to know when, how, and from whom. A man and a woman, Bertha said, were like a key and a lock. If they fitted, all was hunky-dory; if they didn't, nothing clicked.

Bit by bit, Bertha spelled out the particulars she had in mind. She'd never do this for a stranger, but Max was an old friend. She'd known him for over twelve years, and to her, friendship was worth more than gold. Even a friend of a friend was a treasure. Max was, may the evil eye spare him, immensely rich, but he was still young, in the prime of life, well-informed, clever, well traveled, and he understood the world and its ways perfectly. Bertha knew of a man no longer young, in his sixties if not in his seventies, bloated with a fortune counted not in thousands but in millions. He himself had no idea of how much he was worth. He had a bitch of a wife, a vile shrew, and four daughters, all of whom took after their mother. This man's home was in Kiev, but he was a merchant of the first guild, and Jews of that rank weren't confined to the Pale of Settlement [the sixteen western provinces of tsarist Russia where Jews were allowed to dwell without the special permission required to live outside those provinces]; he could live anywhere he wanted in Russia. He'd even had an audience with the Tsar. His family, or rather the animal pack that ringed him round, actually lived in Kiev, but all his business interests were in Lodz, in Warsaw, and abroad as well. When he came to Warsaw he was invited to the Governor-General's mansion. He and Skolan were intimate friends. Bertha had known him for years; he'd confided all his troubles to her.

In her rooming-house he kept a furnished apartment fit for the Tsar. Whether he came to Warsaw or not, she regularly received her rent by mail. For years he'd kept a mistress here, a certain Sofia Mikhailovna, whom he idolized and who idolized him in turn. He, Sergei Davidovitch, was far from handsome, but then a man didn't have to be good-looking. If he didn't look like an ape, it was good enough.

199

Yarme and Keyle: *Chapter 2*

More importantly, a man had to be sharp-witted, have a good heart, be able to love a woman, and heap money on her. Sergei Davidovitch had all these qualities and more. By now he'd have lived out his life with Sofia Mikhailovna, a girl twenty years younger than he was, pretty as a picture, fluent in Russian, Polish, and Yiddish—everything anyone could wish for. But all of a sudden she took to her bed with what seemed to be catarrh and passed away in a week. As bad luck would have it, just when this happened, Sergei Davidovitch had been in Karlsbad, because he suffered from a liver ailment and took the waters there. By the time Sofia gave Bertha permission to telephone Sergei Davidovitch and tell him she was ill, and he managed to get back to Warsaw, Sofia was already laid out in the morgue of the Jewish hospital on Czysta Street.

"Good people, I don't want to pound your ears for long," said Bertha, "but that man fell into the pit of depression. More than depression—he simply broke up and fell to pieces. All this happened two years ago, and because what the earth covers up must be forgotten, I've tried to cheer him up and find him someone to help him pull himself together, but no one's been able to satisfy him. To him, no one's as pretty, as clever, as delightful as Sofia. To tell you the truth, I've been afraid he'll do himself in. In his will he'd settled a fortune on Sofia Mikhailovna, but she left no relatives apart from a husband, a swine who'd never agreed to divorce her and who'd made her life a living hell. It'd be a wicked wrong if money like that fell into this rat's lap. On the other hand, it would be an unforgivable sin if the money were to go to that shrew his wife, and her bitches of daughters.

"A week or so back, when Max fell on me out of the sky after so long and told me about Keyle and his schemes, it suddenly struck me that maybe Keyle could pull it off and put this man back on his feet. By and large, when it comes to things like this you can never know what'll happen."

For a long while no one spoke. Keyle's face flushed unusually red, the kind of flush that sometimes darkens an individual who's drunk too much or is suffering an apoplexy. By comparison with her face, her red hair seemed to pale. Her cheeks, her brow, her throat, everything from the cleavage in her bosom to the roots of her hair, seemed to be steeped in blood. Yarme shuddered and blanched. Stumping Max opened his mouth and forgot to shut it.

Bertha laid a hand on the table.

"If you can still blush like that, girl, you're not among the worst in the world."

"I'm a human being, not an animal," Keyle replied in a muffled voice, while her face was bathed in sweat as though an unseen presence had drenched her with a pail of water. Huge drops streamed down her face.

"Keyle, what's the matter with you?" asked Yarme.

But Keyle mumbled, "Nothing, nothing."

3

Everything turned out as it did in the novels Yarme read in the newspapers. In the morning he went down to telephone from the sausage-shop, and Bertha told him that Sergei Davidovitch was in Warsaw, waiting for Keyle. She was to take a droshky and come right over.

"Why a droshky?" queried Yarme. "It's only two steps from here to the station."

"Tell her to do as I say," said Bertha. "The knot won't come untied over forty kopecks."

When Yarme came back and told Keyle, she began trembling and stammering as though she were an innocent virgin instead of a whore who'd never missed a filthy trick. She baldly demanded that Max accompany her in the droshky and wait for her on a bench in the square in front of the Iron Gate.

"Keyle, stop trembling," Yarme snapped. "That old man lost his virility long ago. He can't manage more than a kiss. We've arranged everything."

"What'll you do?"

"I've got a date with the Queen of Sheba."

"Has Bertha set you up with someone as well?"

"Yes, Keyleshe, a pockmarked widow of fifty."

"Yarmele, mark my words. This Max is our Angel of Death."

"Well, the Angel of Death is for human beings, not for dogs," Yarme replied. "We've got to play around a bit before we croak. I only ask one thing of you — the whole truth."

"I've sworn to you on a prayer book that I won't keep anything from you, Yarmele."

"That's all I want."

"What shall I wear? The red dress or the yellow?"

"The yellow. Don't waste time."

Yarme also dressed up smartly. Somewhere he'd bought a shirt with gold spots, and a tie of the same pattern. Apparently he was nervous as well, since he jerkily puffed at his cigarette.

201

After a while, Yarme and Keyle emerged from their gateway. A plucker from the kosher meat markets herded a flock of turkeys inside the gate. He skillfully manipulated a long rod to keep them from scuttling off to one side.

"To slaughter, eh?" said Keyle.

"Yes, Keyleshe," Yarme replied. "Turkeys must be slaughtered. That's how God wants it."

An empty droshky came by, and Yarme helped Keyle to get in. The louts of the district watched with curiosity as Red Keyle boarded a droshky even though she was carrying no packages. Yarme got in as well, but instead of sitting down, he stood on the running board. On the corner of Gnojna Street he sprang down lightly behind the vehicle. He'd told Keyle that the widow lived on Grzybowska Street.

The droshky turned left and the route made Keyle remember the time she'd first gone with Zaynvl Beanpole to Pesse Pinch's cathouse. She'd been barely fifteen years old and so frightened that Zaynvl had to force her with every new client. Later she grew so coarse and experienced that she outdid all the other tarts with her brazen talk, her mockeries and sharp remarks. Men fought to be with her. They paid her double the price, but for all her impudence she'd remained bashful. How could anyone understand this? Only God, perhaps. In the two and a half years she'd lived with Yarme, she seemed to have forgotten her former exploits. They spoke only of their love. She'd wanted to have a child with Yarme, but then Blind Itche had dragged her back down into the filth, and now evil luck had vomited up Stumping Max.

It was a sunny day just before Rosh Hashonah [the Jewish New Year], the time when Heaven inscribed who would live out the year and who would not.

"This might yet be my last Rosh Hashonah," Keyle warned herself. "Dear God, please let the old man at least have a bottle of whiskey," she prayed silently.

The truth was that she'd endured the shame and degradation of all these years only because of liquor. When she got drunk, she became someone else, another Keyle. When Yarme first came into her life, her dependence on liquor was such that she couldn't stay sober even for a moment. As soon as morning came, even before breakfast, she'd gulp down half a glassful of vodka. Dr. Krummerman, to whom she went every month for her check-up and a certificate confirming that her blood was free of bacteria, had warned her that she'd burn out her guts. It'd been Yarme who, one way and another, had weaned her off the bottle. But now she

Isaac Bashevis Singer

was desperate for a drink; otherwise she wouldn't be able to utter a single word to that rich old man, Sergei Davidovitch.

"Father in Heaven, please don't let him talk to me in Russian!"

Although Keyle had taken on countless Polish Gentiles and Russian soldiers, she'd never properly learned much of their languages except for some dirty words and curses.

The droshky stopped, and Bertha herself was waiting for her at the gateway. She scrutinized Keyle from head to toe, making Keyle so flustered that she forgot to pay the driver the silver forty-kopeck piece she'd been clutching in her fist the whole time. Bertha had to remind her.

Inside the gateway, Bertha said, "Keyle, before we go upstairs I want to tell you a few things. First, keep in mind that this man isn't one of that scum you're used to. Sergei Davidovitch is a cultured man, a merchant of the first guild. He's traveled the world and visited the grandest houses. You must speak to him with the utmost refinement. You must listen to him carefully and not interrupt."

"He speaks Russian?" Keyle asked, feeling her throat go dry.

"Russian, Yiddish, Polish, German — whatever you want to hear and remember. You can speak Yiddish to him. Every Jew knows his mother tongue. Secondly, keep in mind that he's hard of hearing. He's not deaf, but when old age creeps up on you, you're no longer what you used to be. Sofia Mikhailovna knew exactly how to speak to him — not too softly and not too loudly, because if you shout he gets confused. Thirdly, he has trouble with his eyes. Glaucoma, that's what it's called. He isn't blind, but at times he doesn't see. He wears spectacles, but they don't always help.

"I won't tell you to talk to him about world affairs or about the news in the papers because I know you can't, but be polite to him. Hear him out. He likes to talk, to tell stories. You can be sure he'll talk to you about Sofia Mikhailovna. He speaks of her all the time. Don't interrupt him. Show him that you have compassion for him, as they say. You understand?"

"Yes."

"If he gives you a kiss or a caress, humor him. I don't believe he'll do anything like that at your first meeting, but a man's a man even when he's on his deathbed. Don't tell him who you are or what you do. Tell him you're a seamstress from the provinces. That's really where you come from, after all."

"Yes, yes."

Yarme and Keyle: *Chapter 2*

"If a miracle happens and he asks you to go to bed with him, first pretend you're too shy, that you're not used to that sort of thing. But don't be coy too long. He's got neither strength nor patience for long-winded discussions. Sofia Mikhailovna, may she intercede for me, told me that sick as he was, he'd retained his sexual potency. But that was two years ago. Since then he hasn't been the same. He'll obviously ask what your name is, and Keyle isn't a pretty name. It's common as dirt, that name. Why parents give their children names like that I'll never understand—Keyle, Yente, Yakhne, Shprintse, Gele, Grine, Peshe—those ugly old names date back a hundred years! Tell him your name's Sonia. In Russia, every other girl's called Sonia. What was your father's name?"

"My father?" Keyle repeated.

"Yes, your father. If you had a father, he obviously had a name."

"Yes."

"What was it?"

Oddly enough, in her agitation Keyle had forgotten her father's name.

Bertha waited a moment.

"What was his name? Or perhaps he's still alive?"

"No, my father's dead."

"Dead, eh? What was his name?"

"I've forgotten."

"Forgotten? I don't believe it. Just shows you—so what's the reward of bringing children into the world?"

"I'm so confused that—"

"What was your grandfather's name?"

"One grandfather was called Zalman."

"Zalman's fine. Tell him your father's name was Zalman. He'll call you Sonia Zalmanovna. Among the Russians, even among Russian Jews, everyone's called by their father's name. That's their custom."

"I've just remembered my father's name," Keyle said, as though suddenly starting from sleep.

"What was it?"

"Borekh-Yoyne."

"That's an impossible name to say in Russian. Let it be Zalman. He won't look in your passport. As a registered prostitute, you obviously have a yellow passport, eh?"

Isaac Bashevis Singer

"Yes, yellow."

"If you intend going to Buenos Aires later on, that yellow passport's no use. They'll never let you on board ship with a passport like that. We'll make you another passport, but there's time enough to worry about that. Come."

Bertha took Keyle by the arm and found it trembling. Bertha stopped.

"Don't tremble, girl. You're shaking like a hen about to be slaughtered. Sergei Davidovitch is a refined man. He won't do you any harm, God forbid, only good. Sergei Davidovitch was in love with me for many years. When this tragedy with Sofia happened and I brought him the terrible news and went with him to see her in the morgue, he clung to me as if I were his daughter. She wasn't his wife, but he sat down to observe the Seven Days of Mourning for her. Poor Jews came together to make up a *minyan* [a quorum of ten men, a community for prayer] and he gave them charity and asked them to pray while he recited the *Kaddish,* just as one would for a wife. He sat on a low bench and looked into a holy book.

"In the traditional way, I called regularly to comfort a mourner, and one evening he said to me, 'Bertashke my dearest, only you can console me.' And then he told me that even before he'd met Sofia Mikhailovna, he'd been in love with me. He'd taken Sofia Mikhailovna simply because he couldn't get me.

"I told him, 'Sergei Davidovitch, I love you too. Like a friend, like a father, like a brother. But my heart belongs to Hertz Kalashnik.' Sergei understood me. He never brought it up again. Come."

4

Bertha opened a door into a large room with two windows draped in heavy curtains and a carpet on the floor.

"Oh my, a grand salon!" Keyle thought.

Landscapes and portraits hung on the walls; a sideboard, upholstered chairs, a sofa, a cabinet with glass doors were all arranged around the room. Outside the sun was shining, but in here it was as gloomy as twilight. Sitting in a corner, in an armchair with red fringes, was a dwarfish man with a white goatee and a bare skull that thrust up from broad shoulders virtually without any neck, swathed in a floral dressing gown and wearing slippers. He rested his short legs on a plush-covered footstool. The stub of a cigar jutted from his mouth. On a low table in front of him lay half an orange.

"A freak!" flashed through Keyle's mind.

Bertha clutched Keyle's arm tightly, half-leading, half-dragging her along behind. When Bertha had drawn nearer, she said loudly, "Sergei Davidovitch, here's the girl. She's a little bashful, but she'll soon get over it."

With a trembling hand Sergei Davidovitch laid his cigar in an ashtray next to the orange and cupped a hand to his ear. With his other hand he scrabbled in the pocket of his dressing-gown to fish out a pair of gold-rimmed pince-nez on a black ribbon. Through the thick lenses his eyes grew as large and bulging as a calf's.

He muttered several words in Russian, then abruptly changed over to Yiddish.

"Well, well, sit down, sit down. I'm not quite myself, a catarrh, a chill, but never mind, never mind. Bertha Moiseyevna, where ever did you find her? A pretty thing, a beauty. Still young, young . . . How old, eh? We had some refreshments ready here, somewhere, but Zoshke, the maid, has gone off somewhere—doing shopping or something. The telephone rang and I thought that—but when I got to it, no one answered—"

"What? If someone needs you, he'll call again," Bertha said. "Sonia Zalmanovna—the girl's name is Sonia—if you want anything, or if Gospodin Sergei Davidovitch wants anything, everything's in the kitchen: a gas stove, a teapot, tea, sugar, lemon, cookies. I sent Zoshke down to get the prescription filled. She'll also call at the post office after she's been to the market. Would you like tea?" she asked the old man.

"Tea? No."

"There's water in the kettle. All you have to do is light the gas. I'll go back to my apartment and leave you two alone here. My door's just to the left. If necessary, you can knock and call me," said Bertha, turning to Keyle. "Don't ring, just knock on the door. The toilet's in the kitchen. Don't forget to flush."

"Thank you kindly."

"Don't be so scared," Bertha snarled. "No one here's going to bite you!"

Before she left, she winked at Keyle.

As soon as Bertha had left, Sergei Davidovitch said, "Come closer, come closer. Feel at home, at home. I'm not completely well, but I already feel better. A great deal better. What did you say your name is?"

Keyle wanted to answer, but she couldn't remember the name Bertha had just given her. Never before had she been in so luxurious a home. Every moment she spotted new objects she hadn't noticed before. On a small table stood a telephone

Isaac Bashevis Singer

with a bottle of wine or liqueur next to it. A silver casket gleamed inside a glass-doored cabinet in company with a kind of little silver tower engraved with Hebrew letters, and books with leather spines and gilt titles.

"He must be a lawyer," it occurred to Keyle.

He spoke to her in Yiddish but she couldn't make out what he was saying. Was he a Litvak or what? Some years before, when she'd been in the brothel on Tamka Street, an officer had taken her home and she'd spent the night with him. But then she'd been dead drunk and hadn't been aware of anything. All she remembered were marble stairs, and a Slav who'd spoken to her in Russian. He'd balanced a glass of whiskey on her head and tried to shoot it off with a revolver. He'd ordered her to strip naked and take a bath with him. Early the next morning he'd returned her to the place he'd taken her from, and Keyle heard later that the madam had charged him twenty-five rubles for the night. But this was different. The old man here addressed her with respect and treated her as his equal. He invited her to sit down, but she didn't dare to sit in the carved chair with its finials and rattan seat. She barely stopped herself from bursting into tears. She was overcome by a feeling of shame such as she'd never experienced before. She wanted to grab the bottle of liquor and pour it into herself to gain some courage, but she couldn't make herself do this either. She had only one urge: to flee. But what would Bertha say? What would Stumping Max think of her? And Yarme? And even this educated person?

The telephone rang and Sergei Davidovitch slowly rose and picked up the receiver. He spoke Russian, occasionally interjecting a word of Yiddish.

"So sick, yet so clever and educated!" Keyle thought in wonderment.

Something within her wept. Some kind of magic spell had seemingly purged her of all her brazenness, her wantonness, her adult dissoluteness, and she'd once again become a helpless child, a little orphan lost in a great city, while this old man whose life was flickering out was so urbane, so wise, so knowledgeable. Several times he even smiled.

"It may even be that he's talking about me, or mocking me," she thought.

He said, "*Do svidaniya,*" and replaced the receiver. He didn't return to his armchair, but went off to the kitchen. After a long time Keyle heard him flushing the toilet. While he lingered in the lavatory, Keyle decided to uncork the bottle on the table and take a long swig. It was some kind of sweet brandy. After a while she took another swig.

"I'm lost in any case," she mentally justified herself.

In a moment she'd grown more determined and resolute, and even a little bolder.

"Why'm I so afraid? Things can't be worse for me than they already are," she consoled herself.

The two long swigs had restored her confidence. She even reminded herself that her name was now Sonia and that her father's name wasn't Borekh-Yoyne but Zalman, which was her grandfather's name.

When Sergei Davidovitch reappeared at the kitchen door, Keyle ran up to him, took his arm, and helped him return to his chair. As he lowered himself into it, he sighed like someone putting down a heavy burden.

"*Spasibo*. What did you say your name was?"

"Sonia. My father's name was Zalman."

"Zalman, eh? Sonia Zalmanovna. As long as you're young, you imagine you'll stay young forever. But when old age steals up on you, your strength starts ebbing away. Every day some new ailment grips you. Sit down, sit down. That's right. Chairs are for sitting in. I had a great friend in my life; her name was Sofia, Sofia Mikhailovna. I was certain I'd leave the world much, much sooner than she because I was so much older. But fate decided differently. She was also a friend of Bertha Moiseyevna. Those two women sustained my life. I'm the victim of a bad marriage, a false step you make once that can never be reversed. I left her healthy, and when I came back, she was dead. Well, that's how it is. Would you like something to drink? I have some sweet brandy here, women's brandy. I myself dare not drink any alcohol. My stomach, my liver, my bladder . . . The doctor's forbidden me to smoke as well, but I smoke two cigars a day all the same. What harm can it do by now? The body's like a garment. It's strong, strong, but all of a sudden it starts tearing at every seam. No sooner do you mend one tear than three new ones rip open. Pour yourself a glassful. Here's the bottle and a glass."

Only now did Keyle see the glass — one similar to the kind her grandfather used to make *Kiddush* — and she filled it to the brim. She knew full well that there was an expression one used before taking a drink, a Jewish word from the prayer book, but she'd forgotten what it was. She was overcome by an affection for this old man who was chatting so freely, opening his heart, and treating her to brandy. She was afraid that not enough remained in the bottle for a full glass, but she managed to pour one out, and the bottle still wasn't empty. "*Nazdrowie*," she said in Polish,

Isaac Bashevis Singer

draining the whole glassful in one gulp. She even made a gesture as though to hurl the glass against the wall the way soldiers and officers did when they drank. After some hesitation, she replaced the glass on the table again.

"*Nazdrowie, l'khayim* [to life!]," the old man said.

Ah, that was the word she'd been looking for: *l'khayim.* It'd been on the tip of her tongue. At that moment she did something that astounded even her.

She ran up to Sergei Davidovitch, clasped his face in both her hands, and began to kiss his shaved skull once, twice, many times, rapidly and eagerly as though she were afraid the old man would forbid her to do it. It seemed to her that the old man's face grew hot in her hands, or perhaps it was her own heat she was exuding. After his skull, she started kissing his forehead, his nose, his mouth, his little white beard. He didn't return the kisses; he only fidgeted and tried to say something through lips that she covered with her own.

None of this had lasted more than a minute when, trembling, she tore herself away and backed off. Sergei Davidovitch's spectacles had fallen off and dangled on their ribbon. His face was a mottled mass of white and red flecks, his beard disheveled and awry. He stared at her from under white eyebrows and was apparently panting for breath. He mumbled, "Well, so be it. How have I deserved this?"

Keyle wanted to respond, but once again she was at a loss for words. She gasped, "You're a really decent human being." Her own words astounded her.

5

When Yarme told Keyle that Bertha had passed on a widow to him, it was no lie. The widow did indeed live on Grzybowska Street, opposite the Jewish community council. Bertha had shown Yarme a photograph of her: she had a broad nose, a double chin, and appeared to be pockmarked as well. Yarme had heard of her before. Her husband, Nosele Hernia, had grown rich giving ruptures to conscripts to prevent them being enlisted. Nosele had given up the ghost in the Pawiak Prison after one such recruit had denounced him, and he'd left his wife Bronya a fortune.

After Nosele's death, Bronya had been married and divorced twice, and had now confided to Bertha that she had no desire to marry again. Three times under the wedding canopy was enough. Bronya was seeking a lover, she informed Bertha frankly.

"With my pockmarked mug and potato nose, no one will fall in love with me."

Bronya was prepared to pay for love, just like a man.

Stumping Max had paid Bronya a visit, but subsequently told Bertha that even if he were offered a mountain of gold he wouldn't touch that ugly old harridan. Bronya didn't find Max to her taste either: apart from the fact that he was lame, he was stunted. Bertha had then shown Bronya a photograph of Yarme, and after only a single glance, she'd exclaimed, "That's the man for me!"

Yarme allowed himself to be persuaded. Since Keyle was going to fiddle about with Sergei Davidovitch anyway, why should he lie about like a lump at home? After barely three years of living with only one woman, Yarme needed a change, he told himself. Max urged him on. The whole notion of faithfulness between husband and wife wasn't worth a fig. Max had read somewhere that deep in their hearts both men and women longed to be betrayed. But on the way to Grzybowska Street, Yarme felt the wanton power Keyle exercised over him. He was overcome with fear that he'd turn impotent with Bronya. He seemed to have lost his former easy approach to women. He didn't stay in the droshky but walked, stopping every few steps. On Zhabia Street he studied the women's hats in the shop windows. Outside it was still summer, but here they were featuring hats made of felt, cloth, velvet, and fur for the winter season. One shop specialized in hats for women in mourning—the goods were draped in crepe and hung with black veils. Here and there through a window Yarme caught a glimpse of a milliner. The world was alive and thronged with young girls, but he was on his way to some monstrosity, as old as the plague and as pocked as a grater.

"I'll shut my eyes and make believe it's Keyle," Yarme consoled himself. If he intended to become a professional seducer, he couldn't expect love affairs. He had to pretend, just like an actor. Years before he'd been able to manage this very easily, but somehow he'd lost his skill at the tricks of the past. Now he envied Keyle. A female could deceive more easily. She could lie with a hundred men and still remain as cold as ice.

Bronya lived in a luxurious building. Yarme went up to her apartment on marble stairs. He ought to have been bold and playful now, but at the same time he knew he was in a hopeless situation. "Keyle was right," he thought. "That Max is an Angel of Death. Evil luck brought him here to turn everything into filth and slime, and then to destroy us both."

Yarme literally felt two beings wrangling inside him. One argued, "What on earth do you need all these complications for? Better to eat a crust of dry bread

Isaac Bashevis Singer

than to get involved with such a repulsive reptile. Fetch Keyle, haul her home, and don't ever clap eyes on that Max again. He wants to drag you back down into the dirt; don't fall into his net."

The other, the Evil Inclination, countered, "What'll you do? Pluck chickens in a slaughterhouse? Carry baskets of coal from house to house? Sell apples?"

Over the last few years, Yarme had lost his appetite for corrupt dealings. He'd grown soft, timid. He seemed to have split into two people. One ordered him to go home, but the other directed his feet to Bronya's door. Yarme gave a nervous cough and braced himself. He rang and Bronya opened the door to him. She was rouged and powdered, clad in a robe and slippers. She'd apparently had her hair done; perhaps even had it dyed as well.

She measured him up and down, hesitated a moment, and only then let him in. "Yarme, eh? Come in."

She led him down a long passageway into a room covered in maroon wallpaper with a rug of the same color. On a sideboard stood a gramophone with an enormous horn. On the wall hung a portrait of Nosele Hernia with his round face and circular beard. His eyes, smiling as though alive, seemed to be saying to Yarme, "This is what happens to a man when he lies six feet under."

On a sofa strewn with cushions lay a doll decked out in silk and lace. Bottles of wine and liqueur and a bowl of cookies stood on the table. The curtains were drawn and the gas lamps were burning, even though it was now midday. Bronya took the doll off the sofa and motioned Yarme to take its place. She herself sat down in an armchair with a red cover and red fringes. She smiled, showing a mouth full of false teeth, and asked in a mannish voice, "Bertha sent you, eh?"

"Yes, Bertha."

"I know her, I know her like a bad penny. My husband, may he intercede for me, and Hertz Kalashnik were close friends. He called here very often. We played sixty-six together. When Kalashnik made a fool of himself and fell into the hands of the Gentiles, it was Nosele who bailed him out. Now Kalashnik is a big noise in the world and Bertha acts the great lady. But he can't marry her. He has a wife."

"Yes, I know."

"They say he's got another as well," Bronya added.

"Isn't Bertha enough for him?" asked Yarme.

"That's how men are. They've got big eyes, but when push comes to shove, they're worthless. Let's drink a toast. What do you want—brandy? a liqueur?"

"Brandy."

Bronya poured out two glassfuls. It struck Yarme that she had a hand as big as a man's. He gulped the liquor down and felt it scratch his throat and scorch his guts.

"Another?"

"Why not?"

"Don't get drunk. When a man drinks he wants to go straight to sleep."

"Not alone," Yarme said, uncertain of his words.

"Does Keyle know where you are? Bertha told me everything."

"I'm no rabbi, and she's no *rebbetzin*," Yarme replied, astounded at his pert response.

"I like everything to work smoothly. Not the slightest disturbance. I don't want anyone coming to me under false pretenses."

"No pretenses."

"Take a bite of something."

Yarme knocked back the second glassful and rapidly crunched up a cookie. He wanted to behave impudently, to rattle off something smart, but he didn't know what to say. Liquor always made Keyle more lively, but it only made him feel bitter. Bronya gave him a sidelong glance through narrowed, mocking eyes.

"She looks just like a pig," it struck Yarme. He felt not the slightest desire to move closer to this gross beast. "I should never have come here!"

He wasn't so much ashamed of what she would say as of what she would later tell Bertha, who'd pass it on to Max. Yarme was terrified that from now on he'd be impotent with Keyle as well. Keyle had often told him of men who visited whorehouses, couldn't achieve gratification, and then demanded a refund of the ten kopecks they'd paid in advance. Others demanded to be beaten, to be spat on, to have their hair pulled, to be whipped.

Now Yarme sat quietly, gazing intently at the bottle as though deliberating, "Should I pour out another glassful? No, it wouldn't be of the slightest use."

Aloud, he asked: "Where's the toilet?"

"Out in the corridor."

He went out into the corridor, glanced at the front door, opened it quietly, and began racing down the stairs like a frightened schoolboy. Shame raced along with him. He leaped down the stairs two at a time.

Isaac Bashevis Singer

"Well, I'm finished!" something inside him shouted.

He ran quickly out through the gate and rushed down toward Granitszka Street. His legs had grown strangely light. As he ran, he decided that he'd have no more truck with Max. He'd send him to hell and if he refused to stay away, he'd stick a knife in him.

Yarme now felt the urge to lug Keyle out of the slime-pit as well.

"I'll run away to America with her and start living a decent life."

Out of nowhere a passage he'd learned in *kheyder* flashed into his mind: "Naked came I from my mother's womb, and naked shall I return thither." But who'd said that? Moses? Jacob?

He was suddenly overcome by lust for Keyle. He had to have her, now, at once! He was soon back on Ptasia Street and walked through the gateway leading to Bertha's house.

"Please don't let me meet Bertha on the stairs," he prayed to God or whoever was in charge of such matters. But where did Sergei Davidovitch live? Yarme wanted to smash down his door, and if he found Keyle in the old man's bed he'd strangle them both. This was love, true love, and you dared not give away a woman you loved as much as that, not even for a million rubles.

A girl with a triangular freckled little face came down from an upper floor wearing a short dress and down-at-heel slippers over bare feet. Yarme stopped her. He wanted to ask where the old man's apartment was, but at that moment he'd forgotten the old man's name.

"Where does the old man that speaks Russian live? He's sick, he comes from Russia."

"Eh? I don't know."

"Don't you live here?"

"I only work here. I know nothing."

"He's a rich man."

"Ask someone else."

Yarme was seized by a desire to grab the stupid slut and tear her hair out, but he restrained himself. She'd raise an outcry, and he might be hauled off to jail. He stepped aside to let her pass, but in such a way that she had to brush up against him.

"I'm drunk, dead drunk," Yarme mentally justified himself.

6

Stumping Max, or Leon Gempner as he was called in his latest passport, sat in his room at the Hotel Krakowski reading the Yiddish newspaper. For some reason that he couldn't understand and which no doctor had ever explained to him, he always felt hot. In the summer he slept in the nude and didn't even cover himself with a sheet. In the winter he left the transom open both day and night. His lame leg gave him constant pain, and the moment he was alone he took off his shoes and socks. Now he was smoking a cigarette as he read, chattering to himself after every few lines, spewing out words like chickpeas. He didn't know himself whether this was a childhood habit or something he'd picked up in the prisons in which he'd served time—in Warsaw, in Radom, in Buenos Aires. Not only did he talk to himself, he also winked, hissed, grinned, and sometimes even snapped his jaws like a dog catching a fly in the air. Max had reached the point in the serialized novel in which the intriguer and seducer Zbigniew Koczinski had set up a ladder leading to a window in the castle of Count Leopold Kurowicz and had abducted the Lady Helena. Max emitted a thin chuckle. Poppycock, idiocy, completely ridiculous fantasies. There was as much likelihood of this happening as there was of Passover catching Jews unprepared. These scribblers simply wrote whatever came into their heads, building castles in the air.

"As the crackling of thorns under a pot, so is the laughter of a fool," he muttered to himself.

At times Max couldn't believe it himself, but he'd once studied Gemara with *Tosafot* [rabbinic commentaries] in the Piask study house. He'd even been examined by the rabbi. Phrases from the Gemara, from Hasidic teachings, still stuck in his memory. How long ago had he abandoned all that? No more than fifteen years, but it seemed like an eternity. In those fifteen years he'd lived through not one life but a hundred. Had he tried to describe in writing all that had happened to him, no one would've believed him. The very same idiots who read all these newspaper fabrications and took them for Holy Writ would take him for a liar. But then, could all his experiences be put into words, after all? He had sisters, brothers, and children he'd never laid eyes on. He'd deserted wives in Poland, Argentina, Canada. He'd lived for some time in such places as Mexico, Bolivia, Uruguay, Trinidad. He'd gambled in the casinos of Monte Carlo, Mar del Plata, Zapata. Apart

Isaac Bashevis Singer

from Yiddish, Max spoke Polish and Russian, as well as German, Spanish, Portuguese, English. One night in a train traveling from Kiev to Odessa, a general's wife had taken him into a first-class compartment and given herself to him. On a ship sailing from London to Brazil he'd enjoyed liaisons with women from France, Germany, and Italy, as well as with a Black woman whose name and origins he no longer remembered.

Oddly enough, despite all these conquests with women, he was attracted only to men. In the prisons in which he'd served time he'd always found a homosexual. That Saturday evening at the Yiddish theater he'd given the impression that he'd run into Yarme by sheer chance, but in truth he'd longed for him all those years and had actually come looking for him.

"Tsk, tsk, I'm some fruit all right! What goes on in my muddled little head even God couldn't figure out — if He exists at all."

Max finished his cigarette and promptly lit another, striking the match on the floor. He carried with him a gold revolver and kept three different passports — one in a suitcase, and two others, one in each breast pocket of his suit. He had a satchel packed with a vast assortment of sleeping-pills, as well as medicines for headache, stomach ache, constipation, and heartburn.

Five years earlier, a doctor had warned him that he was mortally ill and had ordered him to live a quiet life, to stop smoking, and to cease endlessly chasing after women. The doctor had prescribed electrotherapy, hydrotherapy, alcohol rubs, and had warned him that if he didn't slow down he could drop dead at any moment.

Max laughed. A quiet life! Take better care of himself! How could he live quietly when his brain churned like an engine twenty-four hours of the day and night? Even after he'd fallen asleep, he was assailed by nightmares no words could describe. He soared like an eagle, rolled about in all the punishments of Gehenna. Demons led him astray through desert wastes, cast him on beds of nails and burning coals, buried him in mounds of snow, in pits, in caves. He was shot, hanged, flogged, forced to run a fiery gauntlet as Cossacks battered him with rifle-butts, stabbed him with swords, bayonets, spears. Terrifying monsters appeared before him, half-human, half-animal, with long beaks, pig snouts, burning eyes, half male and half female, with penises and teats, with beards and pigtails. They shrieked at him in piercing voices, bayed like dogs, roared like lions, grunted like wild boars.

Yarme and Keyle: *Chapter 2*

He sank in mires of dung, phlegm, offal. He heard dirges, laments, insane words that couldn't be grasped or remembered beyond the moment. Neurasthenia, the doctor had called it. But what was neurasthenia?

His waking hours were just like his sleep. He was constantly driven to scheme, to fantasize, to build castles in the sky. He was simultaneously rational and mad, compassionate and savagely murderous, pious, superstitious, and blasphemous, bold and cowardly. He spent money lavishly, yet at the same time penuriously accounted for every groschen that passed through his fingers.

He risked his freedom, driving himself into the worst dangers while at the same time living in terror of the evil eye, of black cats, of someone crossing his path with an empty vessel. He carried on his person ivory elephants, amulets, charmed chips of amber. At every opportunity he consulted clairvoyants, fortune-tellers, astrologers who read horoscopes, and mediums who summoned up the dead, displayed images in black mirrors, and brought greetings from those beyond the grave. He'd already found an advertisement in a Warsaw Yiddish newspaper by one Schiller-Skolnik who assisted people in finding lost relatives, mislaid objects, absconded husbands and wives, who offered charms or cures for impotence, arthritis, rheumatism, and chronic hiccuping and who treated patients with magnetism, hypnotism, palmistry, and physiognomy.

"A swindler, a charlatan," Max told himself. At the same time he clipped out the advertisement with a pair of scissors. Who knows? Perhaps this man might be just the one truly possessed of hidden powers. If sorcerers had indeed once existed, why couldn't they exist today?

Max pulled open a drawer and took out an album in which he pasted photographs of all the women and men with whom he'd been sexually involved. It also contained love letters, articles of engagement, marriage contracts. He shouldn't have dared to carry around this damning evidence against himself, but except for these souvenirs he retained nothing of his adventures. For the thousandth time he counted his dupes, scrutinized their faces, spoke to them. Max simultaneously liked and loathed women. They had all disappointed him. In his sleep he dreamed about men. He exploited his lust for men to satisfy women. He called his women by masculine names, sought out those with flat chests, demanded that they shave off the signs of puberty. He often persuaded them to give themselves to other men.

A hotel employee knocked on Max's door to tell him he was wanted on the telephone. Limping heavily, Max sprang up, threw a bathrobe over himself, and

Isaac Bashevis Singer

went out into the corridor where the telephone was located. It was Bertha. She informed him that Red Keyle was with Sergei Davidovitch and that Yarme had gone off to Bronya, the pockmarked widow. Max's spirits rose at once.

"Bertashke, the scheme'll work out just as we planned."

"Max, you could make two walls come together."

"Me? It's all you. If you hadn't let yourself get involved with Hertz Kalashnik, the two of us could've torn down worlds together."

"Bite your tongue, Maxele."

"Bertashke, I'll need a few more passports."

"More? How many do you need? A hundred?" And Bertha laughed.

"She has a mannish voice," Max thought. Aloud he said, "If Jethro had seven names, I need seven times seven passports."

East Central Europe, 1910.

From *Historical Atlas of East Central Europe*, by Paul Robert Magocsi, University of Wisconsin Press: 1993. Reprinted with permission of University of Wisconsin Press and the author.

Appendix

Bashevis Singer as a Regionalist of Lublin Province

A Note

Seth L. Wolitz and Joseph Sherman

Geographically speaking, the prolific output of I. Bashevis Singer is set in a number of locales in Poland, the eastern United States, Israel, and—rarely—a few Western European cities and even South America. Where his major long novels—*The Family Moskat, The Manor,* and *The Slave*—paint vast frescoes depicting the sweeping historical changes that Poland underwent between the seventeenth and the twentieth centuries, his short stories, by striking contrast, tend to be set in specific and narrowly circumscribed topographical locations, the overwhelming number of which are situated in Poland during a very particular period of that country's checkered geographical and political history.

Although Bashevis set a number of his best-known tales in distinctively Jewish areas of Warsaw, all bounded by specifically named streets—Krochmalna (Polish: Krachmalna) Street, the place in which his family's apartment was situated, has become particularly well known to his readers—the majority of his short stories are set in numerous small towns and *shtetlekh* situated in Lublin Province.

This province is named after its capital and most important city, Lublin, a locality that played a highly significant role throughout Polish history and was of particular centrality for the Jews of Poland. Lublin is located southeast of Warsaw; during the halcyon days of the Respublica, the Polish-Lithuanian Commonwealth between the Renaissance and the early seventeenth century, when the city of Krakow was the capital of Poland, Lublin was a far more important metropolitan area than Warsaw itself. Lublin was Poland's major trading city and as such held an important annual trade fair, because it straddled the crossroads between the east-west and north-south trade routes. As a consequence, Lublin attracted merchants from all over Europe, Russia, and the Ottoman Empire. The Jews of Poland inevitably played an important part in this extensive mercantile activity. Many Jewish merchants of considerable substance attended the city's trade fair; eminent rabbis held deliberations there and set up rabbinical courts (*batey din*). Several important Jewish physicians practiced in Lublin in the sixteenth century, one of whom served the king of Poland. And the leaders of numerous Eastern European Jewish communities traveled to Lublin to discuss communal affairs and problems of mutual concern. A substantial Jewish population lived in Lublin, and, given its central location, the city attracted many rabbis and learned Jews who established important yeshivas and printing houses that became renowned throughout Eastern Europe. The most famous of the Rabbinical figures was the Maharam of Lublin, Rabbi Meir ben Gedaliah of Lublin (1558–1616), whose Talmudic Academy drew students from all over Poland and beyond and underscored that Lublin was the major center of religious Jewish thought.

Lublin's committed Jewish character led to its establishment as the administrative center of the Council of the Four Lands (*Va'ad Arba Artsot*), the central institution of Jewish self-government in Poland and Lithuania that endured from the sixteenth century until 1764. (This unique institution served as a model into the nineteenth and twentieth centuries of what many Eastern European Jewish groups sought to restore or re-create on both the political and cultural levels.)

Lublin subsequently also became a creative center of the Hasidic movement which swept Galicia and southern Poland at the beginning of the eighteenth century, a movement which, with its revolutionary reinvigoration of faith, also sparked competing dynastic courts and factional rivalries. Yakov Yitskhok ha-Khozeh (1745–1815), known as the "Seer of Lublin," was the key Hasidic rabbi and miracle worker credited with making Congress Poland and Galicia a great center of Hasidism. This movement continued to exert a profound influence on Jewish life throughout the world right up to the outbreak of World War II.

When Poland as a historical and geographical entity was fragmented as a result of its numerous partitions by foreign powers, Lublin and its surrounding areas first were absorbed by Austria in 1795 and then, after the Congress of Vienna in 1815, passed under the control of Russia, where they remained as part of the tsarist empire until the end of World War I. For nearly a century, therefore, it was the tsarist government that defined the parameters of Lublin Province, and it is this province, so defined, that dominates the geography of Isaac Bashevis Singer's short stories.

In political and historical terms, the actual tsarist province of Lublin stretched southward from the city of Lublin to the Galician Austro-Hungarian border, on which Tarnogrod was the last major town. Its eastern border included the city of Zamosc and the tiny town of Tishevitz (Polish: Tyszowce), which Bashevis characterized in "The Last Demon" (Yiddish: *Mayse tishevits*) as a spot so small and insignificant that "Adam didn't even stop to pee there." In the days of the *Va'ad Arba Artsot,* however, Tyszowce — despite its size — became a central meeting-place for Jewish conferences, like Zamosc and even Tarnogrod. To the west, Bashevis took Krasnik and Yanov (Polish: Janow) as the furthermost boundaries of the Lublin Province he deploys in his fiction. Bashevis's province of Lublin — as readers ap-

Appendix: Bashevis Singer as a Regionalist

prehend it from the cities and towns that he recurrently evokes as settings for his stories—
is considerably narrower than the actual physical territory contained within it during both
tsarist rule and the period of Polish independence between the two world wars. As a result, Bashevis consciously ensures that the reader of his short tales enters specific towns in a
particular circumscribed world that, individually and collectively, carry echoes—for those
who know—of their distinguished past, set in striking contrast to depressing contemporary
evocations of their generally wretched existence in the present.

The center of Bashevis's Lublin Province is not the capital city, Lublin itself, which remains distant and rich in its population and observance of Orthodox Judaism. Instead it is
Bilgoray (Polish: Bilgoraj), the actual town in which his older brother, Israel Joshua Singer,
was born, and where their maternal grandfather, a leading *misnaged* (anti-Hasidic) rabbi,
was a community leader of enormous learning, influence, and power. (Bashevis was born
in Leoncin, in which he sets his story "Son from America.") Bilgoray lies on a direct line in
the southern route from Lublin to Tarnogrod and is one of the larger towns on that route.
Map 2 is the actual map of conquest charted by the Nazi military command to effect the
subjugation of Poland in 1942. It was drawn and used with such deadly precision that the
Germans could note and reach into the most insignificant of Poland's Jewish settlements—
those actual villages and hamlets around Bilgoray which once flourished with a vibrant
Jewish life that was so ruthlessly extirpated. This map presents the normal route the Singer
family would have taken by wagon on its journeys between Lublin and Bilgoray. (Actually,
the family trips to Warsaw and back made use of the train in good part, as Bashevis Singer
notes an alternate route via Lublin in *In My Father's Court.*) Amazingly, a perusal of this
map reveals that many of the towns in which the astonishing events that Singer dramatizes
in his fiction occur in real places near Bilgoray that exist in both physical and metaphysical
dimensions, settings, and times. Consulting the map to follow the road northward from
Bilgoray, one finds that the first stop at which travelers in their wagon would call a halt
would be Frampol, the town in which the events related in both "The Gentleman from
Krakow" and "The Little Shoemakers" take place. Resuming the journey, one then arrives
at the small hamlet of Goray (Polish: Goraj), the setting of Bashevis's masterpiece, *Satan in
Goray.*

Later the wagon would enter Turbin (Polish: Turobin), which serves as the setting for
"The Wife Killer." The wagon would then have stopped at Bechev (Polish: Bychawa), the
location of "Something Is There," before it arrived in the city of Lublin itself, the center
of the rich and animated metropolitan Jewish life which consistently appears throughout
all Bashevis's works. From here, the Singer family on the train went by way of Pulawy and
Ivanogrod (Deblin) to Warsaw, their home and the major city-locale of Singer's work.

Bashevis's fictional absorption of the Lublin Province is not simply confined to the

Seth L. Wolitz and Joseph Sherman

Area around Lublin, Poland, from Übersichtskarte 1:1000000, Warschau-Moskau, 1942. This map was drawn by the German Military Occupation Forces mapmakers in Warsaw during World War II and published in Warsaw. Its bitter and ironic value is that it provides the most complete mapping of the cities, towns, villages, and hamlets available at the time of the Holocaust and shows the road system still intact from the beginning of the century until 1942, which I. B. Singer would have known and traveled. This thorough mapping of all inhabited locations made it possible to reach Jews even in the most obscure locales. The map does not give the definitions of the Polish interwar province of Lublin, for at the top is written "Ehem. Polen" or "former Poland." Thus it is the last image of an Eastern Europe in the Nazi mind but also a most accurate depiction of the human habitations and road system up to 1942.

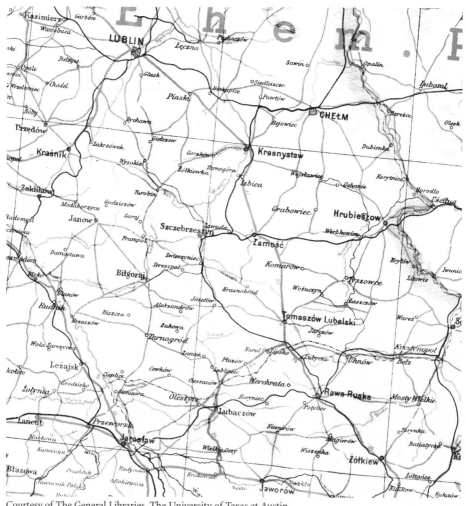

Courtesy of The General Libraries, The University of Texas at Austin.

traveling route taken by the Singer family to and from Warsaw, however. It also includes the area around Bilgoray, stretching as far east as Tishevitz and as far west as Yanov. To the southwest of Bilgoray, Bashevis sets his tale entitled "The Destruction of Kreshev" in the tiny Polish hamlet of Krzeszow; not far away is Byszcz (Polish: Biszcza) and then Radoszyce, where the events recounted in the short story "Passions" are played out. To the northwest of Bilgoray, in Yanov, Bashevis sets the startling and ambiguous events of his famous tale "Yentl the Yeshiva Boy," and further up the road, in the town of Krasnik, the temptation and fall of the widow who is the focus of "The Mirror" takes place. Southeast of Bilgoray is the tiny village of Yosefov (Polish: Jozefow), once the center and court of an important Hasidic dynasty, which serves as the opening locale of "The Unseen" and the early events of "The Old Man." Immediately south of Yosefov is Aleksandrov (Polish Aleksandrow), where "Grandfather and Grandson" partly plays itself out. A little further east, the town of Krasnobrod provides the setting for "A Crown of Feathers." A short way up a narrow road appears the celebrated small city of Zamosc, with its splendid Italianate Renaissance architecture still intact, always an important center of commerce, trade, and learning whose Jews felt a bit superior, if not outright smug, when they compared themselves to their kin in other parts of Poland. Indeed, even in the late nineteenth century, Zamosc was a center of the Haskala, the Jewish Enlightenment movement; it was the birthplace of Y. L. Peretz, one of the fathers of Yiddish literature, as well as of the Jewish socialist activist Rosa Luxembourg. Bashevis Singer detested Zamosc, for it was the spiritual as well as physical home of the "modernists" whose ideologies he found utterly disastrous and destructive. Nearby Komarov (Polish: Komarow), once also the seat of an eminent Hasidic court, is the setting for Bashevis Singer's bittersweet short story "Joy." Komarov was a place name not easily forgotten by those who lived in interwar Poland, for it had been a great battleground of World War I where the Russians were heavily defeated and where the destruction of Jewish life was painfully extensive.

For the sake of precise verisimilitude, Bashevis always takes particular care to describe some distinguishing physical characteristics of the townships, villages, or hamlets he deploys as the settings of his fictions. Usually he notes the location of his chosen milieu by commenting on a local river or the place's lack of natural water, the quality of its soil, or the richness of its surrounding forest. An excellent illustration of this exactitude can be seen in the opening description of "The Destruction of Kreshev." Bashevis's precise knowledge is gained from having once been personally *in situ,* and to this personal observation he adds literary skills of a high order to conjure up, in short vignettes, a realistic picture of the settlement he is calling to mind. Unlike a nineteenth-century writer, Bashevis does not overextend his description; it does not exist for its own sake, or even for the sole sake of documentary realism, but rather metonymically foreshadows the events of the tale that

Seth L. Wolitz and Joseph Sherman

is to unfold. His plot-line integrates the distinctiveness of the town and its inhabitants, their physical appearance, their emotional and social yearnings and their hidden forbidden desires, to merge as a carefully crafted whole. He particularizes his settings sufficiently to provide both the physical and metaphysical dimensions and concerns of the Jewish milieu he describes, which, taken in the broadest perspective, reflect the Polish Jewry of Lublin Province. Topography merges seamlessly into the metaphysical layers of local Polish-Jewish culture, and Bashevis does not fail to point out with sly humor the foibles of the regional Jews he vivifies, especially in their daily dealings with the Gentile population with whom they are obliged to interact.

The narrative voices of Bashevis's tales provide a regional world of Eastern European Jewry quite distinctly and deliberately removed from the Litvak world of northern Poland and Lithuania. This voice obliges the reader to enter the Hasidic life and general culture of the Jews of the Lublin Province and to capture, savor, and experience virtually at first hand its intellectual and religious conflicts. Singer is concerned with fusing the physical and creative imaginary of the Jewish folk in their daily living and in their encounter with the non-Jewish world around them. But the vanished world he portrays is one of an essentially isolated, although markedly distinct, Jewry who are the proud heirs of the great but now lost days of the Polish Respublica and its Jewish Renaissance and of a vibrant Hasidic era now irretrievably in decay. Bashevis makes no real moral judgment, but instead he attempts to provide a world view that goes beyond the merely physical reality to enter into the mindset of a people teetering at the brink of destruction, to which he does not even allude.

Lublin Province, with all its variety of towns, villages, and hamlets, is forever preserved in Bashevis Singer's fiction as a Jewish diasporic world that has rooted itself deeply and made itself comfortably at home. Bashevis presents a picture of a universal Israel in all its truth: a faithful portrait of a culture that was simultaneously linked to an ancient past and yet living in a creation of its own present, all in tsarist Russia's and interwar Poland's Lublin Province. This was a geographical area of Jewish life no less Jewish, accomplished, and real than the Jews of ancient days who lived in the Galilee or who compiled the Babylonian Talmud in Sura and the *Kabbala* in Spain or who live today in Brooklyn or Petakh Tikvah. In his short stories, Bashevis Singer remarkably shows himself as a regionalist in the truest, fullest sense, a writer of genius who, with precision and meticulous care, uses the particular as his chief and best means of reaching the universal.

Appendix: Bashevis Singer as a Regionalist

Glossary

apikoyres: heretic

bezdn: rabbinical court

Erets Yisroel: the Land of Israel (Modern Hebrew: Eretz Yisrael)

ganef: thief, trickster

Halakha: general term for the Jewish religious and ethical laws codified and elaborated in the Talmud

Hasidism: the Jewish populist mystical movement originating in the eighteenth century, like other quietist movements in Western and Eastern Christianity; by the beginning of the nineteenth century more than half of Eastern European Jews were Hasidim or leaned toward its mystical impulses; the rationalists and traditionalists who opposed Hasidism were called *mitnagdim* (opponents) and were mainly centered in Lithuanian territory

Haskala: the Jewish Enlightenment movement imported from Germany at the end of the eighteenth century and prominent among Jews in tsarist Russia in the nineteenth century; it was a Westernizing modernist movement opposed by the traditionalist Jews

Kabbala: the collective term for Jewish writings giving a mystical interpretation of the Bible as well as a praxis

Kaddish: a memorial prayer to honor the dead and comfort the living

kheyder: Jewish religious primary school

khosed: a follower devoted to his spiritual guide, the *rebbe*

koved: honor

loshn-koydesh: biblical Hebrew and Hebrew of religious texts

maskilim: followers of the Haskala (Jewish Enlightenment movement); Westernizers, modernists

melamed: teacher

misnaged: Jewish religious rationalist and opponent of the Hasidim

nar: fool

rebbe: spiritually inspired Hasidic rabbinic leader

rebbetzin: wife of a rabbi

shlemiel: fool

Shoah: the Jewish/Hebrew term for the Holocaust

shtetl: market town

tam: simpleton, fool

taytsh: the Yiddish of old prayer books and tales for women

Va'ad Arba Artsot: Council of the Four Lands (the autonomous governing body of the Jews in Poland during the Polish Respublica)

yeshive: Jewish religious seminary

yeytser-hore: Evil Inclination; erotic desires

yidishkeyt: the distinctive quality of being an Eastern European Jew

amazon.com®

http://www.amazon.com

Your order of January 26, 2002 (Order ID 103–2102347–0025433)

Qty	Item

In This Shipment

1	The Hidden Isaac Bashevis Singer (The Literary Modernism Series) (P–4–B59D15)

As you requested, we've sent this part of your order to en

You can track the status of this order, and all your recent orders, online by

Returns are easy –– even for gifts! Visit http://www.

p 74-75 note 8

p. 75 note 19,20

Thanks for shopping at Amazc

ICY

urn most unused/unopened items within **30** days for any reason, for a full refund. We'll even cost if the return is a result of our error. For full details visit **www.amazon.com**.

YS FROM DELIVERY

than **30** days after delivery, in unsellable condition, or missing parts, we will charge you a restocking fee.

returns more than **60** days after the delivery date (or more than **30** days from the delivery date for Cellular Phones and PCs).

rough our on-site partners or third-party sellers is subject to the returns policy of the partner. See our full returns :om/returns.

gas-powered items.

n was not a result of our error, the return shipping cost will be deducted from your refund.

RNS CENTER - www.amazon.com/returns

st efficient way to return an item is to visit our online Returns Center (even if it was a gift.) Complete , but here's how it works (the whole process takes less than five minutes):

amazon.com/returns

sed the merchandise yourself, enter your e-mail address and password. If you received it as a gift, enter number, which you'll find on the other side of this packing slip (there's even a picture online to help

eturns form, which asks you a few questions about the reason for your return, quantity of items, and so on.

r own mailing label—if you live within the U.S., it's *complete with postage*, saving you a trip to the

the product with this packing slip in the box, tape on the label, and leave it out for your mail carrier om your nearest post office if you are outside of the U.S.).

you an e-mail when we've processed your refund, usually 7-14 days after we've received the item. You'll get our returns policy) the same way you paid for the item (credit card, etc.) —or, if you received it as a gift, certificate.

SE THE ONLINE RETURNS CENTER?

use the Returns Center on our at to do:

Return Form at right.

tire packing slip and the item you ng into a box or package.

ackage securely, add the e postage and send it to this

.com - Returns Center
Mercer Rd., Suite 100
gton, KY 40598 USA

e-mail when we've processed your
4 days after we receive the item. You'll
ject to our returns policy) the same
he item (credit card, etc.) —or, if you
t, we'll send you a gift certificate.

RETURN FORM

DID YOU RECEIVE THIS ITEM AS A GIFT?
If you check "yes", we'll issue you a gift certificate for the refund amount. Don't worry, we won't notify the purchaser that you returned the item. If you check "no", please visit the Returns Center at www.amazon.com/returns.

GIFT NO

GIFT YES

PLEASE CHOOSE A REASON FOR YOUR RETURN:

___ I ordered the wrong item

___ I received an item I did not order

___ Item was not received on time; I no longer want it

___ I found better prices elsewhere

___ No reason—I just don't want it anymore

___ Product performance/quality is not up to my expectations

___ Product is not fully compatible with my existing system

___ Product is missing parts/accessories

___ Product was defective/damaged when it arrived

___ Product became defective/damage after it arrived

DESCRIBE DEFECT/DAMAGE_____

_____

_____

amazon.com®

Thanks for your order!

We hope you're happy with your new stuff. But just in case you're not, our returns policy makes it easy to send it back for a refund or credit.

Visit **www.amazon.com/returns**

y

Description	Format	Our Price	Total
Seth L. Wolitz	Hardcover	$28.00	$28.00

Subtotal	$28.00
Shipping & Handling	$3.99
Shipment Total	$31.99
Paid via Visa	$31.99
Balance Due	$0.00

quicker service. The other items will ship separately.

ting "Your Account" page at http://www.amazon.com/your-account.
zon.com/returns and save a trip to the post office.

om, and please come again!

Earth's Biggest Selection

Notes on Contributors

Monika Adamczyk-Garbowska is professor of English at Marie Curie-Skladowska University, Lublin, Poland. She has translated many of I. B. Singer's works into Polish, including *Satan in Goray* and *The Spinoza of Market Street,* and has published many essays on his work in both Polish and English, among them "Poles and Poland in I. B. Singer's Fiction," *Polin* 5 (1991), and "I. B. Singer's Works in English and Yiddish: The Language of the Addressee," *Prooftexts* 3 (1997).

Alan Astro is professor of languages and literatures at Trinity University, San Antonio. He is a specialist in Yiddish, French, and Spanish literatures. His most recent publication is an important essay related to Bashevis Singer, "Wolf Wieviorka, Parisian Writer and *Forverts* Contributor," *Yiddish* 11 (1998). He was also the editor of *Discourses of Jewish Identity in Twentieth-Century France,* Yale French Studies 86 (1994). He is currently working on Yiddish literature written in Latin America.

Nathan Cohen teaches at both the Hebrew University of Jerusalem and Bar-Ilan University, Tel Aviv, Israel. He is a specialist in Yiddish literature, especially that written during the period of interbellum Poland. He was the last student of Professor Khone Shmeruk and wrote his doctoral thesis on the Warsaw Yiddish writers.

Itzik Nakhmen Gottesman is assistant professor of Yiddish in the Germanic Studies Department, University of Texas at Austin. He is a folklorist and historian and has been elected to the editorial board of the Yiddish *Forverts.* His most recent book is entitled *Defining the Nation: The Jewish Folklorists of Poland* (forthcoming).

Janet Hadda is professor of Yiddish in the Department of English, University of California, Los Angeles. An associate editor of *Prooftexts,* she is a prolific author of many essays and books, her most recent publication being the leading biography, *Isaac Bashevis Singer: A Life* (Oxford University Press, 1997).

Mark L. Louden is associate professor of Germanic studies at the University of Wisconsin–Madison. A linguist of Germanic languages, he has published studies on German and its offshoots like the language of the Amish. Yiddish language and culture is one of his disciplines.

Avrom Noversztern is professor of Yiddish at the Hebrew University of Jerusalem and director of the Bes-Sholem Aleykhem Museum in Tel Aviv, Israel. He has published widely on Yiddish literature and has edited many books. He is an acknowledged specialist in twentieth-century Yiddish literature.

Leonard Prager is professor emeritus of English and Yiddish literature at the University of Haifa, Israel. He has published many studies of Yiddish literature as well as the definitive *Bibliography of Yiddish Literary Periodicals*. Currently he is the editor of the *Mendele Review*.

Irving Saposnik is a professor at the Center for Jewish Studies at the University of Wisconsin–Madison. He has worked and published on Bashevis Singer for many years, his latest essay being "A Tale of an Umbrella: I. B. Singer, Woody Allen, and Their New York Stories," *Modern Jewish Studies* 2 (1999). He is currently completing a new translation of *The Family Moskat*.

Jan Schwarz is assistant professor of Yiddish in the Germanic Literatures Department of the University of Illinois, Urbana-Champaign. Born in Denmark, he has published many translations of Yiddish writing into Danish. His most recent volume is *Den Gyldne kaede: en antologi af jiddisch litteratur* (The Golden Chain: An Anthology of Modern Yiddish Literature) (Copenhagen: Rhodos, 1993). His essays on Bashevis Singer include "*The Family Moskat* in a Cultural and Historical Context," *Litteratur-og-Samfund* (Literature and Society) 38 (1984), and "Isaac Bashevis Singer 1904–1991: A Eulogy," *Ales* (Fall 1991). He is completing a book on the Yiddish literary autobiography, including a chapter on Isaac Bashevis.

Joseph Sherman is associate professor of English in the Department of English, University of the Witwatersrand, Johannesburg, South Africa. He has translated a volume of South African Yiddish stories into English under the title *From a Land Far Off* (Capetown: Jewish Publications, 1987) and has published widely on Bashevis Singer and other Yiddish writers in journals in South Africa, Europe, and the United States. His translation of I. B. Singer's novel *Shadows on the Hudson* (New York: Farrar, Straus, Giroux) appeared in 1998. His most recent publications have been the translation into English and the redaction of the Yiddish text of Dovid Bergelson's *Opgang* (Descent) (New York: MLA, 1999). He has recently organized the Yiddish papers in the Singer archives of the Harry Ransom Humanities Research Center, University of Texas at Austin.

Astrid Starck-Adler is professor of Germanic languages at the Université de Haute Alsace, Mulhouse, France. The editor of a journal on Western Yiddish, she has published widely, including the essay "'Das ma'asse-bukh': Der Platz der jidischen Literatur in der deutschen Umwelt," *Akten des VIII Internationalen Germanisten-Kongresses* 11 (1990).

The Hidden Isaac Bashevis Singer

Seth L. Wolitz holds the Gale Chair of Jewish Studies and is professor of Slavic and French studies at the University of Texas at Austin. He has published widely on both Yiddish and European literatures. His essays on Bashevis Singer are "The Two *Yordim:* Isaac Bashevis Singer Confronts Dovid Bergelson," *Prooftexts* 2 (1982); "I. B. Singer's Debt to Dovid Bergelson," in *Recovering the Canon* (1986); "Satan in Goray as Parable," *Prooftexts* 9 (1989); and "*Der yid fun bovl:* Variants and Meanings," *Yiddish* 11 (1998).

Notes on Contributors

Index

Bosch, Hieronymus, xx
Buchen, Irving, 138
Buchhändler, Yakov, 120
Buenos Aires, Argentina, xvii

"Cafeteria, The" (Di kafeterye) (Singer),
112, 113–114
Cahan, Abraham: family background of,
177–178; and I. B. Singer, xxvi, 173–176,
178–180; and I. J. Singer, 173–178; and
Yiddish language, 65, 68, 74n.6; and
Yiddish writers, 4
Chagall, Marc, xv, xx
Chayefsky, Paddy, xxii
Chmielnicki massacres of 1648–1649, 28,
29, 30–32, 55, 87, 88–89
Chomsky, Noam, 63
Christianity: and Ashkenazic Jewry, 70;
and "Beard, The," 170; and Inquisition,
165; and Man of Dreams, The, 140–141;
and Polish literature, 140; and Satan in
Goray, 48; and "Zeidlus the Pope," 15,
16–19, 21, 22, 23, 24, 126–127
Cohen, Nathan, xxvi
Collected Stories of I. B. Singer, The
(Singer), 154
"Considering Yiddish Prose in Poland"
(Arum der yidisher proze in poyln)
(Singer), 108, 178
"Crown of Feathers, A" (Singer), 223
Cultural imperialism, xx, xxiii

"Dead Musician, The" (Der toyter klezmer) (Singer), xxv, 122, 127, 128, 132n.17
Death: and "Cafeteria, The," 112; and "In
the World of Chaos," 109, 110; and
Singer's worldview, xxv; and "Two
Corpses Go Dancing," 111, 125–126
Demons/demonic imps: and "Black Wedding, The," 128; and Eastern European Jewry, 115; and "In the World of
Chaos," 109; and "Last Demon, The,"
49–58; and Mayse-bukh, 122, 128, 131;
and "Mayses fun hintern oyvn," 95;
and My Father's Court, 169; and Penitent, The, 101; Singer's use of, xix–xx;
and "Taibele and Her Demon," xxv,

129–130; and "Two Corpses Go Danc-
ing," 110, 125–126; and yeytser-hore, 16;
and "Zeidlus the Pope," 24, 126–127.
See also Yeytser-hore (Evil Inclination)
Der Nister, xx, 108; Di mishpokhe mashber
(The Family Mashber), 187
Der zindiker meshiekh (Singer), 174–175
"Destruction of Kreshev, The" (Singer),
223–224
"Diary of the Evil Inclination, The"
(Singer), 110, 113
Diaspora: and Jewish identity, 14, 15, 16;
and Lublin Province, 224; and Yid-
dish language, 72, 73, 99; and Yiddish
literature, 69
Di tsukunft (The Future), 178
Dogs: and Eastern European Jewry, 79;
role of, xxv; and shtetl, 80; and Slave,
The, 80, 83–90; and soul, 85, 86–87, 90,
91
Dolega-Mostowicz, Tadeusz, Kariera
Nikodema Dyzmy (Nikodem Dyzma's
Career), 137
Dos naye vort (The New Word), 152
Dostoevsky, Fyodor, xxii
Drama, 34
Dybbuks: and "Dead Musician, The," xxv,
122, 127, 128, 132n.17; and Mayse-bukh,
119, 122, 127–128; and Satan in Goray,
46–48, 122, 127–128, 167–168; and "Two
Corpses Go Dancing," xxv, 126

East Central Europe, map of, 218
Eastern European Jewry: and assimilationism, 64; and demonic imps, 115;
descendants of, xvii; and dogs, 79; and
Family Moskat, The, 179; and Forverts,
173; and gangster novels, 187–188; and
Lublin, 220, 224; and massacre of Jews,
28–29, 33, 114; and religion, 165; and
secularism, xv; Singer's vision of, xx,
4; and Yiddish language, 71, 72, 73; and
Yiddish literature, 108
Enemies: A Love Story (Singer), xviii, 145
English language: English-speaking Jewry,
xvii–xviii, 6; English translations, xviii,
xix, 4, 119, 136; lexical influence on Yid-

The Hidden Isaac Bashevis Singer

dish, 65, 67–68; and Singer's American characters, 145

English translations of Singer's Yiddish texts: and "Cafeteria, The," 113; as commentary on Yiddish original, 6; and concealment of Yiddish originals, 4–5; and critical/scholarly articles, xx–xxi; and *Family Moskat, The,* xviii, 6, 109–110, 180; and "Gimpel the Fool," xviii, xxii, 6, 11n.4; implications of differences, xiii, xviii, xxiv, 10, 13, 14, 16–17; Jewish and Slavic allusions eliminated from, xxi; and Nobel Prize of 1978, xix; and *Penitent, The,* 94, 98, 102, 103; and Polish language, 144–145; and Polish translations, 137; primacy of, xxi–xxiii, 5; and *Satan in Goray,* xviii, xxi, 31, 36; Singer's role in, xiv, xx, xxi, 6, 11n.2, 151; and Singer's success, 4; and *Slave, The,* 87–89; stylistic differentiation in, xxi, xxv; and "Two Corpses Go Dancing," 111; validity of, xxi, xxvii; and *Yarme un keyle,* 188–190, 192–217; and "Zeidlus the Pope," xxiv, 13, 14, 16, 17, 18–19, 20, 24, 26n.5

Enlightenment. *See* Haskala

Estate, The (Singer), xviii, 135, 219

Evil: and Anski, 167; and Bilgoray, 169; and "Black Wedding, The," 128–129; and "Cafeteria, The," 113, 114; and "Dead Musician, The," 128; and dogs, 80, 83, 84, 86; and "In the World of Chaos," 109; and "Last Demon, The," 52, 54, 57; Literature of Evil, 123–124; and *Maysebukh,* 121–123; and *Penitent, The,* 97, 101, 104; and *Satan in Goray,* 36, 39, 124, 128, 167, 168; in Singer's supernatural stories, 123; and "Two Corpses Go Dancing," 111; and *Yarme un keyle,* 189; and "Zeidlus the Pope," 14, 16, 24. *See also Yeytser-hore* (Evil Inclination)

Existentialism, 95–96, 120

Exorcist, The (film), 167

Faith and Doubt or the Philosophy of Protest (Gloybn un tsveyfl oder di filosofye fun protest) (Singer), 109

Family Moskat, The (Di familye mushkat) (Singer): as autobiographical writing, 157; and Cahan, xxvi, 175, 178–179; English translation of, xviii, 6, 109–110, 180; *Pan Tadeusz* compared to, 138; and Polish language, 141, 142; and Polish literature, 134, 140; and Polish place names, 144; Polish setting, 219; serialization of, xviii, xxvi; and Singer's identity, 5

Farrar, Straus and Giroux, xxi

Farrell, Grace, *Critical Essays on Isaac Bashevis Singer,* xxi, xxii, xxiii, xxvii

Feierberg, Mordecai Ze'ev, *La'an,* xv

Fishman, Joshua, 63, 68

Folklore: and Ashkenazic Jewry, xvi; and autobiographical writings, xxvi, 152, 163, 168–172; and Bilgoray, 167, 168–169; and Jewishness/Jews, 163, 167, 168, 169; and Jewish pope myth, 13; and "Last Demon, The," 55; and morality, 120, 121, 170; and *My Father's Court [Sequel-Collection],* 163, 169–170; and *Penitent, The,* 98; and Polish language, 142; and religion, xxvi, 169, 170, 171–172; and *Satan in Goray,* 167–168; and Singer's style, 115, 119–120, 162; and Singer's use of duplicity of human beings, 122–123; and supernatural storytelling, 119; and time, 120; and Yiddish literature, 13, 162; and Yiddish simile studies, 79–80; and "Zeidlus the Pope," 15, 20, 126

Formalist linguistics, 63

Forverts (Forward): and Cahan, xxvi, 173, 178; and English translations, xviii–xix, 4; and *Family Moskat, The,* xviii, xxvi, 178–180; and folklore, 168; and gangster novel, xxvi–xxvii; and *Man of Dreams, The,* 140; page from, *xxx;* and *Penitent, The,* 93; and I. J. Singer, 174; and Singer's relationship with Cahan, 174–175, 179; and Singer's Yiddish originals, 4, 174; and *Yarme un keyle,* 185, 188; and Yiddish language and culture, 65, 74n.6, 151, 173

Frampol, Poland, *xxxvii,* 6, 8, 221

French language, 64, 68, 72

identity, xv, xvii; Singer's dual identity, 5, 9–10, 190; Singer's Yiddish identity, xiii–xiv, 4, 5, 25; and Yiddish language, 16, 72, 73

In My Father's Court (Mayn tatns bezdn-shtub) (Singer): as autobiographical writing, xviii, xxvi, 154, 157; and child storyteller, 153; and folklore, 163, 164, 170; and Lublin, 221; and Polish language, 141–142

"In the World of Chaos" (Oyfn oylem-hatoyhu) (Singer), 107–109, 110, 113, 114, 115

Israel, xvii, 15, 22, 24, 73

Jewish-American culture, 5, 10
Jewish-American fiction, xviii, xix, 4
Jewish-Americans, xxii–xxiii, 5, 6, 25
Jewish culture, xiii, xiv
Jewish Law, 15, 19, 166
Jewish literature, xix, xxii, 13, 53, 54, 136. *See also* Yiddish literature
Jewish martyrology, 30
Jewish Studies, xxiii
"Joy" (Singer), 223
Judaism: Halakhic Judaism, xv, 16, 34, 35, 36, 41; ideals of, 166; and *In My Father's Court,* 155; and "Last Demon, The," 51–52; and *Mayse-bukh,* 121; and *My Father's Court,* 170, 171; and "Penitent, The," 94–95, 98, 99, 100, 103–104; and *Satan in Goray,* 48; and "Zeidlus the Pope," 20–22, 24–25. *See also* Hasidism
Junosza-Szaniawski, Klemens, 137

Kabbalistic texts, xix, 20, 123–124
Kaminska, Esther-Rokhl, xv
Karpluk, Maria, 142–143
Katz, Eli, xxiii
King of the Fields, The (Der kenig fun di felder) (Singer), 137, 138–139, 143
King, Robert, xxvii
Kock, Rabbi, house of, *xxxvi*
Konopnicka, Maria, *O Janku Wedrow-niczku* (On Yash the Wanderer), 136
Kosinski, Jerzy: *Being There,* 137; *Painted Bird, The,* 137

Krall, Hanna, 138
Kraszewski, Jozef Ignacy, 143; *Krol Chlo-pow* (King of the Peasants), 139; *Stara basn* (The Old Fairy Tale), 137, 138–139
Kresh, Paul, 8; *Magician of West 86th Street, The,* 188–189
Kulbak, Moyshe, *Meshiekh ben Efrayim,* 34

Labov, William, 63
Landis, Joseph, xxiii
"Last Demon, The" (Mayse tishevits) (Singer): and Lublin, 220; and messianic/apocalyptic motifs, 49–51, 53, 55, 56–58; and Yiddish language and culture, 51–52, 130; and Yiddish literature, 51–54
Latzk-Bertholdi, Wolf, 29
Leivick, H., 34
Leyeles, Arn, 34
"Little Shoemakers, The" (Di kleyne shusterlekh) (Singer), 178, 221
Louden, Mark, xxiv–xxv
Love and Exile: An Autobiographical Trilogy (Singer), 107, 109, 110
Lublin, Poland, 219–220, 222
Lublin Province, Poland, 219–224
Luxembourg, Rosa, 223

Magician of Lublin, The (Der kuntsn-makher fun lublin) (Singer), xviii, 95
Maharam of Lublin, 220
Maimonides, 19
Malamud, Bernard, xviii
Malin, Irving, xxvii
Manger, Itzik, xvii
Mann, Thomas, *Magic Mountain, The,* 95
Man of Dreams, The (Der man fun kha-loymes) (Singer), 140–141
Manor, The (Singer), xviii, 135, 219
Markish, Perets, 34; *Di kupe* (The Heap), 42
Mark, Mendl, 79–80
Mark, Yudl, 79
Maskilim, 14–15, 20, 73
Masson, Jeffrey, 90
Matthews, Brander, 68–69
Mayn tatns bezdn-shtub (Singer), 154, 157

Mayse-bukh: "Black Wedding, The" compared to, 128; and dybbuks, 119, 122,
127–128; and evil, 121–123; and Middle
Ages, 120, 121; *Satan in Goray* compared
to, 124; and supernatural storytelling,
xxv, 119, 124–125, 130, 131; and women,
121, 129; "Zeidlus the Pope" compared
to, 126–127
"Mayses fun hintern oyvn" (Singer), 95
McFarlane, James W., 83
"Menashe and Rachel" (Singer), xxvi, 154
Messianic/apocalyptic motifs: and Asch,
33; and Holocaust, xxiv, 49, 50, 55, 57–
58; and "In the World of Chaos," 109;
and "Last Demon, The," 49–51, 53, 55,
56–58; and *Mayse-bukh,* 124; and *My
Father's Court [Sequel-Collection],* 171;
and Peretz, 33–34, 43, 55–56; and *Satan
in Goray,* 31, 32, 34–46, 48–49, 55, 124;
in Yiddish literature, xxiv, 33, 36–37, 41,
43, 49, 50, 53, 54–55, 56, 57, 58
Miami Beach, Florida, xiv
Mickiewicz, Adam, 137; *Pan Tadeusz,* 134,
138
Miller, David Neal, xxvii
Milosz, Czeslaw, 134
Miron, Dan, 98, 114
"Mirror, The" (Singer), 223
Modernism: and Cahan, 173; and narrative
devices, xix; and *Satan in Goray,* 36, 39,
41; and Singer, 36, 60n.11, 115, 173; and
Zamosc, 223
Modernity: and *Penitent, The,* 93, 100, 101;
and Polish Jewry, xvi
Morality: and animals, 90; and Asch, 187;
and "Cafeteria, The," 114; and "Dead
Musician, The," 128; and folklore, 120,
121, 170; and "In the World of Chaos,"
109; and "Last Demon, The," 51–52;
and *Mayse-bukh,* 121, 122, 124, 130; and
Penitent, The, 94, 96–97; and *Satan
in Goray,* 35, 47, 49; and Singer's early
works, 151; Singer's personal morality,
175; in Singer's supernatural stories,
123; and *Slave, The,* 87–88; and "Two
Corpses Go Dancing," 113; and Yiddish language and culture, xvii, xix;

and Yiddish literary criticism, 35; and
"Zeidlus the Pope," 14, 15, 20, 21, 24, 113
Musil, Robert, *Man Without Qualities,
The,* 100
My Father's Court [Sequel-Collection]
(Mayntatns bezdn-shtub [hemshe-
khimzamlung]) (Singer), 163, 164–171
"Mysteries of the Cabala, The" (Singer),
153
Mystical traditions, xvi, xx

"Naftali the Storyteller and His Horse,
Sus" (Singer), 154
Nahman of Bratslav, *Seyfer sipurey mayses*
(The Holy Book of Tales), xx, 113
Narrative devices: and "Cafeteria, The,"
112–113, 114; and folklore, 119, 120; and
Fun der alter un nayer heym, 153; and
In My Father's Court, 170; and "In the
World of Chaos," 109, 115; and *Man
of Dreams, The,* 140; and modernism,
xix; and *Penitent, The,* 98; and *Satan
in Goray,* 38, 39, 40–43, 45–48, 49; and
Shosha, 154; and "Two Corpses Go
Dancing," 125; and "Zeidlus the Pope,"
14
New York City, xiv, xvii, 9, 151
New Yorker, xxi, 4
Nietzsche, Friedrich, 124
Niger, S., 35
Nobel Prize of 1978: and "In the World
of Chaos," 108; and Polish literature,
134; and Singer's life, 9, 10; and Singer's
persona, xix, 25; and Singer's views on
Yiddish language, 62, 74; and Yiddish
language and culture, 151
Noversztern, Avrom, xxiv

"Old Man, The" (Singer), 223
Opatoshu, Joseph, xix; *A roman fun a ferd-
ganef* (Romance of a Horse Thief), 187;
Fun nyu-yorker geto (From the New
York Ghetto), 187; *Untervelt* (Under-
world), 187

Pappenheim, Bertha, 119
Partisan Review, xviii

The Hidden Isaac Bashevis Singer

"Passions" (Singer), 223

Penitent, The (Der bal-tshuve) (Singer): and choice, 95–96; and morality, 94, 96–97; and religion, 93–95, 98, 100, 101, 102, 103–105; and Yiddish language and culture, 98, 99, 103

People along My Path (Mentshn oyf mayn veg) (Singer), 157, 163

Peretz, Yitskhok Leybush: *Bay nakht afn altn makr* (Nighttime in the Old Marketplace), 42, 44, 51; "Bontshe shvayg" (Bontshe the Silent), 111; "Der kuntsn-makher" (The Conjurer), 39; *Di goldene keyt* (The Golden Chain), 37, 42, 44–45, 107, 108; "Di toyte shtot" (The Dead Town), 110; as emerging writer, xix; and Hasidism, xx; and messianic/apocalyptic motifs, 33–34, 43, 55–56; and modernism, 115; *Monish*, 39, 55–56, 58; neo-Romanticism of, 186; and Polish language, 136; and Polish literature, 140; and secularism, xv, 113; symbolist tales of, 108; and Tsaytlin, 137; and Zamosc, 223

Poe, Edgar Allan, xxi, 109

Poetry, 34, 37, 42, 43, 52, 55–56

Poland, xvi–xvii, 8, 9, 219–224

Polish Gentiles, xvi

Polish Jewry, xvi, 31, 108, 158, 224

Polish language: and fictional translation, 140–141; and first and family names, 142–143; and Kraszewski, 138; proverbs and sayings in, 143–144, 145; and Singer, xxv–xxvi, 135, 136, 146n.4; symbolic function of, 141–142; and translations of Singer's work, 137, 144–145; and Yiddish language, 144–145, 146

Polish literature: and *Family Moskat, The,* 134, 140; and fictional translation, 140–141; Jewish characters' readings in, 139–140; Singer's knowledge of, 134, 135–136; Singer's literary polemics against, 138–139; Yiddish literature compared to, 136–137, 139

Pollack, Yakov, 120

Portuguese language, 64

Postmodernism, xxi, 101

Prager, Leonard, xxv

"Problems of Yiddish Prose in America" (Problemen fun yer yidisher proze in Amerike) (Singer), 69, 98–99, 178

Prus, Boleslaw, 135; *Pharoah,* 134

Przybyszewski, Stanislaw, 140; *Homo Sapiens,* 138; *Outcry, The,* 134

Ravitch, Meylekh, 175

Religion: and folklore, xxvi, 169, 170, 171–172; and "In the World of Chaos," 110, 113; and Lublin, 220; and *My Father's Court [Sequel-Collection],* 164–166, 170–171; and *Penitent, The,* 93–95, 98, 100, 101, 102, 103–105; and Polish literature, 139, 140; and secularism, xv, xvii; Singer on, 13, 14–15, 16, 18, 24–25, 25–26n.2, 94; and Singer's early works, 151; and *Yarme un keyle,* 191; and Yiddish language, 72, 73; and "Zeidlus the Pope," 16, 21

Reymont, Wladyslaw, 134; *Ziemia obiecana* (The Promised Land), 136–137

Rischin, Moses, 177

Rise of David Levinsky, The (Singer), xxvi

Robak, A. A., 86

Romanticism, 167

Roth, Henry, 5

Roth, Philip, xviii, 5

Rubenstein, Ida, xv

Russia, 220

Russian language, 65, 137, 145, 185

Russian Silver Age, xvi

Rymkiewicz, Jaroslaw Marek, *Umschlagplatz* (Deportation Place), 137–138

Sabbateanism, and *Satan in Goray,* 32, 34, 35, 36, 40, 41, 45, 48

Sade, Marquis de, 97, 127–128

Saposnik, Irving, xxiv

Sartre, Jean-Paul, 96

Satan in Goray (Der sotn in goray) (Singer): and Cahan, 174; and Chmielnicki massacres of 1648–1649, 28, 29, 30–32; dybbuk in, 122, 127–128, 167; English translations of, xviii, xxi, 31,

Singer, Joseph, 189
Singer, Pinkhes Menakhem, 152, 154–155, 158, 176–177
Singer Yiddish archive, xxvii, 185
Slave, The (Der knekht) (Singer): and autonomy of animal life, 81–84; and dogs, 80, 83–90; and dog's name, 84–86; and dog's symbolic role, 86–90; and Gentiles, 84–85, 87, 89, 91; and Polish language, 145
Sloan, Jacob, xxi
Slowacki, Julisz, "Smutno mi Boze" (I'm Sad, God), 136
Sociolinguistics, 62–63, 73–74
"Something Is There" (Singer), 221
"Son from America" (Singer), 221
Soviet Union, 72
Spanish language, 64, 72
Spektor, Mordkhe, *Aniim ve'evyonim, oder gliklekhe un umgliklekhe* (The Poor and the Miserable, or the Happy and the Unhappy), 186
Spicehandler, Ezra, 84
Starck-Adler, Astrid, xxv
Stereotypes, 143
Strauss, Ludwig, 119
Supernatural storytelling: and "Cafeteria, The," 112, 113–114; and evil, 123; and folklore, 119; and "In the World of Chaos," 107; and *Mayse-bukh*, xxv, 119, 124–125, 130, 131; and "Two Corpses Go Dancing," 111, 113; and Yiddish literature, 115
Sutcliffe, Thomas, 94–95
Sutzkever, Avrom, "Tsu poyln," 136
Svive, 178

"Taibele and Her Demon" (Taybele un hurmiza) (Singer), xxv, 123, 129–130
Taytsh, 38, 121
Teller, Judd, xxiii
Telushkin, Dvorah, 168
Truth: and "Gimpel the Fool," 7–8, 9; and "Zeidlus the Pope," 21, 24
Tsaytlin, Arn, 34; *Esterke,* 137, 139
Tuszynska, Agata, 3
Tuwim, Julian, 136

"Two Corpses Go Dancing" (Tsvey meysim geyen tantsn) (Singer), xxv, 110, 111, 113, 125–126, 128

Ukraine, 29
Ukrainian language, 145
Unger, Maria, 134–135
"Unseen, The" (Singer), 223

Varshavski, Oyzer, *Shmuglyars* (Smugglers), 186–187
Varshe 1914–1918 (Singer), xxvi, 152–158

Warsaw, Poland: and *Family Moskat, The,* 144, 179; Jewish quarter map, *xxxiv;* Krochmalna Street photograph, *xxxv;* and *My Father's Court [Sequel-Collection],* 163, 164; and Prus, 134; as setting, 219; and Singer's Yiddish-speaking milieux, xiv; and *Varshe 1914–1918,* 154–156; and *Yarme un keyle,* 185, 190–191
Weininger, Otto, 109
Weinreich, Max: *Bilder fun der Yidisher literaturgeshikhte* (Images from Jewish Literary History), 48; and Yiddish language, 16, 62, 70–71, 72; and YIVO, 69, 71, 75n.15
Weinreich, Uriel, 63, 71
Weissenberg, I. M., 187; *A shtetl,* 186
Westernization, xv–xvii
"Wife Killer, The" (Singer), 221
Wisse, Ruth, 93–94, 98
Wittlin, Jozef, 136
Women: and *Mayse-bukh,* 121, 129; and *Penitent, The,* 96–97, 101, 103–104; and Polish literature, 140; and *Satan in Goray,* 42–43, 46–48; and Singer's supernatural storytelling, 129
Writers' Club, 9
Writers' Club, The (Der shrayber-klub) (Singer), 157, 163
Wyspianski, Stanislaw, 136

Yarme un keyle (Yarme and Keyle) (Singer): English translation of, 188–190, 192–217; and *Forverts,* 185, 188;

The Hidden Isaac Bashevis Singer